I0825532

Endorsements for

Leading from the Heart

"In this brilliant, sensitive, and provocative challenge to your future, Young shocks typical self-help books that wallow in self-centeredness. Instead, he puts your future in the context of caring relationships with others as an antidote to narcissism."

—Richard E. Boyatzis, PhD, Distinguished University Professor, Case Western Reserve University, and Author of *The Science of Change: Discovering Sustained, Desired Change of Individuals to Teams, Organizations to Communities*

LEADING FROM THE HEART

LEADING FROM THE HEART

EVIDENCE-BASED · NEUROSCIENCE-INFORMED
THE ESSENTIAL GUIDE TO SELF-EMPATHY AND
SELF-COMPASSION IN COACHING AND CLINICAL PRACTICE

DR. D. IVAN YOUNG,
MCC, NBC-HWC

A POST HILL PRESS BOOK
ISBN: 979-8-89565-529-0
ISBN (eBook): 979-8-89565-530-6

Leading from the Heart:
The Essential Guide to Self-Empathy and Self-Compassion in Coaching and Clinical Practice

Cover design by Amy Jane Made

All people, locations, events, and situations are portrayed to the best of the author's memory. While all of the events described are true, many names and identifying details have been changed to protect the privacy of the people involved.

Although every effort has been made to ensure that the personal and professional advice present within this book is useful and appropriate, the author and publisher do not assume and hereby disclaim any liability to any person, business, or organization choosing to employ the guidance offered in this book.

This book, as well as any other Post Hill Press publications, may be purchased in bulk quantities at a special discounted rate. Contact orders@posthillpress.com for more information.

Post Hill Press
New York • Nashville
posthillpress.com

Published in the United States of America
1 2 3 4 5 6 7 8 9 10

Contents

Foreword
by Carrie Abner

WE LIVE IN A WORLD that moves at the speed of light. Rather than reducing our work, technology increases our expectations of productivity. Communication with others is often a mix of initialisms, acronyms, and chat speak sent in quick texts. Between remote work and online collaboration tools, keyboards are now among our closest colleagues. In this world that pushes us to do more in less time, the opportunity to stop, reflect, breathe, and relate sometimes feels, well, *indulgent.*

But it shouldn't. And it doesn't have to. There is a different way.

Empathy invites us to pause, to witness, to connect. It is a quiet, unhurried force that creates and builds bridges between us. At a time in which we increasingly interact with technology and artificial intelligence, practicing empathy allows us to be and feel truly human *with* one another.

Today, empathy is more vital than ever. The ability to be present with each other, to relate emotionally, and to connect at a deeper level is fundamental for our well-being.

But empathy is not just a natural, innate "feeling" or sentiment. It's a skill, an intentional practice, and a way of being that can be shaped, molded, and expanded over time. And while we often think about empathy as a practice with others, we cannot fully hone this skill without beginning internally and being able to demonstrate empathy with ourselves.

Empathy has the power to transform our relationships, our communities, and our lives. But its impact transcends the personal sphere, as well.

According to the World Economic Forum, empathy is among the top ten core skills for the future workforce (Future of Jobs Report, 2025). It allows leaders to connect more deeply with their teams, listen beyond words, support diverse perspectives, communicate with compassion and clarity, and more effectively resolve conflict. It's a skill that is purely human, unlikely to be replaced by technology.

This book is a guide and a companion designed to help us build, reinforce, and practice empathy in our lives. It weaves together research and experience, along with practical tools, to support the reader in embodying empathy more fully with themselves, their personal relationships, and their professional practice. Whether you are a seasoned coach or counselor seeking to hold space for your clients or someone simply seeking to live more compassionately with those around you, you will find meaningful insight, support, and inspiration.

May this book help you listen more deeply, connect authentically, and lead with empathy.

—Carrie Abner, Head of Credentialing for the ICF

Foreword
by Margaret Moore

DR. D. IVAN YOUNG'S *Leading from the Heart* arrives at a critical moment, showing how we are too often focused outwardly while neglecting the inner work that enables genuine transformation. What Dr. Young illuminates is the power—and necessity—of self-compassion and compassion as foundational competencies and daily habits.

When Dr. Young describes empathy and compassion as "precision instruments" rather than "soft, gauzy feelings," he echoes what researchers have been showing for two decades. Self-compassion downregulates the sympathetic nervous system, our threat response, to reveal the parasympathetic nervous system which relaxes the brain and body to support learning, growth, and resilience. We are able to lift out of stress cycles that deplete our capacity to show up fully.

What makes this book unputdownable is that Dr. Young earned every word through direct experience. His journey through cancer, documented with unflinching honesty, transforms the book from a theoretical treatise into a survival guide forged in life-threatening illness. When he writes about choosing between the "omniscient self" and the "obnoxious self," he's describing the daily choice each of us faces in being present to our own mortality, fragility, and humanity.

The framework offers a roadmap for developing "sustainable presence." This is the capacity to show up fully, day after day, without burning out, numbing out, or checking out. It requires what Dr. Young so eloquently describes: the ability to wield compassion as both internal and external tools.

Leading from the Heart shows us how to operationalize compassion in high-stakes environments where "failure is not an option." Drawing from hostage negotiation, crisis leadership, and his own medical emergency, he demonstrates how self-compassion and compassion function as cognitive strategies that enhance decision-making, strengthen relationships, and literally save lives.

I encourage you to read this book multiple times. Allow yourself to be moved by Dr. Young's story. Engage with the exercises and self-reflection prompts. Think about how you can help others using the book's lessons.

May this book serve as both mirror and mantra. As a mirror, it will reflect back to you the compassion you already possess. The mantra? Self-compassion is not self-indulgence. It's neurobiologically smart and professionally essential.

With my deep respect, appreciation, and compassion,

Margaret Moore, aka Coach Meg, MBA
Executive Coach, Thinkers50 Coaching Award winner, Founder, Wellcoaches Corporation, Co-Founder, Institute of Coaching, Co-Founder, National Board for Health and Wellness Coaching

A Message from Me to You

JUST A FEW YEARS AGO, I began writing this book. At that time, I'd convinced myself that I was creating an astute playbook for everyone who guides others through high-stakes, high-pressure environments where failure is not an option. My intention was to write a calming, go-to field guide for those in leadership roles, like executive coaches and clinicians, that could also benefit the average person. Then the ground split, and I fell right between the cracks as all hell broke loose.

Illness, upheaval, and a parade of unexpected detours rewrote every tidy outline I had taped to my office wall. I'll unpack those storms soon, but keep this in view: What tried to bury me ended up forging the cognitive weapon you're now holding in your hands. Out of that upheaval emerged a survival map on how to flourish while salvaging what's left of your life, with an emphasis on creating and maintaining transformational relationships with yourself and others.

My promise is straightforward: By the final page, whether you read these words or let me whisper them through your earbuds, you'll be equipped with some new tools. You will know how to handle empathy and compassion the way a samurai wields a sword. Yes, a sword. Empathy and compassion are not soft, gauzy feelings; though you may think otherwise, they are more like weapons likened to precision instruments. Sharpen them, and they open locked boardrooms, heal cracked marriages, and cut through the noise of self-doubt. Leave them dull, and they can wound if not seriously debilitate you, manifesting as burnout, resentment, and performative kindness that fools no one while making a complete fool out of you.

Empathy has become a conference-room buzzword, but its true power lives in two arenas:

1. **Internal mastery**: The discipline of seeing yourself clearly, extending mercy inward, and calibrating your motives before you act.
2. **External influence**: The strategic art of reading a room, diagnosing quiet pain points, and delivering exactly what moves people to trust, decide, and change.

History's most magnetic leaders—heroes and villains alike—have perfected both arenas. They know when to sheath empathy as a balm, and when to unsheathe it as a blade. That duality is why entire nations rally behind a single voice, why teams sprint through brick walls for the right manager, and, yes, why some charismatic tyrants bend crowds to their will.

You'll learn to spot the difference.

Along the way, we'll tackle a nagging truth: Most people, especially in the West, taste only a thimbleful of the peace and joy they're built for. If you sense a quiet ache you can't name, you're not defective; you're simply due for recalibration. Picture your life as a grand piano that's ever so slightly out of tune. My job is to hand you the tuning fork, guide your ear, and help you tighten each string until the melody is unmistakable.

Here's what our journey will cover:

- **Self-Compassion Without Self-Sabotage**: How to pour into your own cup without drowning in self-absorption.

- **Weaponized Empathy**: Case studies of leaders who used compassion to heal…and those who used it to manipulate.
- **The Science of Connection**: Why mirror neurons, oxytocin, and cognitive empathy set the stage for every successful negotiation—personal or professional.
- **The Relationship Rescue Kit**: A step-by-step method to repair strained partnerships before they fracture for good.

By the end, you'll be able to pull empathy and compassion from their scabbards at will, temper them with discernment, aim them with integrity, and change every room you enter. No more background hum. Full symphony.

Ready? Let's sharpen the blade and begin.

MY STORY

I was only a few months into drafting the first part of this book when I was diagnosed with stage two retromolar cancer. Like most people who are confronted with a life-threatening illness, I most certainly wasn't ready for that, let alone all the stress and anxiety that came with it. In one gut-wrenching instant, my life was completely disrupted. My ability to control my thoughts, emotions, and even my day-to-day schedule was stripped from me. As disconcerting as that was, the diagnosis was the easy part. In no way was I prepared for the nightmarish emotional and psychological rollercoaster ride that life would take me on for the next several months.

Anyone who knows me will quickly tell you how prayerful and spiritually grounded I am. Up until that season, my default mode was Zen. Little did I know the extent to which my convictions and spiritual beliefs would be tested over the months that followed.

Before this experience, it was second nature for me to support and encourage others I saw suffering while suppressing my own inner turmoil. I'd mastered the art of assuring people that no matter how bad whatever they were going through, they could always count on one simple truth—everything is working for your good. That rhetorical statement rolled off my tongue like olive oil poured from a decanter. Isn't it interesting how my "usual" way of thinking ended up coming back to bite me in the ass when it was my turn to ingest my rhetoric? I must admit, life found one hell of a way to force me to confront my own beliefs. It was as if divine intervention forced me to sign up for an introspective journey that I was in no way prepared for.

As I became the one going through hades, it wasn't so easy to connect the dots and truly believe those comforting words that once flowed so freely from my lips.

I remember asking myself, "How in the hell is this working for my good? I might be dead by the time it's all said and done."

At that moment, it became clear to me that I had to confront every philosophical, spiritual, and cognitive part of myself, particularly those that were fundamental to my public persona and brand. I understood that my faith and hope were all I had to help me move forward. During this transformative period, I came to a profound realization that self-compassion and empathy were not just integral to my core values, but they also wielded a formidable influence on how my brain functioned, how I used my mind, and my psychopathology. This revelation has entirely transformed my beliefs, emotions, and perspectives on human mental and emotional functioning.

Mastering self-compassion and empathy is crucial for resilience, self-efficacy, and forming meaningful relationships with oneself and others.

GOING DEEPER

Although my inner circle is small, I was fortunate to be surrounded by people who genuinely cared about me. I had an excellent interdisciplinary team of extremely dedicated and talented physicians at MD Anderson Cancer Center in Houston, Texas. MD Anderson is recognized as one of the world's top cancer treatment centers. In addition to that, I had a supportive staff, a loving partner, mentors, and friends who sincerely had my best interests at heart. Honestly, I had no idea how much I would need this support until later. However, the one thing I needed most to survive this ordeal was the ability to connect with the most significant part of myself intentionally. What part is that? It's the self, or more specifically, my relationship with my mind and spirit.

> "Only when you reach the limits of your mortality can you truly confront the profound duality that plagues human nature: the struggle between the omniscient self and the obnoxious self."
>
> —Dr. D Ivan Young, MCC, NBC-HWC

This dichotomy reflects a deeper spiritual battle that many spiritual traditions seek to illuminate.

In Christianity, the Apostle Paul speaks of the "inner conflict" in Romans 7:14-25 (NIV), where he describes the struggle between the desire to do good and the tendency toward sin. This mirrors our own duality: the omniscient self, which strives for grace and understanding, and the obnoxious self, which succumbs to cynicism and despair. In the Christian religion, Jesus embodies the omniscient self, offering hope and healing to the broken, reminding us that when we surrender to love and compassion, we transcend our limitations.

Similarly, in Islam, the concept of the *nafs* delineate different aspects of the self. The *nafs al-Ammarah* represents our carnal, base instincts—our obnoxious side—while the *nafs al-Mutma'innah* signifies the tranquil, enlightened self that finds peace in submission to the divine. The journey toward recognizing which side we align with is a spiritual pilgrimage toward surrender and understanding, a theme echoed in the teachings of the Prophet Muhammad, who emphasized the importance of inner purity and the pursuit of righteousness.

Hindu philosophy introduces us to the concept of "Atman"—the true self that is eternal and omniscient, in contrast to the "ego" or *Ahamkara*, which binds us to illusion and suffering. The Bhagavad Gita teaches us that in recognizing our true nature, we can rise above the dualities of existence. As one of the primary characters in the Bhagavad Gita, Arjuna's struggle reflects our own, as he learns to discern between his higher self and the distractions of fear, doubt, and despair.

From a more worldly perspective, consider the journey of an agnostic individual grappling with purpose and meaning in a complex world. They may find themselves at a crossroads when facing adversity, unsure about where to turn for answers. In those moments, the obnoxious self can manifest as doubt and nihilism, leading to a sense of disconnection. However, through introspection and the pursuit of knowledge, the agnostic can tap into a deeper understanding of their own values and motivations, embracing the omniscient self that recognizes the inherent meaning in human connections and experiences. This awakening often fosters empathy and compassion, illuminating a path forward even in the face of uncertainty.

When I was diagnosed with cancer, that season of my life forced me to pick a side. I chose to embrace the intentionally omniscient self, understanding that true power lies not in dominance, but in humility and connection to the unseen. As I navigated this path,

I held fast to the belief that by nurturing the omniscient within I could transform the obnoxious into a source of growth, facilitating not just personal healing but also contributing to a collective awakening. In a quest like this, we are not merely choosing sides; we are answering a call to transcendence, seeking unity in our shared humanity.

My awakening was based on coming to terms with the fact that the compassion and empathy I'd been demonstrating and freely giving to others would play a critical role in my ability to sustain and heal myself.

A WALK IN THE PARK

The moment I stepped into MD Anderson, I was enveloped in a warm, inviting atmosphere. The staff radiated kindness and compassion, their smiles easing some of the tension that had settled in my chest. Despite all of that, I knew that this was no ordinary appointment—it felt like a confrontation with my own fragility.

It had been two months since my cancer diagnosis. Today was the day that we would discuss my impending surgery. I remember when Dr. Patrick Garvey entered the room, I felt a wave of comfort wash over me. Over the past few weeks, he and I had established a genuine rapport, and his humble demeanor put me at ease. As he sat down, I could sense the care behind his gaze, yet the weight of what we were discussing loomed large.

"Do you ski?" he asked, trying to lighten the mood, and although I thought it seemed trivial, his friendly tone gave me a moment of relief. I managed a small smile, my mind racing—was this really the time for such a question? I replied, "Bro, I'm Black, hell no, I don't ski." Then we both laughed. Yet, despite my attempt at humorous banter, it didn't mask my anxiety, and he definitely sensed my discomfort about the subject at hand.

With a tone that was both gentle and serious, he explained the complexities of my upcoming surgery, the free fibula mandibulectomy that was soon to be part of my immediate future. He did it in a way that was clear and relatable, using colors to describe the difficulty: green for easy, blue for slightly easy, red for intermediate, and black for difficult. When he uttered the words, "black diamond," suddenly the reality of what we just discussed hit *hard.* I felt my breath clasp the back of my throat; that's when the reality of my situation began to sink in. *What the hell did I do to deserve this?* I thought to myself, grappling with the unfairness of it all. Despite my commitment to lead a healthy lifestyle, I was now facing a life-altering surgery.

Hearing that my cancer had progressed to stage four in three months due to wrestling with what my exorbitantly priced insurance company would cover felt like a crushing blow. Until now, I had never undergone anything more invasive than a routine dental checkup, and the thought of being sedated, vulnerable, and unconscious filled me with dread. I was overwhelmed—seven surgical teams, eight hours (original approximation), turned into over twelve hours in the operating room, and a recovery that hovered on the horizon like an uncharted path. The fear that I might not wake up or that this could be the beginning of a long, grueling fight for my life was, to say the least, paralyzing.

In that moment of despair, I sought solace in the hospital chapel. I sank to my knees on the cool tiles, feeling the weight of my fears as I poured out my heart in prayer, tears streaming down my face. The pain was palpable, a deep ache that wrapped around my soul. I cried not just for myself, but for the life I had fought to maintain, now hanging by a delicate thread. I'm not sharing this to elicit your sympathy, but I do want you to feel the intensity of what a void that only compassion and empathy can fill felt like for me. I also want you to understand the fear and vulnerability that enveloped me—a poignant reminder of how fragile life truly is. Above all, I want you to remember that, no matter how strong you, your patients, or your team members are, we are all vulnerable to the ups and downs of life.

DIVINE INTERVENTION MEETS SELF-COMPASSION AND SELF-EMPATHY

By default, I didn't turn to people first. I looked deeper within. My long walks in the park became intently focused on conversing with the two entities that most impacted my life. One was me and the other was the source of our creation, which I call God.

On one of my more difficult days, I was at the park walking and praying about my struggle with this cancer diagnosis. To make matters more interesting, I had just finished doing a live broadcast on one of my social media platforms, which regularly received over half a million engagements every twenty to thirty days.

During the broadcast, I proclaimed that I knew God was allowing me to have this experience *for a reason.* I passionately told my audience and myself that the reason I was going through this was because it was meant to teach me something about true transcendence and the greater part of myself. I boasted how strong my faith was and how I knew that no weapon formed against me, including this cancer, would prosper. But, truth be told, when nobody was looking, I had more than my fair share of moments weighed down by fear, sadness, disdain, and inner turmoil.

Right after I finished the live broadcast, I remember having these contradictory feelings. I was a living example of cognitive dissonance. On the one hand, I meant everything I said. On the other hand, a part of me was terrified of the unknown. I had never undergone an operation, let alone been diagnosed with a disease that had a significant chance of ending my life.

Between the fear of dying during a long, complicated surgery and the chance that even if the surgery succeeds, this disease could come back and possibly cause my premature death, it's no surprise that I was plagued with doubt and hopelessness.

That's when I realized the importance of being empathetic and compassionate toward myself and others. It sounds simple, doesn't it?

Trust me, it's anything but.

EMBRACING EMPATHY

If somebody had told me I would be writing a book about empathy, I would have assumed they'd lost their damn mind. I'm no Mr. Congeniality. Although I possess compassion, a kind heart, reasonable emotional intelligence, and good self-awareness, I was never aware that empathy and self-compassion were essential tools for my survival. I always thought of those things as aspects of one's character or persona. Never did I consider them to be tools or cognitive strategies, or, in my case, weapons that I would someday use to fight depression and anxiety.

Before my epiphany, I believed that empathy was a performative act. It was a tactic employed by people who desired acceptance or likability from others. Likewise, I thought compassion was something you gave to other people, not something you needed for your own sanity and survival. That's until I started digging deeper.

It was in a pivotal moment of reflection that I began to embrace empathy, not just toward others but also toward myself. For a long time, I had viewed compassion as a luxury reserved for others, believing that to be kind to myself was a sign of fragility. However, as I migrated further into my cancer journey, I realized that this mindset was not only limiting but counterproductive. Recognizing that self-compassion is, in fact, a profound strength, opened my eyes to the importance of vulnerability in my growth and especially in my recovery.

Now, more than halfway through my cancer journey, I uncovered the profound power of empathy and its role in enhancing our healing experiences. This realization ignited a determination in me to confront my diagnosis head-on. I learned that embracing empathy and compassion for both myself and others is vital for navigating one's emotional landscape.

In my many moments of uncertainty, I recognized that true emotional intelligence involves fostering meaningful connections with what's going on within oneself and being mindfully present for others' challenges. This deeper appreciation transformed my self-perception and opened new avenues for healing.

Empathy became a guiding light, reminding me I was never alone in my struggles. By sharing my story with fellow warriors, I drew strength from our shared experiences, nurturing my emotional well-being and enriching my overall health.

Through this journey, I discovered that to truly empathize is to connect with our humanity. It highlighted the importance of community and support, empowering me to face the unique challenges of cancer. Embracing self-empathy and self-compassion allowed me to transform my fears into actionable steps toward healing and renewed hope. When externalizing this to others, together, we uplift each other, celebrating resilience and the remarkable journey of healing.

As I embraced this new understanding, I found that my capacity for empathy expanded, enriching not only my interactions with others but also my relationship with myself. This growth allowed me to let go of the notion that being vulnerable was synonymous with weakness. Instead, I began to see vulnerability as an essential component of genuine self-acceptance and emotional resilience. With this evolving perspective, I fostered a deeper connection to both myself and those around me, leading to a more compassionate and fulfilling life.

Once I began considering the relevance of empathy, I quickly discovered that it's one of the most critical skills demonstrated by influential leaders, diplomats, and hostage negotiators. It's consistently used by people who masterfully control high-tension, dangerous, and problematic situations and circumstances where failure is not an acceptable outcome.

I learned the same was true about compassion. My deeply embedded view of compassion was that it was something we gave to others. I never saw it as a clinically proven process that could produce transformational, lifelong results.

EMPATHY COMBINED WITH COMPASSION: THE LETHAL PUNCH

Only in recent years did I realize that empathy, combined with compassion, possesses the same power as a lethal punch from the most highly skilled mixed martial artist. Contrarily, I surely didn't realize the consequences that can result from misuse. A lack of empathy isn't just a mere blind spot or oversight. Mismanaged empathy is the equivalent of handing a samurai sword or a loaded high-caliber assault weapon to a sloppy drunk. It's going to cost you. More than likely, you will seriously regret the price you'll pay for being either careless or self-serving.

Empathy is a powerful tool, but it is often overlooked or misused. In the hands of intelligence agencies, elected officials, and crisis negotiators, it can become a weapon hidden in plain sight. This manipulation turns empathy from a means of connection into a tool of control.

By the time you recognize that you are being influenced, your thoughts, emotions, and environment are shaped by others, the decision has already been made. You find yourself in a precarious position, trapped in a checkmate where your vulnerability has already been exploited.

This dynamic is evident in the political landscape, where a significant percentage of Americans is always susceptible to manipulation. Politicians skillfully craft messages that make the less informed feel seen, validated, and safe. Yet, beneath this façade lies a troubling truth: these leaders exploit people's fears and vulnerabilities, cleverly activating vulnerable emotional triggers to achieve their own ends. This is a cautionary tale of how empathy can be wielded in ways that undermine genuine connection and understanding.

I understand that the examples I just used may seem assertive, but when used ethically and accurately, empathy can be a tool for positive and measurable change. When combined with compassion, it can help you develop a kind, nurturing inner voice that encourages healthy behaviors that can significantly increase your cognitive capacity.

Empathy and self-compassion foster emotional resilience, alleviate suffering, and promote psychological growth. There is an immeasurable competence that results from harnessing the "power of intention" to be more self-aware and emotionally vulnerable.

Taking this a step further, a plethora of evidence- and research-based content validates how the appropriate and well-applied use of compassion and empathy can have measurable effects on psychopathology. The presence or absence of empathy significantly impacts all stages of human development and behavior, not to mention well-being and even neurochemistry. That's right. This often-overlooked character trait is so much more than what it appears to be. It's a finely honed skill.

I was so impressed with the potential of its use that I was compelled to write this book.

When used appropriately, empathy can catalyze measurable and lasting change when used with skill and deliberate intention. When deployed in the most stressful of circumstances, empathy can change how you're perceived and how you interact and relate to others. As you master using it on yourself, it also becomes an unlimited source for increased self-efficacy and self-evolution.

I'm proof of this hypothesis. Empathy got me through one of the most critical seasons of my life. Self-empathy was the main source material for my healing and continued evolution.

So, what is empathy, and how can *you* use it to improve every area of your life, as well as the lives of those around you?

Get ready, because we're going to cover a lot in the next ten chapters.

Chapter One

WHAT EMPATHY IS AND ISN'T

LIFE HAS A WAY OF humbling you. In the last few years, I've been forced to confront betrayal, disappointment, and even myself in ways that stripped me down to the core. Those experiences showed me that real leadership doesn't come from titles or strategy; it comes from leading from the heart. Leading from the heart requires something most of us avoid until crisis makes it unavoidable: self-empathy and self-compassion. That's what this book is about.

This is not another motivational pep talk; it's an essential guide to facing yourself honestly, so you can stop sabotaging your relationships, your work, and your well-being. If you've ever wondered, "Why me?" in the middle of your struggles, I want you to know this—those struggles aren't proof that you're broken. They're the raw material for growth, and together we're going to forge them into strength.

When we mistakenly think that we're alone and unique in our struggles, we tend to get stuck in a cycle of self-pity. The two things we need the most during these times are empathy and compassion.

Some of the toughest lessons I've recently learned are ones I didn't ask for and certainly didn't want to learn from firsthand experience. However, they ended up bringing me the greatest awareness and growth.

It's not an accident that you're reading this book right now. You've probably asked yourself, "Why me?" I know I have. These last few years have taught me lessons about betrayal, disappointment, self-sabotage, being taken advantage of, and experiencing losses when I expected gains. These experiences are not what anyone, including myself, wants to go through at any point in life. Yet the experiences we least desire are the same ones that increase our tenacity, resiliency, and self-awareness, and, most importantly, put us on the path toward self-actualization.

If you're like me, odds are you've been betrayed by people you trust, love, and depend on. However, the person who has betrayed you the most is actually the one who looks back at you in the mirror—*you*!

I've learned something about myself: I can be tough on other people, but I'm even tougher on me. Maybe that sounds familiar to you. When we don't see ourselves clearly, we end up fighting battles we don't need to fight, and sometimes, we block the very opportunities meant for us. Now, if you believe in a higher power, you might call those opportunities blessings; if you don't, think of them as the good things life already has in store. Either way, this isn't a religious book. It's about something bigger—how self-reflection and awareness can become your sharpest tools for building stability in your health, your wealth, and your relationships. Add in self-compassion and accurate empathy, and you gain the power to stop sabotaging yourself and start unlocking your full potential—whether you're leading a team, building a brand, or just trying to strengthen the relationships that matter most.

Self-compassion and empathy aren't just nice ideas you toss around in a classroom or on social media; they're game-changers.

Think of them as the hidden gears that keep your life running smoothly. Without them, it's easy to get stuck in cycles of self-sabotage: snapping at people you care about, blowing up opportunities, or running yourself into the ground. However, when you actually practice them, they flip the script. Suddenly, conflicts that would have wrecked a relationship can turn into moments of deeper trust. Business conversations that were headed for disaster can find common ground. Perhaps most importantly, you stop carrying stress as if it were a permanent weight on your back. Self-compassion and empathy don't make you soft—they make you strong enough to face life without destroying yourself in the process.

Imagine navigating your interactions with a deep understanding and kindness toward yourself and others. This approach not only fosters healthier relationships but also cultivates an environment that enables growth and progress. In business, empathy allows you to connect with others on a deeper level and facilitate agreements that might otherwise seem impossible.

Moreover, self-compassion acts as a shield against the relentless pressures of life, enabling you to maintain resilience and clarity even in the most challenging circumstances. By nurturing these qualities within yourself, you create a foundation for a more fulfilling and balanced life. Embrace their power and let them guide you toward a future shaped by intentionality and profound connection.

To truly grasp the intricacies of others and navigate your life with purpose, you must first embark on a profound journey of self-discovery. Many of us wander through life with a distorted lens, unable to see ourselves clearly or objectively. This lack of self-awareness often leads to a failure to cultivate genuine respect and love for ourselves in a way that fosters growth and fulfillment.

Without this essential knowledge, we risk living in a perpetual cycle of misunderstanding and disconnection—both from ourselves and those around us. We may find that we're reacting to situations based on fear or insecurity, rather than authenticity, which can result in strained relationships and missed opportunities for meaningful connection. The consequences can be profound: a life marked by regret, unfulfilled potential, and a deep sense of dissatisfaction.

Conversely, the potential that lies in embracing self-awareness is transformative. By confronting our inner truths, we unlock the ability to engage deeply with others and foster relationships built on empathy and understanding.

Reflect on this: understanding yourself is not just a prerequisite; it is a fundamental act of courage that lays the groundwork for a life lived with intention. The choice is yours. Will you delve into the depths of your being, or will you continue to drift in the shadows of an unexamined existence?

FACT: If you lack self-compassion and empathy for yourself, life becomes much harder to navigate and can turn lonelier and more miserable than necessary. In summary, this first chapter focuses on gaining clarity about yourself.

KNOWING AND UNDERSTANDING YOURSELF

Before we begin, I would like you to grab a pen and a piece of paper. That's right, this is one of *those* books.

We're going to dive deep. You can't truly understand yourself unless you embrace introspection and examine all the ways you've contributed to your painful outcomes, whether in harmful or less-than-desirable ways.

It's critical that we begin this process objectively. You may believe you have a clear understanding of yourself and others. I'll let me be the first to tell you, as a clinician with over twenty years of experience, that we often see ourselves in a distorted or even false way. Depending on what has happened in your life, your perspective may be biased at best or, worse, damaged and delusional.

Let's get into it.

1. How old are you? Which generation were you born into? (Baby boomer, Gen X, and so on)
2. What is your gender? Race? Nationality?
3. What's your current socioeconomic status compared to what you were born into? How did your socioeconomic status influence how you were viewed in society as a child, and how does it continue to affect the way you live today?

These are some of the core filters through which we interpret and experience life. In this chapter and the next, we'll explore how these factors shape the way you see yourself, others, and the world around you.

In fact, even these basic demographics play a powerful role in shaping how you think, feel, and show up in everyday life.

The following details we need to dive into are your actual life experiences.

4. What kind of environment influenced you from birth through adolescence? What was going on in your home, community, and among the people around you? How do you notice the imprint of the past showing up in the way you think, act, and relate to others today?

There's a reason I'm asking you these questions. While your experiences are unique, certain patterns in how you think and act will probably emerge based on parts of your childhood and teenage years.

Did you have a single parent, or were your parents together? Was your home life loving, dysfunctional, or inconsistent?

During the early years of our lives, our parents and guardians act as our role models for behavior. However, this doesn't necessarily mean they are great examples of functional behavior. Adolescents are especially vulnerable to parental influence, or the lack thereof, particularly between the ages of twelve and fifteen.

Your role in the family doesn't disappear once you grow up. It subtly shapes how you present yourself in adult relationships, both romantic and otherwise.

You've probably heard of "only-child syndrome." Perhaps you recognize it in yourself as well. The youngest is often seen as the baby who gets away with everything, while the middle child is remembered as the one who always got overlooked. If you have siblings, ask yourself: were you the oldest, the youngest, or somewhere in between? If you were the firstborn, especially with several younger siblings, you may not have had much of a childhood at all. Instead of being cared for, you may have been drafted into the role of caretaker long before you were ready.

YOUR SOCIOECONOMIC BACKGROUND

What about your socioeconomic background? Did your family move often, chasing stability, or did you grow up surrounded by abundance and certainty? These early conditions do more than set the stage for childhood. They subtly shape how you perceive yourself, how you interact with others, and even how you navigate success or struggle today.

If you grew up in a home where turning on the lights and opening a full fridge were never in question, you likely escaped the weight of a scarcity mindset. However, for many people, scarcity leaves lasting impressions that never fully fade. Even when life improves, there's often a lingering anxiety, an instinct to brace for the rug to be pulled out from under you, even when you're standing on solid ground.

On the other hand, if you were raised in affluence, privilege brings its own blind spots. Comfort can create a cushion so soft that you miss the hard edges others live with daily. It's easy to take consistency for granted or undervalue the small, everyday things, such as stability, loyalty, or even the simple ability to rest without worry. Without realizing it, abundance can dull your appreciation for resilience in others, or blind you to the quiet strength it takes just to survive when resources are scarce.

Both paths shape the stories we tell ourselves. Scarcity can breed grit, but it can also breed fear. Privilege can foster confidence, but it can also lead to complacency. The question isn't just where you start—it's how is that start still echoing through your choices, your relationships, and the way you measure success today?

How did your parents or caregivers interact with you?

Did your parents affirm and praise you, or did you find yourself begging for affection until you finally gave up? Were they balanced, firm but fair, holding you accountable without being overly strict? Or perhaps you were left to fend for yourself, overlooked in the chaos of daily survival. Some children get lost in the shuffle because their parents had more month than money, or simply weren't ready to be parents in the first place—and it showed. The harsh truth is this: just because you had both a mom and a dad in the house doesn't mean you had good parents.

The way your caregivers show up for you—whether consistently, inconsistently, or absent—sets the stage for how you develop autonomy, resilience, and self-efficacy. A child who is affirmed learns that effort leads to reward, which builds confidence and the ability to trust themselves. A child who is ignored or dismissed often learns the opposite—that their needs don't matter or that relying on others is unsafe. That lesson can carry over into adulthood as people-pleasing, low confidence, or self-sabotage.

Strict but supportive parents often raise children with resilience: kids who learn to take responsibility, bounce back from failure, and persist under pressure. Parents who were harsh without warmth may have bred compliance without confidence, producing adults who struggle to take initiative, avoid risk, or doubt their own competence.

Meanwhile, those who grew up neglected may have developed autonomy by necessity, but it often came with a heavy cost: anxiety, hyper-independence, and difficulty trusting others.

Every environment leaves its fingerprints. Whether those marks built your confidence or fractured it, the effect is real. The question now is whether you're still living under those old patterns—or whether you're willing to rewrite the script and build the resilience and self-efficacy your parents couldn't give you.

Your home life isn't where the formation of your beliefs and behaviors ends.

5. How was your environment outside of your home?

Were you ever made to feel like an outsider? Maybe you were the token Black kid in an all-white school, carrying the weight of representing an entire race in every classroom interaction. Perhaps you were taunted for your sexual or gender identity, shamed for simply being who you were. Maybe your family didn't look like the families around you, and that difference became a spotlight you never asked for.

On the flip side, maybe you weren't mocked—you were isolated. Raised in a bubble where your worldview was filtered through the narrow lens of whatever media your household consumed, whether CNN, Fox News, or another one-sided narrative. That kind of environment can leave you believing you've seen the whole picture when, in reality, you've only been shown one angle.

The truth is, each of us has been influenced by stereotypes and expectations. Some of these stick to us like labels we never chose; others become invisible barriers that quietly restrict our thinking. Here's the good news: you don't have to accept them as your reality. You can question them, challenge them, and rewrite the story. That's the purpose of this book—to question the lenses you've been given, so you can take full responsibility for who you are and, more importantly, who you want to become.

So, take some time to write your answers down, because we're going to look at how *all* these experiences shaped you and your perceptions, filters, expectations, and beliefs. As my son used to say in his three-year-old voice, "It's going to get gooder and gooder from here."

If you'd like professional support and are ready to invest in yourself while exploring your origins, contact my office at info@drdivanyoung.com to schedule an appointment.

THE RELATIONSHIP BETWEEN EMPATHY AND YOUR EXPERIENCES

Every claim and piece of advice in this book is meant for you to analyze and determine if it's relevant to you or someone you deeply care about. Whatever your situation, I'm simply presenting facts, offering explanations, and recommending solutions in the hopes that you will revisit your preconceived notions about yourself, your circumstances, and others. Your success with developing self-compassion and wielding empathy will come from humbling yourself while doing deep introspective work.

GENERATIONAL BEHAVIOR AND EMPATHY

Later, we'll discuss the link between your experiences and your ability to empathize. However, I also want to touch on a few key ideas in this chapter, as the potential for impact is enormous.

Let's explore how different generations approach parenting as an example.

The "gentle parenting" approach has garnered considerable attention in recent years. I won't go into too much detail here, but this is an important topic because empathy is one of the key drivers behind this parenting approach.

Let me be clear: I am not advocating for or against this parenting style. Every child is different, with varying emotional and physical needs. Gentle parenting may work well for one child, but a modified approach might be better for another. As with any other parenting approach, there are advantages and disadvantages. However, empathy is one component of gentle parenting that I fully advocate for.

I come from a generation of parents who believed physical discipline was the best way to teach respect and accountability. Did this approach teach us anything about ourselves and how to express our feelings properly? Maybe, maybe not.

Alternatively, the gentle parenting approach is centered on empathy and understanding to teach children self-awareness and emotional regulation. It's a complicated topic, but there's a balance to be had in teaching your children respect and consequences, as well as empathy and compassion.

While this book isn't about parenting, compassion and empathy are crucial in building strong relationships with everyone, including your children. If you weren't shown empathy as a child, you probably have a lot of work to do to unlearn certain limiting beliefs and patterns of behavior.

EMPATHY AND YOUR HOME LIFE

Throughout your childhood, your relationship with self-compassion and empathy is greatly shaped by two factors:

1. How your parents, caregivers, or family members treated you.
2. How they interacted with and treated other people.

We've seen the impact of chaotic relationships with parents or guardians time and time again.

Children exposed to a turbulent, unempathetic relationship between their parents may struggle with communication and empathy in their own adult relationships. This experience can lead them to feel unworthy of empathy, since they never witnessed healthy self-care or respect. They may have seen one parent tolerate mistreatment from the other. Consider how your parents or caregivers coped with their challenges—did they turn to drugs, alcohol, religion, work, unhealthy relationships, or self-degradation?

Of course, it doesn't always happen the same way for everyone. Familial relationships aren't the only influence on our ability to recognize and demonstrate empathy.

Even if you have a decent track record with empathy, that doesn't mean you don't have to be intentional. Our habits and old patterns have a way of sneaking up on us when we get too comfortable. Therefore, self-evolution requires a steadfast commitment to wielding empathy and self-compassion with intention.

HOW YOUR GENDER MIGHT INFLUENCE YOUR ABILITY TO EMPATHIZE

In this section, we'll be talking about individuals who are born male or female.

There appears to be differences in how men and women develop empathy across cultures and generations. This goes deeper than stereotypes. Women are typically expected to be more empathetic, compassionate, and emotional, while men are expected to be more logical and less emotionally driven.

It's crucial to recognize that stereotypes can be harmful to both men and women. Men are not emotionless, and women are not devoid of logic. Bias is detrimental. Ultimately, two things can happen. You may miss out on the positive contributions someone could bring to your life, or you may hinder your own growth by allowing biases to obstruct your progress. It is essential to remain open-minded, as you never know who might offer answers and solutions to challenges you weren't even aware of.

That being said, when it comes to compassion and empathy, there are some fascinating gender-related differences to consider. I'm sharing this with you for one reason: I want you to consider these ideas as you work to gain more clarity and self-empathy.

Meta-analyses of decades of research indicate that women are generally more accurate than men in decoding emotional expressions across face, body, and voice, a pattern closely tied to empathy-related brain and emotional intelligence processes (Hall and Goh, 2025). In one study, men were more accurate in detecting happy body language, while women were more easily able to recognize angry and neutral body language (Sokolov et al., 2011). Although other studies show no difference when accounting for gender, I encourage you to consider how your nature, gendered experiences, and the way you were raised based on your gender contribute to your views toward yourself and others, inasmuch as these instincts are more primal in nature and are more a matter of brain function and hard wiring.

Body language recognition is only one small aspect of empathy. On its own, it doesn't reveal a significant difference in the development and exercise of empathy between the two genders. Anyone can show empathy, but on average, women tend to engage in more altruistic behaviors, such as donating or volunteering. Men also engage in prosocial behaviors, but their motivations tend to differ. Along the same note, often women are more motivated by empathy, while men are more motivated by social norms and expectations. Again, these are only a few studies, and everyone is capable of accurate empathy. I'm not giving you an excuse if you aren't empathetic. I encourage you to examine how your gender expectations and experiences influence your relationship with empathy.

THE INFLUENCE OF RACE AND NATIONALITY

There are several reasons our deep dive into empathy involves considering the impact of race and nationality on your relationship with yourself and how you connect with others.

Let's pause on something that often gets overlooked—the intersection of race and empathy.

Racism and discrimination don't just wound the body; they also reshape the heart. Experiencing them can distort how you empathize with others, sometimes dulling your ability to connect with people who share your race, and at other times hardening you against those who don't.

The absence of empathy in how you were treated can quietly bleed into how you see yourself, how you interpret your own worth, and whether you can extend compassion inward.

I've seen this up close. Within my own community, I've watched the wounds of systemic oppression harden into self-hatred—people absorbing the hostility of the outside world and turning it inward.

Racism and marginalization don't just divide groups. It quietly separates people from their own sense of identity.

The relationship between race and empathy is rarely simple. Prejudice is brutal, without question. Yet the very pain it causes can awaken something deeper. For some, suffering leads to isolation. For others, it becomes a doorway to compassion and unity.

So the real question is this: when injustice touches your life, will it close your heart—or will it open it wide enough to change not only you, but the world around you?

THE EXTERNAL FORCES PUSHING YOU TOWARD OR PULLING YOU AWAY FROM EMPATHY

Of course, we know that empathy and compassion aren't black and white. Many people grew up with the odds against them and still emerged as kind individuals. They were never shown empathy as children, yet they're now able to treat other people with respect and compassion. However, that doesn't mean their circumstances won't affect their relationships with themselves and others.

Conversely, some people never receive kindness and appreciation, so they don't treat others kindly. Some individuals bully others because they were bullied. Their bullying isn't always overt.

As we discussed, you have several examples of how to behave. You pick up on these cues whether you're directly involved or not. Your mother or father might have had a negative self-view. Maybe they talked badly about themselves in front of you. The simple act of observing their behaviors and words gets absorbed into your subconscious, whether you like it or not.

So, how do you make the shift from being a victim of your circumstances to taking responsibility for your life and who you become? How do you take responsibility while also treating yourself and others with compassion and empathy?

We're going to go over all of that.

First, we will address one of the main issues in trying to show empathy: confusing it with sympathy.

THE DIFFERENCE BETWEEN EMPATHY AND SYMPATHY

We often get empathy wrong. We confuse it with sympathy, pity, or compassion. It's not as simple as sending a "get well soon" card to a friend or encouraging your employees to take their PTO. If it were that easy, friends would stay friends, nobody would ever break up, and leaders wouldn't have any unhappy employees.

I believe empathy is about being aware of the "significance of the moment." The impact can be transformational, whether you're applying this awareness to yourself or others. It can change relational outcomes, whether you're engaging with your children, supporting a friend going through a difficult time, managing an angry customer, or simply reassuring yourself. Empathy might not alter what's in front of you, but it *will* greatly influence how you handle it. The most impactful outcome of using empathy correctly is that it can change how whatever you're dealing with affects you.

Compassion and sympathy are components of empathy, but empathy is more than simply being aware of how a person feels or being kind to them. It goes beyond feeling sorry for someone.

Empathy is feeling *with* someone. It's the ability to sense, feel, and understand the emotions, thoughts, and experiences of others. Empathy is what bridges the gap between acquaintances and true friends, failed relationships and healthy, lasting unions, and being stuck and realizing your potential. It's a skill that requires a lot of effort to effectively harness and utilize in various circumstances.

It's nearly impossible to put empathy into practice if you don't have any empathy for yourself. I'm not saying you can't be a caring, kind, and helpful person if you don't empathize with yourself. There are plenty of people who prioritize the well-being of others, often sacrificing their own well-being to make sure others have what they want and need because it gives them a purpose. While it's noble to take care of others, showing yourself empathy is the best thing you can do if you truly want to make a difference in your own life, let alone others.

Why is this?

Giving others empathy without ever giving yourself any often leads to resentment and a lack of fulfillment.

This book will help you learn to show yourself empathy so you can extend it to others at home, work, and everywhere else.

Once empathy becomes an intentional practice in your everyday life, you'll notice a shift in the way you think and behave. You'll likely feel happier, more fulfilled, and more capable than ever before. Most people around you will too.

The next five chapters will help you figure out how to implement empathy to achieve your goals, whether you're:

- A leader who's trying to lead more effectively
- A partner who's trying to better themselves and improve their relationship
- Someone who wishes to reconcile with a loved one
- A person who wants to be accountable and in control of their life and happiness

THE THREE MAIN TYPES OF EMPATHY

To wield empathy properly, it's helpful to be aware of the different types. You might be improperly practicing one or more of these without knowing the potential pitfalls for you and others.

The three types of empathy, established by psychologists Daniel Goleman and Paul Ekman, include:

- Cognitive empathy
- Emotional empathy
- Compassionate empathy

Cognitive empathy is the ability to understand another person's perspective and comprehend their emotions. This type of empathy can be used to communicate more effectively with those who are close to you, as well as with those who are not part of your immediate circle, such as your employees.

However, you can fall short of accurate empathy with this type if you don't internalize the other person's emotions. However, empathizing with others' emotions also carries risks.

Emotional empathy is the ability to tune into and share the feelings of another person. While this helps you connect emotionally with others, it can also cause exhaustion or burnout if you're not careful. We often see the negative effects of this type of empathy in "helping" professions, such as medicine, nursing, psychological practice, and coaching.

Finally, compassionate empathy is focused on understanding someone's situation and feeling with them, but it goes beyond that. This type emphasizes taking action and offering help where you can. This is where you want to be, because this type is holistic and rooted in emotional intelligence, allowing you to share others' emotions without taking them on as your own.

EMPATHY AT PLAY IN THE REAL WORLD

Let's look at the advantages and disadvantages of all three types of empathy with some real-world examples. Of course, there are many more potential pros and cons for you and the people with whom you care about and must interact with, but I hope these will help you start to understand how different empathetic approaches can affect all involved.

1. An employee comes to you and tells you they're experiencing personal issues that are starting to affect their work.

A possible cognitive empathy approach involves expressing concern for your employee. You give them some time to talk more about what they're going through and thank them for sharing their concerns with you. You offer a few words of support, and that's the end of the conversation.

Pros: You've shown that you care about them and that you're appreciative of them confiding in you. They might feel better because they were able to get it off their chest.

Cons: They might not feel supported entirely because you didn't offer any potential solutions or assistance. Your employee might feel like that's the end of it, and they can't bring it up again because it's their problem and you're already aware of it.

Possible emotional empathy approach: You do all of the above, but you also take the time to try to relate to them with one of your own experiences. You tell them they can talk to you at any point if they feel like their situation is becoming more difficult.

Pros: You've connected with them on a deeper level, and they likely feel comfortable talking to you again in the future. You can make sure they're doing okay by keeping the lines of communication open.

Cons: If you've gone through something similar, you might internalize their experience, which could lead to emotional burnout for you.

A possible compassionate empathy approach involves demonstrating a mix of cognitive and emotional empathy, while also offering help. You suggest they take some time off (or consider it if things worsen). You could check in with them daily to see how they are. Depending on your existing relationship with them, you may want to take a more personal approach, such as bringing them a home-cooked meal or spending time with them outside of work.

Pros: They likely feel supported and that they're able to talk to you again if they experience further issues. You can stay up to date with their professional progress and offer extra support when needed. You're fostering a work culture based on empathy, compassion, and good communication.

Cons: Maintaining professional boundaries may be challenging in the future. If you have a personal relationship with them outside of work, it may be challenging to strike a balance between being their supervisor and their friend. Other employees may feel as if they're treated differently.

2. Your friend confides in you about their struggle to start a family with their partner.

Possible cognitive empathy approach: You try to console them. You validate their feelings and let them know you're there for them.

Pros: They likely appreciate your kind words and expression of support. They may feel like they can talk to you because you didn't immediately offer solutions, and they were simply looking for a compassionate ear.

Cons: You're connecting with them and their feelings mainly on a superficial level.

Possible emotional empathy approach: You listen to them and ask what they need from you. You try to relate to their experience, even if you haven't gone through something similar. This may seem like validating their feelings or discussing someone close to you who has gone through a similar struggle.

Pros: They feel like you understand them and want to help. You've created a safe space for them to share their feelings, both positive and negative.

Cons: They may want to vent without hearing about your experience or someone else's experience. Asking what they need from you might overwhelm them further.

A possible compassionate empathy approach is to validate their feelings and emphasize that they can talk to you anytime. You ask them if they would prefer you simply listen or give advice. You relate to their feelings and experiences, even if you don't know exactly what they're going through. You actively check in on them.

Pros: They know they can count on you if they need to get their feelings out in the open. They feel supported and like they can tell you anything. You checking in takes the pressure off them, so they don't feel like a burden.

Cons: If you've experienced something similar and take a compassionate empathy approach, you might project feelings and advice based on your experience onto them. Even if you haven't gone through the same thing, but they're a close friend, you might feel like it's your responsibility to make them feel better and neglect your mental health and the feelings that are coming up for you.

3. Your child is being bullied at school and is experiencing mental health problems as a result.

Possible cognitive empathy approach: You let your child vent to you and tell them that you're there for them, but you don't take the conversation further. Maybe you believe it's a normal part of being a kid. You encourage them to resolve the situation on their own.

Pros: Your child might have their own ideas on how to handle the situation, and you're giving them a chance to solve their problem. They may want you to simply listen and not offer solutions.

Cons: Your child is in a vulnerable position, and they're still learning how to handle conflict. In this situation, it may be best for you to actively assist them in resolving the issue. If their mental health is suffering, the problem is already too serious to ignore.

Possible emotional empathy approach: Once you're aware of the situation, you let your child know you're there for them. You validate their feelings and let them know that bullying is never okay. You say you'll have their back no matter what.

Pros: They'll know you care, and they're justified in feeling this way. You're giving them a chance to resolve the problem, knowing they have your full support.

Cons: As a parent, this situation might require you to intervene. Since they're experiencing mental health issues, they need support *now*, possibly even professional support.

Possible compassionate empathy approach: You talk to your child and encourage them to come to you in the future. You offer solutions based on your knowledge of the situation and possibly your experiences.

Pros: Maintaining open lines of communication with your child is essential for a healthy relationship with them. They likely feel supported by you, and they'll talk to you as they experience other challenges.

Cons: Based on your own experiences, you might be projecting your feelings onto them. There's also a chance that your idea of how they should handle it might not be the best way. It's probably a good idea to talk to the teachers or principal at your child's school before the situation escalates further.

4. Your coaching or therapy client has a mental breakdown during your session together.

Possible cognitive empathy approach: As a clinician or coach, you understand the importance of validating the client's feelings. If you're experienced, understanding how and why your client might be feeling this way is not only crucial to their progress, but second nature to you in your line of work.

Pros: You're able to remain calm and objective, providing your client with a clear, bird's-eye view of their situation.

Cons: The coachee may not feel as if you're invested in them and their progress. Of course, you're not responsible for others' feelings, but you do have a duty as a leader, coach, clinician, or mental health professional to demonstrate empathy and connect with those in your care.

Possible emotional empathy approach: You encourage them to explore why they feel the way they do. You ask the person in your care questions and try to get to the root of their struggles. You validate their feelings first.

Pros: You're truly interested in understanding them and where they're coming from in the first place.

Cons: You could get burned out or struggle with feelings that bubble up due to your past experiences. You might not be able to distance yourself in a way that allows you to see the best path forward for your client clearly. You may have had similar experiences like this one, and odds are, many of your other clients have too. Given that, you may take on their feelings and have a hard time viewing their situation objectively.

A possible compassionate empathy approach involves asking the person you're supporting questions and offering them support.

You try to get them to a place where they see their situation more clearly. You encourage them to slow down, check in with their feelings, and talk it through. Before they leave, you come up with some methods to help them be proactive if they feel this way in the future.

Pros: The person seeking help feels supported and like they're able to solve problems on their own, which is the goal of your sessions together. They likely know you care about them and want them to succeed.

Cons: You must be careful not to cross the professional boundary when interacting with your clients. It's also imperative to make sure your personal feelings aren't impairing your judgment. Checking in with yourself after working with clients is essential to make sure you're emotionally stable and able to remain objective.

All these examples demonstrate the power of empathy when utilized in different situations.

Accurate, compassionate empathy can help you deepen your personal and professional relationships. It can also increase your efficacy as a leader or professional. However, it's critical to set boundaries and have self-awareness so you can prevent burnout.

SETTING BOUNDARIES WITH COMPASSIONATE EMPATHY

All these empathy approaches involve setting boundaries. If you can master compassionate empathy, you'll be able to connect with others on a deeper level without endangering your well-being, professional integrity, and health.

Here are some simple habits that will help you maintain boundaries with empathy in both your personal and professional life.

1. Check in with yourself.

You'll see this advice throughout this book. You can't perform well in a personal or professional capacity if you don't know what's going on with yourself and your biases, limiting beliefs, and feelings.

2. Do a relationship audit.

Some relationships are simply not healthy or beneficial for you. Some people will take advantage of your empathy, either intentionally or unintentionally. If there are people in your life who don't want to be helped or want to exploit you for your compassion, do yourself (and them) a favor and let them go.

3. Acknowledge your limits.

Sometimes we can't give someone else our full attention or empathize with them in the way they need. It's okay to step away for a while and take the time you need to recharge. Then, you can revisit the relationship or situation when you feel emotionally ready.

I'll acknowledge that there are times when we're struggling, but we need to be there for the people in our lives. If someone needs you and you're in a vulnerable spot, you can still be there for them *and* take care of yourself. Ensure you have the support *you* need, even if it's in the form of professional help. If you and your partner, friend, or family member are leaning on each other, make sure you're not codependent. Remember: Misery loves company.

MAIN TAKEAWAYS FROM THIS CHAPTER

⇒ While your experiences and circumstances are unique to you, you're not alone in what you're feeling.

Don't make the mistake of assuming that you're alone in this world. This often leads to a victim mentality or an inflated sense of self.

Each one of us is important, but the world doesn't revolve around any one individual.

Some of us need to focus less on ourselves and more on others. For some, the opposite is true. There must be a balance between showing ourselves empathy and extending that empathy to others. The saying "You can't pour from an empty cup" is applicable here.

⇒ You can be kind and compassionate toward others without understanding and loving yourself, but self-empathy is crucial for accurate empathy.

True empathy becomes possible when you understand who you are and all the factors that contribute to your identity, beliefs, and behaviors. Your experiences have a huge impact on how you view yourself and others, as well as how you behave and respond to events in your life. Once you're aware of this, you gain more control over the way you treat yourself and how you interact with others.

⇒ There are significant differences between empathy, sympathy, and compassion.

Empathy includes sympathy and compassion, but it also involves understanding others' emotions and feeling *with* them. Empathy is a skill that requires deliberate action and practice.

⇒ When done correctly, empathy can improve your life, as well as the lives of those around you.

Empathy is becoming a more popular topic, with many personal development materials focusing on its importance. There's a good reason for this. Empathy contributes to positive change.

It's essential to your happiness, success, and the greater good.

⇒ There's more than one type of empathy.

It's essential to be aware of the advantages and disadvantages of each. When done right, empathy should not:

- Burn you out
- Make you feel resentful
- Be shown at the expense of your health or happiness

You must show empathy to yourself *and* others. That's when true growth is possible for all involved.

Chapter Two

THE DANGERS OF EMPATHY

IN THE PREVIOUS CHAPTER, we explored the potential consequences of misusing empathy. However, we need to dig deeper to truly understand the detrimental effects of a lack or misuse of empathy before discussing how to overcome our challenges with empathy.

Does the knowledge that empathy can be dangerous challenge your perception? It certainly clashed with mine. It's jarring when you've been told to put yourself in others' shoes your whole life, only to find out that it can sometimes be harmful to you and the other person if you do. In that way, empathy is no different from any other well-intentioned emotion or action. Despite your benevolent intentions, it can sometimes go too far and have unintended consequences.

When navigating situations that require empathy, you must be aware of potential pitfalls and how to steer clear of them. While it's natural not to always make the perfect empathetic choice, honing your awareness and skills can help reduce the likelihood of encountering further challenges.

EMPATHIC CONCERN AND DISTRESS

Empathy can lead us toward empathic concern or empathic distress.

Empathic concern helps us demonstrate compassionate empathy and alleviate others' problems and pain. Alternatively, empathic distress is getting trapped in our own suffering and being unable to take action to help ourselves or others.

Empathic distress often leads to burnout, withdrawal, apathy, and other mental and physical health issues. This is what causes life coaches, healthcare workers, and other professionals in "helping" industries to become detached, drained, or burned out from their jobs. It typically results from a lack of emotional regulation, which is why I'm focusing so much on mastering self-empathy.

In the healthcare field, particularly in internal medicine, professionals often emphasize the significance of maintaining a reasonable psychological distance to effectively handle high-pressure situations without feeling overwhelmed. Similarly, it's crucial for individuals to avoid becoming overly enmeshed in others' emotions, while still acknowledging and responding to those emotions effectively. Striking a balance is pivotal, as becoming emotionally detached can hinder empathy and the ability to maintain healthy and respectful personal relationships. It's also essential to consider how a certain level of objectivity contributes to effectiveness in these situations.

Empathic distress isn't reserved for health professionals. If you're a caring person in general, based on your experiences, you may tend to give too much to others and not enough to yourself. Self-neglect and a lack of self-awareness are among the most significant contributors to empathic distress.

The boundary-setting process we discussed in Chapter One is helpful for avoiding empathic distress or other unintended consequences of inaccurate empathy.

Another potential pitfall of empathy is becoming codependent or helpless because you're unable to maintain boundaries.

CODEPENDENCY AND LEARNED HELPLESSNESS

Codependency often results from becoming overly involved with other people's problems. This might happen while you're also in a vulnerable state.

It can be challenging to have compassionate empathy for someone while maintaining healthy autonomy if you're not fully aware or in control of *your* current emotional state. Internalizing others' perceptions and feelings, and putting their needs before yours, can lead to the formation of codependency and other toxic habits. Moreover, it can significantly inhibit your ability to remain objective. You can't see the other person's needs accurately if you view them through the lens of your biased perspective.

Examples of codependency and learned helplessness include a coach enabling you to rely on them for external feedback or approval. This is harmful because it's a coach's job to empower their clients to develop self-efficacy and solve their problems without external validation. There are many reasons why this might occur. An unethical coach might try to make you dependent on them because they want power or want to continue making money off you. Another possibility is they don't realize they're creating a codependent relationship by blurring personal and professional lines. If the clinician is not in touch with their own emotions, it will prevent them from effectively empowering their client.

Another example is an overbearing parent who does everything for their child and doesn't teach them the relationship between responsibility and consequences. While the parent may act from a place of care and empathy, the result is usually a child, and eventually, an adult, who doesn't try to do anything for themselves and inappropriately relies on others to validate and complete them.

Oftentimes, this stems from the parents' own experiences, limiting beliefs, and fears. We talked about the different effects your upbringing has on your ability to empathize with others effectively, so it's unsurprising that a codependent relationship can stem from a parent either wanting a similar relationship with their child or wanting to do things differently than their parents did. Though their intentions are good, the outcome often isn't.

While these consequences of inaccurate empathy are mostly unintentional and passive, empathy can also be intentionally used as a weapon. It's crucial to be aware of this when you're going through a difficult time in your life or even when you're thriving. This might shed light on your current relationships and help you make decisions about who and what you'll tolerate as you become the best version of yourself.

EMPATHY AS A WEAPON

Remember this: lacking empathy is dangerous, but convincing yourself you're empathetic when you're not is even more destructive. One blinds you to the needs of others; the other blinds you to your own blind spots, and that illusion of competence can cause more harm than outright ignorance.

> "Out of all the essential skills you need to succeed, like academic achievements, experience, and exposure, honing perfected empathy stands out as the most crucial. It demands unwavering, intentional effort to master!"
>
> —Dr. D Ivan Young, MCC, NBC-HWC

When I began my journey with this subject matter, my preconceived notions about empathy were intertwined with sympathy and compassion. While these are elements of empathy, true empathy and emotional intelligence require ongoing practice and learning.

If there's one thing that we all have in common, it's the need to feel safe, secure, connected, and validated. In today's world, acknowledging that you don't feel this way is easy to avoid because of technology and automation. People are prone to isolation and only identifying with fringe elements of society, especially introverts.

On one hand, it's easy to ignore feelings of insecurity and unfulfillment because you get a dopamine hit at your fingertips. On the other hand, the comparison game that happens when you see the highlight reels of everyone's lives or when their delusional beliefs seduce you allows irrationality to creep into your mind, making you more vulnerable, prone to exploitation, and less confident in who and what you are.

This can be emotionally and physically dangerous. We see the harmful effects of this with the recent increase in mental health problems, especially among young children and teenagers. It's also evident in the forms of religious and political extremism that target those desperate to belong. This can impact an entire nation, as well as your team members, clients, and loved ones. Even the most intelligent individuals can remain vulnerable to exploitation, especially when someone knows how to make them feel valued, recognized, and included. That's why self-serving elected officials tend to favor and target those who are isolated, less educated, cognitively challenged and willfully ignorant.

The period from 2019 to 2022 revealed the need for empathy more than ever. Due to the pandemic, America became even more polarized. Certain countries, politicians, and political parties took advantage of individuals' need to feel seen and heard.

When you live as part of a perceived minority, you're especially vulnerable to emotional manipulation. "Minority" doesn't only refer to race; it can also mean your socioeconomic status, nationality, core values, or religious beliefs. Anyone who feels outnumbered or unseen is vulnerable when someone clever enough taps into that longing for recognition or influences others to blame their challenges on the targeted group.

At our core, we all want to belong. We all yearn to be part of something bigger than ourselves. Here's the danger: if you haven't learned to understand and empathize with yourself, you become like an open wound, eager for healing, but vulnerable to infection. What often shows up looks like medicine, sounds like medicine, even smells like medicine, but it's actually poison dressed as a cure.

History shows us the cost of falling for false belonging. Again and again, exploitation has divided communities that could have stood stronger together. When our deepest need to feel safe and accepted is twisted by leaders or movements with selfish agendas, it doesn't just threaten our individual well-being—it fractures our collective humanity.

As we explore the contents of this book, I'll discuss techniques that will help you heal the wounded parts of yourself and hopefully start to mend our culture as a whole.

WHEN YOU START WITH NO OR LITTLE EMPATHY

The last thing I want to do is scare you off by talking about the potential dangers of zero empathy or misusing empathy. Keep in mind that we all make mistakes, and you're already ahead because you're here making the effort to understand them. Even those who know how to show genuine empathy will make mistakes sometimes. After all, we're all human.

If you're reading this book because you struggle with being empathetic toward yourself and/or others, overcompensating is another threat you must be aware of.

If you believe you used to be a jerk in the past, or you just recognize you weren't the most caring individual, it can be difficult to know when to protect yourself and when to set boundaries. If you feel harshly toward yourself because of someone or something in your past, that's a vulnerability some might want to exploit.

This is why I have you start with self-awareness and self-empathy. The introspective exercises in this book will help you identify your biases, patterns, and blind spots. They are not meant to make you feel bad about yourself or give you an excuse to throw a pity party. Self-awareness should never be a self-bashing exercise.

Perhaps your experience is different, and you used to show too much empathy without knowing how to utilize it effectively, which led to compromising situations. Now, you tend to detach yourself or keep your guard up.

Regardless of your previous experiences, I encourage you to be disciplined in your quest to evolve as a person using accurate empathy.

Don't forget to empathize with yourself first!

ON THE RECEIVING END OF EMPATHY

Empathy works like breathing. You exhale when you extend compassion outward, and you inhale when you welcome the same kindness back into your own lungs. A healthy rhythm requires both. In other words, this book doesn't just teach you how to breathe out empathy—it also nudges you to pause, draw in a deep, nourishing inhale, and truly feel supported. The more freely you accept empathy, the more effortlessly you can share it and vice versa.

Since belief influences reality, the air you choose to breathe is important. When you believe you deserve love, respect, and understanding, you naturally draw in people who provide those qualities. Conversely, if you lack self-compassion, you might find yourself holding your breath in relationships that leave you gasping. Simply put, your inner narrative creates the atmosphere that you and everyone around you will breathe in. Of course, there is always a root cause for restricted breathing. If accepting help or empathy feels suffocating, it indicates a deeper block—that resistance merits gentle exploration.

The reflections in Chapter One offer a starting point, and the next exercise builds on that work. Step by step, you'll observe your inhale-exhale pattern of empathy - both giving and receiving. With deliberate practice, it can increase self-awareness and provide you with newfound ease.

THE CURSE OF YOUR ORIGINS

Let's continue where we stopped with the introspection from Chapter One and focus a bit more closely on the "settings" that influence your empathy. Picture your identity as a sound-mixing board in a recording studio. Each slider represents your generation, age, race, gender, and socioeconomic status. Even where you live adjusts the tone and volume of how you perceive others and how clearly you hear their stories. When one slider is pushed too high or too low, the whole song drifts off-key.

Now, swap the mixing board for a pair of prescription glasses. The lenses you wear are shaped by every life experience and personal attribute you carry, including childhood memories, career milestones, cultural traditions, triumphs, and hardships. If the prescription is accurate, the world comes into crisp focus; colors pop, details sharpen, and you can read the subtle emotions on another person's face. When those lenses are scratched, outdated, or the frames sit crooked, everything blurs. You might miss cues, misread intentions, or overlook your own needs entirely.

As you move through the next exercise, gently identify where your "frames" may be bent or your prescription off. Note the attributes, formative moments, or lingering beliefs someone could exploit or that make you doubt your worth. By naming these vulnerable spots, you can schedule a "vision check," ensuring your empathy, both given and received, remains clear, balanced, and truly in focus.

If you can't think of any off the top of your head, you can come back to it. We're going to go over certain characteristics now.

WHICH GENERATION ARE YOU PART OF?

We already touched on this in Chapter One, but now we'll go deeper. The generation you belong to doesn't just mark the year you were born—it profoundly shapes how you see yourself, how you connect with others, and even how you practice empathy. Each generation carries its own advantages, blind spots, and biases, shaped by the culture, technology, and social forces of its time.

Baby Boomers (1946–1964)

If you're a Boomer, you came of age before the internet and smartphones. You memorized phone numbers, built relationships face-to-face, and likely place high value on loyalty and direct, personal engagement. For you, a phone call or visit feels more meaningful than a text message—and when those gestures don't show up, it can feel like neglect.

- Advantages: Resilience, strong work ethic, loyalty, and appreciation for tangible connections.
- Blind Spots: Can struggle with rapid cultural shifts, may dismiss digital communication as shallow, may expect younger generations to "earn" what they themselves had to fight for.

- Alignment/Conflict: Boomers and Gen Z often clash over communication (calls vs. texts), but both care deeply about legacy—Boomers in what they leave behind, Gen Z in the change they're determined to create.

Generation X (1965–1980)

Gen X grew up during the transition—the Cold War, MTV, and the dawn of the personal computer era. Many were "latchkey kids," coming home to empty houses, which fostered independence but also a lingering skepticism of authority.

- Advantages: Independent, resourceful, adaptable to both analog and digital. Often act as cultural translators between older and younger generations.
- Blind Spots: Cynicism, detachment, and reluctance to fully trust institutions.
- Alignment/Conflict: Gen X values independence like Boomers, but resonates with Millennials' desire for authenticity. They often play a bridge role in conversations across generations.

Millennials (1981–1996)

Millennials are the first true "in-between" generation—raised with analog childhoods and digital adulthoods. They remember dial-up internet and playing outside until dark, but they also became early adopters of social media. Their worldview was shaped by economic recessions, rising student debt, and the collapse of traditional career promises.

- Advantages: Collaborative, adaptable, value-driven, tech-comfortable but not dependent. Seek meaning and impact in work and relationships.
- Blind Spots: Burnout, comparison culture fueled by social media, disillusionment with authority. Sometimes perceived by older generations as entitled or fragile.
- Alignment/Conflict: Millennials resonate with Gen Z around inclusivity and activism, but may frustrate Boomers or Gen X by questioning traditional workplace hierarchies.

Generation Z (1997–2012)

Gen Z has never known life without smartphones, Wi-Fi, or global connectivity. Communication is fast, text-based, and often digital-first. They grew up with social justice movements, climate change headlines, and unprecedented access to information.

- Advantages: Tech-native, globally aware, outspoken about causes, and resilient in navigating uncertainty.
- Blind Spots: Struggle with anxiety, shorter attention spans, and balancing online presence with real-world connections. Sometimes, mistake visibility online for genuine influence.
- Alignment/Conflict: Gen Z may feel worlds apart from Boomers, yet both generations have a mission-driven lens—one rooted in institutions, the other in disruption. They align closely with Millennials on inclusivity but are often bolder in demanding change.

Generation Alpha (2013–present)

Alphas are still young, but they're the first generation fully raised in a world of AI, streaming platforms, and algorithm-shaped experiences. Their worldview will be influenced as much by screens and digital ecosystems as by parents and schools.

- Advantages: Global exposure from an early age, access to unprecedented learning tools, and being comfortable with diversity and fluid identities.
- Blind Spots: Risk of over-reliance on technology, shallow digital connection, and curated realities that blur with truth.
- Alignment/Conflict: They'll share Gen Z's fluency with digital culture but may struggle even more to balance human connection with machine-driven life.

THE BIGGER PICTURE

Every generation carries unique strengths: Boomers offer loyalty and resilience, Gen X independence, Millennials adaptability and collaboration, Gen Z urgency and innovation, and Gen Alpha digital fluency. However, each also carries blind spots: rigidity, cynicism, burnout, anxiety, and over-reliance on tech.

The challenge and the opportunity are to see these differences not as barriers, but as bridges. Generations may clash over communication styles, values, or trust in institutions. Yet, at the core, they share universal needs: to be seen, to belong, and to matter. The more we acknowledge these dynamics, the better equipped we are to empathize across divides and learn from those who see the world through a different lens.

I raise these issues not to divide us over our differences, but to explore how these experiences shape your perspective on empathy and your capacity to empathize.

1. What is your gender, and what does that mean for you?

In the twenty-first century, gender has evolved beyond the traditional binary of male or female. The spectrum of gender identities has expanded, resulting in a more nuanced understanding of gender. It's crucial to reflect on how your own gender identity and perceptions of gender impact your relationships with others and yourself.

A variety of cultural and social factors make up your view of yourself. Consider:

- How much of your views on gender were shaped by your culture?
- What about your social interactions and the different roles you've played in your family and community?

In the first chapter, we discussed the differences between females and males in their ability to understand others' physical and emotional states. Now, we will explore how your gender experiences in today's world influence your relationship with empathy.

Our communities are becoming increasingly accepting of individuals who identify as a gender different from the one they were assigned at birth. However, these individuals still encounter numerous challenges that impact their relationships with themselves and others.

If you are such an individual, now is a good time for some deep introspection.

- How have you been treated by others, especially those whose approval you seek?
- Have you been accepted or excluded simply for being yourself?
- How have these experiences influenced your identity and self-worth?

Transgender youth experience disproportionately high levels of bullying and discrimination, which in turn are strongly associated with elevated symptoms of depression, anxiety, and lower self-esteem (Sares-Jäsk et al. 2023). If they have external support or are already well-developed adults, some can develop a healthy sense of self; however, others are unable to cope with these challenges. Self-empathy is much harder to develop when your sense of self is threatened, marginalized, or in flux.

Generally, men and women experience the world in different ways. There are many double standards that influence our perceptions of self and gender. For instance, women are often seen as "slutty" or promiscuous if they sleep with several men, whereas men usually receive a pat on the back for the same behavior. These unspoken gender rules can lead to identity issues, self-loathing, and other mental health issues that hurt your capacity to empathize with yourself and others.

If your identity and self-empathy are solid, you might be able to block out negative feedback like this and move on without a dent in your perception of self. However, if you're going through a vulnerable time, or you're vulnerable because of where you are in life (i.e., your adolescent years), then you might be more sensitive to rejection and others' opinions. In these cases, checking in with yourself and cultivating self-empathy is crucial. It's also wise to seek professional help (or get help for your child), so you/they have a well-qualified, unbiased support system and an outside perspective with your best interests at heart.

2. Where are you from, and where do you live?

In other words, what's your nationality, and how does it affect the way you view the world? How does it contribute to your view of others who don't look like you, or those from different countries?

I identify as an African-American man and take pride in being American. However, I must recognize the ongoing history of racial bias, institutional bigotry, and cultural and political hypocrisy in the United States. The color of my skin often causes a range of feelings, from self-hatred to underlying stress and anxiety. Being well-informed about the world around me makes it increasingly difficult to witness the systemic impact of two centuries of social deprivation and racial oppression on my community. It's noteworthy that many Americans tend to exhibit a sense of superiority and dismiss less economically developed people and countries, despite the potential to learn valuable lessons from them. Interestingly, my experiences have shown that I encounter less bias, racism, and bigotry abroad compared to what I experience here in the United States.

I'm least proud of the ways in which America is such a hypocritical country. As a nation, we fail to live up to many of the values we claim to stand for. As a Black man, I experience the pain of cognitive dissonance and underlying anxiety more than others.

Since we are more privileged than many other countries, we can fall into a pattern of indifference. We ignore what's happening elsewhere because it's "not our business." While we don't always have much power over what's happening in other places, we can connect with our compassionate empathy and take action in any way we can to be more considerate of ourselves and others. This might look like volunteering or donating to organizations that support other countries, but I believe such altruistic behavior should begin within the confines of our own hearts and minds. What good is physically protesting and fighting for human rights everywhere else if we don't treat ourselves and others with more empathy and compassion at home?

Never neglect empathy because you feel like your efforts won't make a difference. Empathy toward even one person has a ripple effect that can change the course of countless lives for the better.

3. What race(s) are you?

How does this filter affect your view of yourself and life?

I'm an African-American male, born in 1961 into a racist, hateful, bigoted America. In my childhood, it was normal for me to see dogs being sicced on people who looked like me simply because they wanted access to fair housing, voting rights, and a decent education for their children. Having experienced these challenges, I am acutely aware of the struggles faced by other marginalized communities.

Today's political climate is not just unraveling the hard-won civil rights advancements of the past fifty years; it is actively widening the wounds of injustice. America is grappling with divisive leadership that fuels a resurgence of racism, which seeps into our political and judicial systems. This reality deepens the scars for those who are already marginalized, reminding us all that the fight for equality and dignity is far from over. It calls each of us to stand in solidarity and advocate for a more just future.

I understand how it feels to be judged and mistreated. It's disappointing that in 2025, America is still grappling with racial issues. When Donald Trump was elected president in 2016, it seemed as though every gain for civil rights and equality achieved over the past fifty years was undone in less than thirty-six months. The Voting Rights Act was effectively dismantled, and a woman's right to make decisions about her own body was heavily restricted by a Supreme Court dominated by ultra-conservative justices, which did not reflect the diverse and progressive perspectives of modern America. From 2016 to the writing and publishing of this book in 2026, the greatest threat to democracy came from homegrown white supremacists who had the full support of then and re-elected President Donald Trump.

At the same time, there are so many in the majority who are far from racist and are some of the most empathetic, kind, and supportive people I've ever met.

Alternatively, I've also met people who still believe that not everyone is equal. Some in privileged positions want to hold onto their advantages. Others even pretend to care while secretly working against equality.

I've also seen the effects of self-loathing within my own race because of institutionalized racism. They believe those who look like them aren't as deserving or capable as others. I'll say a lot more about this in this book because it's what I want you to remember if you don't remember anything else: You can't fully and accurately empathize with others if you have no self-empathy.

Examining your racial origins and assumptions can help you identify your blind spots and biases, both against yourself and others.

4. What was/is your socioeconomic status?

People tend to bond in suffering, as well as in privilege.

Our circumstances shape the attitudes we hold, and they can influence our level of optimism and faith. Often, individuals facing socioeconomic challenges demonstrate resilience and strength in their mental, emotional, and cultural aspects when confronted with difficulties. However, it's important to note that this is not the case for everyone.

Individuals experiencing economic hardships may harbor resentment toward those who are more privileged, perceiving themselves as lacking. This perspective can create limitations in their opportunities, as well as negative self-fulfilling prophecies.

Maslow's hierarchy of needs explains this phenomenon. Until one's safety needs are met, it's nearly impossible for them to focus on

> "Conversely, those with more than adequate resources may lack awareness of the challenges faced by the less fortunate. As a result, they might unintentionally appear insensitive or lack reasonable emotional intelligence due to being out of touch with the realities of everyday life for those facing hardship. It's important to recognize that this isn't just a concept; it's a reality that warrants our mindful consideration."
>
> —Dr. D Ivan Young, MCC, NBC-HWC

higher-order thinking. People don't consider things like giving back or making life meaningful as much as they focus on simply surviving.

Imagine society as a vast landscape dotted with elevated terraces and low-lying valleys. Individuals born or who now stand on the higher terraces enjoy a sweeping view, free from many of the obstacles that wind through the valleys below. From that altitude, the path looks smooth and obvious. However, the daily detours, ravines, and fallen branches that impede valley travelers can be nearly invisible to those looking down from the ridge.

Likewise, privilege can function much like polarizing sunglasses: it filters out certain harsh glares, yet it can also dim or distort the very details—poverty, discrimination, and health inequities, that require urgent attention. Unless we pause to lift the lenses and look again, we risk misreading the terrain altogether.

Only a small portion of the wealthy population realizes that their vantage point is not just a perch but a platform for meaningful change. To be sure, wealth alone does not guarantee wisdom; nevertheless, resources *do* grant the power to fund equitable initiatives, amplify the voices of the marginalized, and model inclusive practices in boardrooms, classrooms, and communities. Therefore, the question shifts from "Why should I help?" to "How will I use what I have?"

Your upbringing, education, and present circumstances act as the settings on your internal empathy dial. Naturally, having walked a difficult road can heighten sensitivity to another's pain, yet shared experience is not the sole route to accurate understanding. Empathy is less about identical footprints and more about careful listening, honest curiosity, and the courage to sit with discomfort.

Moreover, cultivating empathy requires deliberate acts of perspective-taking, such as reading diverse narratives, engaging in courageous conversations, and—when possible—inviting people with lived expertise into decision-making circles. In short, empathy grows when we leave the comfort of our terrace to explore someone else's valley with humility and respect.

Ultimately, awareness paired with intentional action becomes the birthplace of collective progress. Think of empathy as a bridge-building toolset: awareness locates the gap, intention supplies the blueprint, and courageous practice lays each plank across the divide. Consequently, every mindful step you take toward understanding another person strengthens the structure beneath both of you.

Thus, the call is clear:

- Acknowledge the real power embedded in privilege.
- Listen for the stories hidden by height or filtered by familiar lenses.
- Act through equitable policies, inclusive language, and shared opportunities to ensure the bridge remains open and safe for all who cross.

By choosing to look beyond ourselves and adjusting our vantage when necessary, we transform empathy from a feel-good concept into a force capable of reshaping the social landscape for everyone.

As we consider the following chapters in this book, I encourage you to take a deep, introspective dive so you can focus your attention on the ones that will help you the most. My goal is to help you make the necessary internal shifts to become the person you were created to be by evolving beyond the person you are now.

BRINGING IT BACK TO YOURSELF

Your commitment to personal growth is commendable. As you travel this road of self-evolution, remember that the word *self* is part of the journey's name. Think of empathy like the safety instructions on an airplane: you secure your own oxygen mask first, so you have the breath to help the passenger beside you. In the same way, the compassion you offer outward must be balanced by the compassion you allow inward; otherwise, your well-intended generosity will eventually run out of air.

Everyone you meet is worthy of a moment of understanding, yet it's equally vital to refill your own emotional tank. Imagine an empathy "fuel gauge": every time you extend patience, kindness, or support, the needle dips. Purposefully accept those same gifts from others so the gauge doesn't hover on empty. Giving and receiving are two gears in the same engine; when one stalls, the whole vehicle slows down.

That said, carry a healthy awareness of your boundaries. While many people will respect your time and energy, a few may test the limits. If someone repeatedly shows you they can't or won't reciprocate, consider it a flashing warning light on your dashboard. Address the issue directly, and if necessary, pull over and recalibrate the relationship.

Finally, notice whether the company you keep is also committed to growth. Just as gardeners tend the soil around budding plants, surround yourself with people who cultivate their own character. When someone's true colors become clear, believe what you see. Loving others and practicing empathy is a beautiful calling, but never let it uproot your own well-being. Vigilance ensures your benevolence remains a strength, not a liability.

THE DANGERS OF EMPATHY FOR CLINICIANS, COACHES, AND MENTAL HEALTH PROFESSIONALS

Empathy is the heartbeat of effective helping professions, yet, like any powerful tool, it carries hidden edges. Picture yourself as a finely tuned radio tower at a busy airport: you receive clients' emotional signals and broadcast understanding back to them. When the frequency is clear, healing, meaningful messages flow in both directions. However, without carefully calibrated boundaries, those same waves can distort, creating subjective emotional feedback that drowns out the true signal no matter how good your intentions are.

One of the clearest examples of this distortion is transference neurosis—the moment a client projects feelings tied to someone else directly onto you. Sometimes the projection is warm: a client begins to see you as the only person who truly "gets" them, or even experiences romantic attraction, as one of my own clients once did. Other times, the projection is scorching anger and resentment, or deep distrust surfaces, seemingly aimed at you rather than at its true source.

To extend the metaphor, think of your office as an airport runway. Your empathic presence guides each client's plane toward a safe landing. Yet, if the runway lights blur together because you've dimmed your boundaries, the plane may overshoot, veer off course, or attempt to taxi straight into your control tower, threatening your reputation and your well-being. That is why balanced empathy requires both generous illumination *and* clearly marked limits.

BOUNDARIES MATTER

So, what do you do when a client's or team member's projection crosses the professional line? First and foremost, you check the cockpit of your own inner aircraft. In practical terms, that means practicing self-empathy: pausing to assess your emotional fuel level and honestly evaluating whether you can continue on this route. As you have learned throughout this book, self-empathy is not indulgence, but maintenance. This is similar to the crucial pre-flight checklist that a pilot uses. Whether you're a coach, clinician, or mental health provider, being mindful of your engagements and how you manage your relationship with the person seeking your help keeps your *and* their objectives grounded, moving forward, and safe.

Occasionally, a client's hostility or over-attachment becomes unsafe. In those cases, the ethical course is to "close the airspace" by terminating care (divorcing the client with compassion and empathy) and, whenever possible, referring the individual to another professional. More often, though, the danger is subtler yet still draining. A client may pepper sessions with low-grade frustration or blur personal boundaries with constant texts. Here, clear communication, ground rules about scheduling, confidentiality, and professional scope act like sturdy fencing at the edge of your runway: visible, firm, and non-negotiable.

Of course, you cannot prevent every unexpected landing, yet you *can* refine your radar. By noticing early signs of projection, sudden idealization, repeated flirtation, or hostility that seems out of proportion, you can gain precious seconds to redirect the approach if done properly. Gently naming the dynamic ("I sense you may be feeling unheard outside these sessions; let's explore that feeling together") invites insight without shaming the client.

Ultimately, empathy with boundaries transforms from a potential hazard to a reliable collaborative navigation system. It guards your energy, models healthy relationships for those working through their challenges, and ensures the therapeutic journey remains a collaborative process, not a collision course. Remember: When your empathy stays balanced, you help others soar while keeping both feet firmly planted on the runway of professional integrity.

IT'S TIME FOR A CHECK-IN

Now that you've done some introspection and started looking at who and what contributes to your sense of self, I want you to take some time to check in with yourself. After all, we've determined that checking in with your thoughts and emotions can help you move forward with clarity.

I invite you to reflect on the following questions:

1. How do I feel about myself after considering and answering these questions? Do I feel worse or better about myself and my abilities than I did before this process? Do I feel the same?

It's completely normal to struggle with negative feelings when you first consider your areas of improvement. It's also okay to not feel much different. This is only the beginning. As you get further along in this book (and this process), you'll likely feel a wide range of emotions. Be present with them and listen to what they're telling you.

2. What have I learned about my relationship with myself?
3. What has this process taught me about my relationships with others?

Introspection often reveals judgments and beliefs that we didn't know we had. These thoughts influence our actions and dictate the course of our lives, so analyzing them may involve recognizing patterns and habits we have. Odds are, you'll start to notice which behaviors and beliefs support your growth and which ones you need to shed to become your best self.

4. What's one small way I can improve my relationships with myself and others today?

As I've said multiple times, self-evolution is an ongoing journey. You can't expect to always get self-empathy and empathy toward others right away because you're only human. Don't let that scare you. Start taking small, intentional steps today so you're even better tomorrow.

5. Am I willing to do what it takes to master accurate empathy toward myself and others?

Mastering accurate empathy requires a commitment to taking consistent action to better yourself and your relational skills. If you get discouraged or overwhelmed along the way, step back and remind yourself that the importance of empathy can't be overestimated. Learning empathy will improve every area of your life.

MAIN TAKEAWAYS FROM THIS CHAPTER

⇒ Empathy can lead us to empathic distress, empathic concern, or apathy.

Being aware of your feelings, biases, and experiences helps you maintain a healthy emotional distance as you extend accurate empathy toward others.

If you're not careful, empathy can turn into overload. When you get swallowed up by your own emotions—or the pain of others—you slip into empathic distress. In that state, you're too consumed to help yourself, let alone anyone else. Compassionate, accurate empathy simply isn't possible when you're drowning.

On the other end of the spectrum, overwhelm can push you toward apathy. Instead of feeling too much, you shut down and stop feeling altogether. Apathy becomes a kind of self-protection, but it distances you from others and keeps you from building the healthy, reciprocal relationships we all need.

⇒ Empathy can be intentionally used as a weapon.

Staying in touch with your emotions and developing self-empathy will make you less susceptible to others taking advantage of you. If you understand what empathy truly looks like, you're more likely to recognize when someone wants the best for you or when they're trying to exploit you.

It's important to learn how to use empathy accurately so others can't use your compassion and kindness against you.

⇒ Your age, gender, location, race(s), and socioeconomic status heavily contribute to your view of the world and your place in it.

By now, you should be getting the big picture regarding your experiences and how much they influence your ability to empathize with yourself and others.

I don't want you to read these chapters and start self-diagnosing yourself with beliefs you may not have. I simply want to bring attention to the factors that *could* be affecting your ability to understand and feel with yourself and others.

⇒ As a coach or healthcare professional, the stakes are often higher when it comes to practicing empathy.

You have to set firm boundaries without distancing yourself too much. It's important to be aware of your own experiences and feelings when working with clients so you can identify any vulnerabilities that may prevent you from being objective and showing accurate empathy.

Trying to ignore your feelings can lead to projection that affects your ability to properly counsel the person trusting you with their truth.

⇒ Don't forget to start and continue with self-empathy.

To demonstrate accurate empathy, you must cultivate self-awareness and self-empathy as an ongoing part of your process.

Being aware and present with your own beliefs and feelings can help ensure you won't head toward apathy, empathic distress, codependency, or learned helplessness.

Chapter Three

ACCURATE EMPATHY AS AN ACTION AND SKILL

BY NOW, YOU UNDERSTAND THAT nobody is born with the ability to show accurate empathy. Much of what you see about empathy on social media, TV, or other public platforms downplays what empathy truly is. Empathy is a skill that must be intentionally cultivated. It is a conscious action we choose to take. Perfecting its use requires intention and insight. Though you may not be great at it now, not only can you improve your abilities, but you can also master them. Some people think they already understand what empathy is and how to use it properly, but trust me, no matter how much you *think* you know, there's much more for you to learn. Mastering accurate empathy is crucial for coaches and clinicians, as it directly impacts client outcomes.

The concept of accurate empathy was established by American psychologist Carl Rogers, one of the founders of humanistic psychology (Moyers and Miller 2013). He contributed to the development of person-centered psychotherapy. His model is also referred to as "client-centered," as he discusses accurate empathy specifically in the context of psychotherapy.

> "Here's what I found most interesting. Rogers' idea of accurate empathy wasn't based on one's ability to sense what someone else is feeling. He saw accurate empathy as a way of actively understanding another's perspective as precisely as possible. He encouraged a curiosity that extended beyond simply listening to someone's story."
>
> —Dr. D Ivan Young, MCC, NBC-HWC

I agree with Rogers; we're more likely to wield empathy appropriately when we deliberately take listening a step further and use imagination and acceptance to expand our understanding of a person's story and feelings.

To do this effectively, here are some questions that I encourage you to consider asking your team members or clients as you dig deeper:

- What is their relationship with the subject at hand?
- What factors are shaping this person's emotions and experiences? As we discussed in Chapters One and Two, how might their background, upbringing, and natural temperament be influencing what they feel and how they respond today?
- What deeper context is shaping this person's perceptions? Look beyond the surface—what core values, beliefs, or even the absence of them—might be influencing the way they see and interpret the world?
- Why does "it" matter? Why is this important to them?

Accurate empathy involves welcoming curiosity and accepting that being right or wrong about someone's feelings is irrelevant. The idea is to ask questions and be open to learning something new about them and their situation while avoiding the propensity to project your feelings onto them or allow your preconceived notions to dictate or influence your response.

Of course, we're only human and can't avoid this completely, but we can approach the process more deliberately and maintain an open mind. This significantly increases our ability to improve as we learn to empathize in different contexts.

Rogers' instructions to ask questions and keep an open mind stem from the idea that the coachee or team member is the expert in their life. You may be an expert in your field, but the average person knows what's inside of them better than anyone, including you. They might not understand the full picture of why they're feeling the way they are, but that's where you come in. Your sincere concern and curiosity can help them probe deeper, discover new perspectives, and find answers to their questions from within. Your ultimate goal is to help the individual get to know themselves better, even if the individual is yourself. Masterful coaches make it their mission to build self-efficacy and resilience in their clients.

Another important aspect of accurate empathy is the belief that we all have an inherent desire to attain positive psychological functioning. While some of us may get in our own way through self-sabotaging and other damaging tendencies, everyone wants success and happiness in some form or another.

Therapy and coaching are meant to help you meet and exceed your goals of success and happiness, but it's not a therapist's or coach's job to tell you what to do. Person-centered therapy and compassion-focused coaching can help you gain a deeper understanding of yourself and your life from a non-judgmental perspective. The goal of a good clinician is to help you tune into your inner resources while co-creating a plan to better equip you to achieve your goals.

WHY IS ACCURATE EMPATHY A STRUGGLE FOR MANY?

The ability to wield empathy accurately is yet another example of the interplay between nature and nurture, illustrating that neither is guaranteed by either. Some people are empathetic because they received compassion and empathy early in their lives or at some point throughout their adulthood, while others are empathetic because they never received it and refuse to be like those who didn't give it to them. It's important to remember that those who didn't receive empathy during childhood are still capable of showing it to others. However, many of these individuals struggle to fully understand and accept their own feelings without being overly self-critical. To overcome this blind spot, they must learn to demonstrate empathy toward themselves to develop accurate empathy toward others.

Other people aren't empathetic because they were given empathy without proper boundaries. They weren't disciplined or taught that their actions have consequences. As a result, they care too much about themselves and not enough about others. We see this when an indulgent parent raises a child. An entitled child will, in most instances, become a callous adolescent and fail miserably at showing compassion and concern for others.

Trauma and abuse survivors often struggle with self-compassion—a capacity that is crucial for developing accurate empathy toward others (Germer and Nef 2015). Like self-empathy, self-compassion is the basis for treating others with compassion. You can still be a kind and caring person if you haven't learned self-empathy and compassion, but cultivating these skills is necessary to ensure that accurate empathy becomes a regular part of your interactions with others.

If you find it difficult to be kind and understanding to yourself, it can lead to engaging in behaviors that are detrimental to your well-being. What's worse, having low self-worth can lead to getting involved in harmful relationships. This happens because when you don't take care of yourself, have a predominantly negative opinion of yourself, and/or believe others perceive you negatively, it becomes difficult to recognize or appreciate when someone treats you with empathy and respect. Moreover, it can be challenging to offer compassion and understanding to others when you're unable to do so for yourself.

Some people may not be empathetic because they were never shown empathy during their formative years. These adolescents become adults who consciously or subconsciously believe they don't owe anyone empathy because, at a subconscious level, they feel unsafe, unloved, and misunderstood.

A significant example of this is how young boys are raised to be tough and suppress their feelings and emotions. At a very young age, they are taught that "real men" don't cry, make themselves vulnerable, or experience fear. They are constantly told that "strength" is what defines manhood. However, the reality is that it takes much more courage to acknowledge one's fears and express one's true feelings. By conditioning young men to internalize these emotions, we are setting them up for major challenges as fathers, husbands, and friends. The inability to connect with one's own emotions hinders psychological well-being. Consider this: If you teach your son or daughter to disregard their own feelings, how can you expect them to care about, respect, or value the emotions of others?

As we discovered in Chapters One and Two, your experiences and identity heavily influence your ability to empathize with yourself and others. However, I must reiterate that regardless of your background and current relationship with self-empathy and empathy, you *can* become better at receiving and giving empathy.

THE APPLICATION OF ACCURATE EMPATHY FOR COACHING AND HELPING PROFESSIONS

In this book, we discuss the use of accurate empathy by coaches and clinicians; however, remember that the advice provided can be useful across various situations and disciplines. Empathy can transform your perspective on life, your overall well-being, and your most cherished relationships.

Accurate empathy for a coach, health professional, or clinician is at the core of successful client outcomes. Many of us, especially early on in our coaching or medical careers, make the mistake of dealing with our clients rather than engaging with them. We put them in boxes and depersonalize them instead of truly connecting with them. We're either taught to approach our careers in this manner, or it happens along the way as we struggle to cope and succeed.

It's imperative that coaches and clinicians understand the significance of their contribution to someone going through a tumultuous period. Not observing someone's pain and feeling with them is nearly equivalent to malpractice.

> "As coaches and clinicians, we either embody transformation or model hypocrisy—there's no middle ground. A 'do as I say, not as I do' mindset corrodes trust and credibility. Practicing what you preach isn't optional; it's the very foundation of your credibility. If you want to thrive in this profession, start by leading yourself with the same discipline and compassion you demand of others."
>
> —Dr. D Ivan Young, MCC

To excel in clinical practice, it's crucial to be mindful of how and why we integrate our personal lives into our work. One core aspect of mastering accurate empathy is understanding the driving force behind why we chose a helping profession in the first place. Most of us entered our field because we wholeheartedly wanted to create a positive impact in the lives of those in our care. By staying connected to our initial motivations, we can position ourselves for personal success while effectively supporting our clients in achieving their goals.

BURNOUT IS REAL

Many of us strive to have a positive impact on the lives of those we interact with and coach. However, over time, it's common for most people, especially highly skilled coaches, clinicians, and licensed professionals, to feel disheartened and worn down. This can happen due to various reasons we've talked about, such as struggling to follow our own advice. Often, the result is misdirecting empathy toward our clients, team members, or loved ones, while stretching ourselves thin between work and personal commitments. The challenges of everyday life can sometimes become overwhelming, making it even more difficult for us to effectively assist those who need our help the most. While I primarily speak to coaches based on my own experiences, this advice applies to all.

It's common for all human beings to experience moments of discouragement and exhaustion. We may find ourselves preaching self-care and mindfulness to our clients and team members while neglecting to prioritize these practices in our own lives. It's not unusual for a good leader, coach, or clinician to pour excessive emotional energy into supporting others while neglecting their own needs.

Financial concerns, relationship issues, and health challenges can all add to the burden that providers carry. These challenges can marginalize our ability to effectively intercede for our clients. When this occurs, it becomes essential for us to undergo deep introspection. This process involves taking an objective look at our thought processes, beliefs, and behaviors. It allows us to identify areas where we may be holding ourselves back or perpetuating unhealthy patterns.

Only through this process of introspection can we accurately demonstrate empathy toward ourselves, our clients, and those we hold dear. As we begin to understand our own struggles and limitations fully, we can develop a more profound sense of compassion and understanding for others. This self-awareness enables us to provide more comprehensive support and guidance to those we serve. It's crucial to recognize that seeking support from colleagues, mentors, or mental health professionals can be beneficial even if you're a clinician yourself. These individuals can offer a fresh perspective and provide valuable insights that can facilitate personal and professional growth.

Remember, taking care of ourselves is not a sign of weakness, but a necessary step toward maintaining our ability to serve others. By prioritizing our well-being, we create a solid foundation from which we can extend our support to those in need.

INTROSPECTION, MINDFULNESS, AND CHANGE

Nowadays, we don't have to look far to find advice on being mindful and present. However, these tips and tricks usually lack context.

The truth is that most clinicians lose their motivation or sense of connection to their purpose over time. This doesn't usually mean you're not cut out for your profession. It's simply a sign that you must be more intentional with self-empathy and self-compassion while engaging in the workplace, in clinical practice, and in client sessions, as well as in every other area of your life.

If you once loved helping people, but now you're losing that spark, take a step back and consider what's changed.

It's no secret that working with people, especially people who are hurting, can cause us to do one of two things.

1. We can develop what I call *shared morbidity*—when we absorb so much of our clients' struggles that their burdens become our own. In this state, we aren't just supporting their challenges; we're carrying them, and the weight leaves us mentally and emotionally depleted. Instead of guiding from a place of clarity, we risk drowning in the very waters we're supposed to help them navigate.
2. We can become numb to other people's feelings—not because we don't care, but because life has left us jaded or we're quietly carrying our own anxiety. When that happens, empathy doesn't disappear overnight; it erodes slowly, leaving us disconnected from the very people we're meant to understand.

Neither of these is helpful.

So, how do you accurately direct your empathy to the person in the mirror and the people in front of you? Let's talk about it.

HOW TO START SHOWING ACCURATE EMPATHY TO YOURSELF (AND OTHERS BY DEFAULT)

There are a few best practices for getting in touch with your ability to show accurate empathy.

1. Check in with yourself.

Coming to the table wounded as you attempt to help the wounded is *not* a good idea. Take ownership of your brokenness and vulnerabilities.

Own up to the parts of your life that are distracting you. These might include trauma, unmet needs, relationship and financial struggles, or any other difficult events that might impact your ability to accurately empathize with yourself and the people you're treating.

Assess where you are and where you're not. We're often much better at taking care of others than ourselves. This is especially true when we care for others for a living. The consequences of this are dire. Just like you're told to put your mask on first before helping others do so on a flight, you must take care of and nurture yourself first. If you fail to support yourself and engage in self-empathy, you're putting your reputation, the individual you're working with, and your license or certifications at risk.

Accurate empathy involves a great deal of self-care. Oftentimes, we feel that self-care is selfish, but it's quite the opposite. When we focus on bettering ourselves, our clients, loved ones, and acquaintances also reap the benefits of our growth and self-improvement.

2. Understand that ongoing education is a requirement *and* a preference.

Take yourself and your goals seriously enough to put extra time and work into your profession or practice and be intentional about increasing your cognitive capacity and emotional competence. Be selective about your continuing education. Make it your mission to take classes and workshops that help you be more effective for yourself, your team members, and your clients/patients.

This form of self-improvement enhances your skills and capacity to demonstrate accurate empathy.

It's easy to get too comfortable and stop exploring new ways to improve. While you don't have to set a goal to make more money or get another degree, you should always seek to learn more about what you do and improve upon how you apply what you learn.

A learning mindset also applies to your relationships. The world is ever-changing. You and everyone else are constantly changing with it, whether you're aware of it or not. By paying attention to the ways you change and grow, you'll be able to understand when others change as well. This is particularly important for long-term relationships, because your loved ones will change a lot throughout their lives. Don't hold anyone to the person they used to be. Try to understand and empathize with who they are now.

What drove you in one season of life may not serve you in the next. Perhaps you started out as a nurse and discovered a deeper passion for geriatrics. Maybe you began as a life coach and now feel called toward health and wellness coaching. The path doesn't have to stay the same, but wherever it leads, empathy—especially accurate empathy—is the bridge that keeps you aligned with the people you serve. Your priorities must reflect not only your growth but also the needs of your audience.

The same applies in your personal life. Maybe you once swore off children, only to realize later that you want to build a family. You wouldn't just "wing it." You'd do your homework, prepare, and commit to being the best parent you can be. That drive to do your best is powerful—but so is the wisdom to adjust when life asks for change.

Excellence isn't about perfection; it's about alignment. It's the courage to pause, revisit your *why*, and count the cost of the path you're on. Sometimes that means taking two steps back so you can take four forward. True excellence is a living standard—one that evolves as you do.

3. Be honest about your limits.

There's no shame in admitting when you don't have the emotional capacity to empathize with situations that overwhelm you. Too often, we push forward out of guilt or pride, when the truth is we're only hurting ourselves and the very people we're trying to help by forcing what we can't sustain. If a particular client or type of work drains you beyond repair, the most honest and compassionate choice is to step back.

Yes, this is especially hard when money is tight. However, one of the hardest lessons in this profession is also the most freeing: not all money is good money, and not every client is meant to be yours. Clarity requires courage—the courage to protect your energy, your health, and your professional integrity. Accurate empathy isn't just about tuning into others; it begins with extending that same empathy to yourself.

Start small. You don't have to master this overnight. Practice assessing your limits with honesty, and allow yourself to grow step by step. Over time, you'll find that your best work, both personally and professionally, flows not from pushing past your breaking point, but from aligning with what you can give wholeheartedly.

MY OWN EXPERIENCES WITH WRONG-FIT CLIENTS

Early on in my practice, I made the mistake of ignoring my limits a few times. All of us are familiar with those friends and family members whom we see out of obligation. I had a relative who caused me a lot of distress as a client. Whenever I put them on my calendar, I wanted to resume smoking marijuana, which was a bad habit I had long abandoned. Just scheduling them would raise my heart rate and give me severe stress and anxiety. If this was my reaction to seeing their name, you can imagine how I felt when I had sessions with them.

I came to realize that I should consider referring some of my clients to another clinician. I've learned that I can't help everyone, and sometimes trying to help other people ends up hurting me. As a clinician and as a human being, it's important to accept that I can't be a superhero for everyone. I've had to develop the courage to free myself from certain people and situations.

It's not your responsibility to be all things to all people. You must set boundaries. Not doing so is a disservice to you and the people that you're attempting to accommodate. What good does it do for others to profit from your gifts if you're losing your peace of mind in the process?

It's vital to recognize that you may not be showing enough empathy toward yourself in your career. Here are some ways you might be holding back on self-empathy and not setting boundaries that would benefit both you and the person you're supporting.

4. Not setting specific work hours and sticking to them.

The people you support should *not* have access to you twenty-four hours a day. This is the quickest path to burnout. Honor yourself and your downtime by stipulating your work hours in your contract and client conversations. This ensures that your clients understand when they can expect to reach you and when you're unavailable. It also sends a message that you value your personal time and that you're not always on call.

Unfortunately, many people struggle to set these boundaries due to a lack of self-empathy and respect for themselves and their time. This often stems from deep-seated beliefs about ourselves, others, and the world around us. For example, we may believe that we are not worthy of rest and relaxation or that we need to always be available to our clients in order to be successful.

These beliefs are often reinforced by today's "hustle culture." We are constantly bombarded with messages that we need to work harder, faster, and longer to achieve success. This can lead us to feel like we can't take time off, even when we're exhausted. As my grandma would say, "The devil is a lie."

It's important to challenge these beliefs and develop a healthier and more sustainable approach to work. This means learning to set limits, saying no to additional work when necessary, and taking regular breaks. It also means practicing self-compassion and understanding that we are all human and that we need time to rest and recharge. This is especially true if you work for yourself or with a small group practice.

5. Allowing clients to steamroll you.

We talked about transference in Chapter Two and how clients may project negative feelings onto you. You must be firm and stand up for yourself when necessary. You don't always need to let a client go in these situations. However, if you choose to keep working with them, you must have respect and empathy for yourself in these situations to better manage your emotions and still help them.

6. Taking on too many clients (or responsibilities).

You may be taking on too many clients at one time for several reasons. Two of the most common reasons are a scarcity mindset and the belief that you aren't valuable if you're not busy. Working hard is admirable and necessary, but overwhelming yourself and burning out aren't commendable or practical outcomes.

We tend to compare ourselves to others, especially in our careers. We think we should be able to work the same number of hours, take on the same number of clients, and make the same amount of money as others at our level. All these comparisons do is lead to discontent and limit your potential. Cultivating self-empathy helps you halt these harsh comparisons and forge your own way forward based on your needs, goals, and values.

This process of boundary setting and relationship auditing doesn't only apply to your work. Part of self-empathy is surrounding yourself with people who don't try to manipulate, use, or drain you. You cannot effectively practice self-empathy if you tolerate those who lack empathy toward you and themselves. You'll either intentionally or unintentionally allow them to interfere with your ability to care for yourself, as well as the relationships and responsibilities you need to prioritize.

HOW TO SHOW YOUR CLIENTS YOU'RE EMPATHIZING WITH THEM

As we have come to realize, words are not enough to accurately display empathy toward someone. It's essential that the person sitting across from you feels supported and understood so they can fully open up to you and help you help them.

One way to show the person you're guiding that you're empathizing with them is by being fully present. If you've checked out because of personal reasons, they can tell. If your client feels like they're a burden to you or you feel like you're doing them a favor, they can sense it. Most people can feel when they're unwanted or unappreciated, especially those who are already going through a traumatizing and tumultuous period. Odds are, a lot of your patients struggle with their self-worth, which makes your ability to empathize with them even more crucial to their evolution.

Let's be real. Working with certain clients can sometimes feel like walking through a minefield. You never know when something they say or do might set something off inside you. Here's the thing: they can feel it too. Even when you're not saying a word, your body is speaking volumes.

In fact, verbal communication is just the tip of the iceberg. The real story lies beneath the surface in your tone, pitch, facial expressions, posture, and even the energy you bring into the room. It's kind of like being around a dog—ever notice how they can sense when you're tense or uncomfortable? Humans aren't that different. We pick up on subtle cues, especially when our nervous systems detect a potential threat, whether emotional or relational.

So instead of pretending everything's fine and trying to camouflage your discomfort, consider taking a different route. If a client regularly pushes your buttons or leaves you feeling drained, it's okay to refer them to someone who's a better fit. That's not failure, it's wisdom. Another approach? Let them know, gently and honestly, that you don't have the current capacity to support them in the way they deserve.

Of course, how you do this matters. With the right tone and care, setting a boundary doesn't have to feel like rejection. When you frame it as doing what's best for them, and for yourself, it becomes an act of compassion, not dismissal.

On a related note, showing empathy isn't just about being kind; it's about being curious without steering the conversation. Carl Rogers nailed this idea: Ask questions that open doors, not ones that funnel people into answers you expect. Steer clear of assumptions or inserting your own feelings. Instead, create space for them to explore what they're truly experiencing.

Ask to understand, not to respond. When you listen to learn, not to fix or defend, you build trust. In that space, real transformation begins.

While every person is different, these are two essential elements of accurate empathy that should be applied in every situation, personal or professional.

EXAMPLES AND NEXT STEPS

A huge element of accurate empathy is trying to learn and understand more about the person in front of us. Let's look at how we can put accurate empathy into use in the real world. We'll expand on the examples in the last chapter and use some additional examples as well.

1. An employee comes to you and tells you they're experiencing personal issues that are starting to affect their work.

Don't assume anything. Jumping to the conclusion that your employee wants time off or any type of special treatment is a bad idea. Instead, ask them how they feel their personal issues are affecting their work. Maybe they want to try something new to get their productivity back on track. They might need someone to help them with certain tasks as they sort out their situation at home, but never assume.

As a boss, you have to balance your responsibility to the company with your responsibility to your employees, who are human beings first. It's understandable if one of your concerns is the potential impact on the success of the company. However, failure to show empathy toward individual employees can be even more detrimental to the company, especially in the long run. Neglecting empathy can create a toxic environment and undermine morale.

2. Your friend confides in you about their struggle to start a family with their partner.

This is a somewhat common situation, so you might assume you know what your friend wants or needs to hear, either based on your experience or the experiences of others in your life.

However, everyone's responses, needs, and desires are unique and ever-changing. Your friend might need comfort one day and seek your opinion the next. If you don't try to find out, you might miss the mark with your responses.

3. Your child is being bullied at school and is experiencing mental health problems as a result.

This is a situation that's incredibly delicate. Your child is still developing their sense of self and their interpersonal skills. This is an opportunity to show them what accurate empathy looks like. How you respond to the situation will influence the way they view and treat themselves. Give them grace and understanding so they can learn to show these things to themselves.

It's more important than ever to validate their feelings and not dismiss them or the situation. As a parent, you have so much influence over how your children feel about themselves and whether they treat themselves with love and empathy. That's not meant to scare you. Odds are, you already know this, but I want to emphasize how important it is to lead by example in these situations.

4. Your coaching or therapy client has a mental breakdown during your session together.

While you're trained to help the people you're supporting with these situations, that doesn't mean you're always in the right headspace to handle it in the best possible way. It also doesn't mean that you'll know what to do right away, because every client is different.

In these scenarios, asking questions to understand them better is a must. They may need someone to listen, but you're also there to guide them so they can find answers for themselves.

As we talked about earlier, it's also essential to your success and theirs to make sure that they're a good fit for you and your services. Otherwise, your lack of presence and commitment will show up in how you care for that client and will likely affect their outcomes.

5. Your partner expresses how they feel about something you did or didn't do.

In romantic relationships, especially long-term ones, it can be easy to become comfortable and complacent. Being comfortable can be a good thing if we're talking about feeling safe and being able to openly express our feelings. However, it can also be a bad thing if it means we stop putting in effort. Accurate empathy requires intentional effort.

If your partner is open and tells you how they feel, they should be met with nothing less than empathy. You might feel defensive at first if they're talking about something you did or didn't do. When this happens, ask yourself why you're feeling that way. Then ask them questions that shed light on why they're feeling the way they are and if there's a deeper root cause. It's okay if you feel resistance at first, as long as you validate their feelings instead of dismissing them. They may be wrong about your intentions or the reasoning behind your actions, but their feelings are real and present.

If the topic is a repeated conversation, it's usually a sign you need to dig deeper. Are you really trying to understand them, or are you trying to end the conversation and placate them for a period of time with promises to put in effort?

Sometimes we don't realize we're not showing empathy toward those we love in a way that will deepen our relationships. This is why consistently engaging in introspection and doing relationship audits are two of the best things you can do for your health, happiness, and success.

PRACTICE MAKES PERFECT

By now, you probably recognize some patterns in the examples we've gone over. It can still be challenging to put accurate empathy into practice because we all have unique beliefs, behaviors, and relationships. Some we're aware of, and others we haven't noticed yet. Hopefully, the introspection we did together in Chapters One and Two revealed some of your most relevant and impactful beliefs and behaviors. You'll be well on your way to mastering accurate empathy if you take the time to go through those exercises and start practicing self-empathy.

However, to make this process more actionable and accessible, here are some practice scripts for everyday situations that might occur for you as a parent, partner, coach/therapist, boss, or friend.

I should note that these are incomplete conversations. They're meant to show you how to demonstrate accurate empathy with just a few lines within different roles.

1. You and your partner have a disagreement.

Partner: It bothers me when you do (or don't do) *insert issue.*

You: I'm not sure why it bothers you. Can you help me understand why it's so important to you?

Partner: It makes me feel like you don't care about my needs. I feel neglected and like I'm not a priority.

You: So, it seems like you feel loved and appreciated when I take small actions to reduce your stress. Is that right? What can I do to show you that you and your needs are my top priorities?

Partner: I don't expect you to always do this or that. It's more about me wanting you to tune into my needs every once in a while and share some of the emotional load.

You: So, if I did *insert example of a caring action*, would it make you feel prioritized?

Partner: Yes, that would help me feel like my needs are being met.

This may feel weird at first, and it's a general script, but the intention to understand where your partner is coming from and how they're feeling is clear. It's also crucial to remember to show empathy to yourself, even when you're showing it to others. If something is bothering you, make sure to communicate how you feel once you've taken the time to properly understand their position. Don't jump right into your feelings, but also don't let the conversation end before you address your concerns.

2. Your child wants to do something, but you tell them no, and they're upset with you.

You: You seem upset about not being able to go on the class field trip. Are you angry or hurt, or is there something else going on?

Your child: I'm the only person in my class who's not going.

You: Does that make you feel like you're missing out on something?

Your child: Yes, it's embarrassing. All my friends are asking why I can't go.

You: I understand why that would be disappointing. I'd love for you to be able to go, but *insert reason.* (Give them a better reason than "because I said so.") If another field trip comes up, we will try to make it work.

Of course, this conversation can look a lot different, especially depending on your child's age. It's important to validate their feelings and try to understand them, as most children aren't yet in tune with how they feel and reasons behind those feelings at a young age.

Also, give yourself grace, because parenting isn't easy, and every child is different.

3. The person sitting across from you is stuck in a cycle of self-pity.

Client: It feels like everything is falling apart, and it's all my fault.

You: I noticed when you said that, your face twisted and you balled your hands up, but I want to understand more. Are you feeling angry, or are you more disappointed?

Client: I'm angry at myself. I mess everything up all the time.

You: What makes you feel that way? Do you have an example of another time you felt like you messed up?

Client: I just always mess up in one way or another.

You: Let's do something. I want you to think of one time when you were proud of yourself. Can you recall just one time?

Client: Yes, I have one in mind.

You: So, you don't mess *everything* up. Now, try to think of another time you felt like you messed up. How did that go? What led you there, and how did you move on?

By asking questions like these, you're encouraging the person trusting you with their truth to step back and see the bigger picture. If they can recall having overcome a similar situation, they'll learn from past experiences and feel more confident about solving problems going forward.

4. You need to speak with your employee about their performance, which has been going downhill for weeks.

You: It seems like you might be struggling to get your work done. I want to make sure you feel supported and understood. Do you feel that you are?

Employee: I've been having a really hard time at home. I'm sorry, it won't happen again.

You: I'm sorry to hear you've been going through a tough time. Is there anything I can do to make you feel more supported here? First and foremost, I want to make sure you're okay. I know that you're a hard worker.

Employee: My situation at home is making work feel overwhelming right now. Thank you, but I don't think there's anything you can do at the moment.

You: Would adjusting your work slightly to include *insert suggestions that would still work for the company but give the employee more flexibility* help you feel less overwhelmed?

Notice how in this situation, your employee might feel like they're being reprimanded at first, depending on your existing relationship. They might try to dismiss their difficulties by simply promising to do better. If you let the conversation end there, you're missing out on an opportunity to truly connect with them using accurate empathy. It's unlikely their work will improve, and even if it does, they'll likely still be struggling personally, and it will show up in their work once again. It's possible to miss the opportunity to connect in any of these situations, so you must learn to recognize when there's an opening to show empathy.

There's also the aspect of offering suggestions to help, which is an example of compassionate empathy. You're not leaving it up to *them* to ask for a solution, which they're probably likely hesitant to do as an employee.

5. Your friend is going through a difficult time.

Friend: I don't know what to do anymore. It's been so challenging every day and it's been consuming all my time and energy.

You: That must be so overwhelming.

Friend: I'm just frustrated because I feel like I've tried everything.

You: I would be frustrated too. Do you want to come up with some ideas together?

While all these examples sound straightforward, we know that conversations rarely go as smoothly or directly as these ones.

However, what I want you to pay attention to is the way questions are asked. While you might make some assumptions from time to time, follow-up questions can reveal thoughts and feelings you weren't aware of before. When you truly understand how they feel, you'll be better equipped to offer appropriate solutions or take helpful action.

It's also a good idea to reflect on how help or thoughtful suggestions are offered in some of these examples. While you may not be responsible for the outcome of a situation or how the other person handles your responses, these approaches will deepen your connection with the people who are meant to be in your life. It's essential to show those you truly care about that you're invested in their experiences and how they're feeling. Accurate empathy is the only way to do this.

MAIN TAKEAWAYS FROM THIS CHAPTER:

⇒ Accurate Empathy involves trying to understand someone's perspective as much as possible so you can connect with them and their feelings.

This concept, developed by psychologist Carl Rogers, can be applied in coaching, therapy, parenting, marriage, and any other personal or professional relationship. It's the key to building and maintaining genuine, meaningful relationships. Having accurate empathy toward yourself first is a crucial step toward self-improvement, the betterment of your community, and ultimately, a better world.

⇒ Even if you already know the basics of showing empathy, there is always room for improvement.

While our ability to show empathy toward ourselves and others is heavily influenced by our upbringing and experiences in adulthood, it's a skill we can all develop and strengthen. It may come naturally to some and not to others, but we're all capable of it, as long as we're open to introspection and self-improvement.

⇒ One of the main ways to show others you're engaging in accurate empathy is to be present and actively listening.

Whether you're helping a client or talking to a loved one, the other person can tell if you're not fully present or invested. Make sure you're listening to understand instead of to respond or move the conversation along.

Be particular about the relationships you cultivate, because a disconnect is one of the reasons you may struggle to be present.

⇒ Here are four habits to start with to demonstrate empathy toward yourself and others: check in with yourself, welcome learning and growth, be open to change, and be honest with yourself about your limits.

All of these require being fully, and sometimes brutally, honest. You can't change for the better if you're pretending to be someone or something else. You won't get far in your relationships if you aren't honest with yourself and others about who you are and what you want.

⇒ To understand someone and show them accurate empathy, you have to be willing to set your assumptions aside and keep an open mind.

Asking questions to gain a deeper understanding of someone's feelings and experiences is an essential aspect of accurate empathy. We often miss the opportunity to connect with others on a deeper level because we assume we know or understand how and what they're feeling.

⇒ **Accurate empathy is intentional, authentic, and specific.**

Even if empathy isn't something you possess yet, you can develop it if you truly want to make a difference in your life, as well as others' lives. It may feel foreign and inauthentic at first, but it will become genuine once you realize its true power.

Accurate empathy is an action and a skill. Once you develop it, you must continue to be active and intentional in your pursuit of empathy.

Chapter Four

THE DOS AND DON'TS OF ACCURATE EMPATHY FOR HIGH-CAPACITY COACHING

AS LEADERS, COACHES, CLINICIANS, AND healthcare professionals, our primary goal is to facilitate significant, lasting, and meaningful transformations in the lives of our clients and patients. The most fulfilling aspect of my work is hearing clients (who came to me struggling in most areas) express how our collaboration has positively impacted their lives. I strongly believe that consistently achieving this outcome relies on the skillful integration of empathy, compassion, and emotional focus coaching techniques in a seamless client-centered approach.

I penned this chapter because most coaches struggle to navigate client sessions effectively, especially with more challenging clients. Paradoxically, it's these clients who can immensely benefit from your skills and often provide the most compelling testimonials. In essence, the greater the challenge, the greater the potential for reward.

To kick off this conversation, let's use an unusual example. Let's compare working with challenging clients or team members to removing particles and plaque buildup from your teeth. Granted, there are a few ways to accomplish this. You could brush your teeth or, you know, use a hammer. Using a hammer would definitely get the job done, but you'd be in a great deal of pain and toothless afterward! Similarly, some coaches try everything from consulting to mentoring and even chastisement to deal with a problematic client or team member. Not only do none of those things work, but those strategies can also derail the coach-client relationship and ultimately do far more harm than good to both parties in the long run.

Coaching is about helping people tap into underutilized reserves and overlooked capacities that are indigenous to them, not fixing them. Consulting is more about giving business clients templates and advice. I'm not saying it's never appropriate to shift roles. I used to make fun of practitioners who would say, "I'm going to take off my coaching hat now," or something along those lines. However, the more I reflect on my experiences as a coach, the more I realize how true it is that sometimes you need to take one hat off and put on another—with your client's permission. Their permission is key to avoiding crossing boundaries that shouldn't be crossed and applying empathy in an inaccurate manner.

An example is when you and the coachee are discussing a subject in which you have a great deal of expertise, either from experiences with previous clients or from personal experiences. If the person sitting across from you is open to it, asking their permission to step out of your coaching role and brainstorm together can be useful.

What does this do?

It allows the person you're guiding to cultivate awareness and think through their situation without you taking over and making it about you and your experiences. Although your experiences are valid, your related feelings can get in the way of your ability to engage in accurate empathy.

Brainstorming is a cognitive earthquake. It shakes things up and moves them around until you're facing a different direction with a new perspective. I often tell other clinicians that disruption is a constituent of lasting change, and a necessary one at that.

Coaching is a collaborative pursuit. During that collaboration, the pursuit of empathy significantly contributes to the desired outcomes for the person uncovering their potential.

Another example of when you need to step back but still show empathy is when the individual engaged in self-discovery gets stuck. They'll naturally look to you for answers. They might even ask you to tell them what to do. There are two problems with this:

1. If you tell them what to do, and even if you're right, they won't learn anything.
2. If you give clear instructions regarding what to do and things still go wrong, they more than likely will blame you, if not sue you, for the resulting mess.

Either way, they won't learn anything!

This kind of dynamic can quietly create an unhealthy dependency where the client begins to look to you not just for guidance, but for approval. It may not happen in one session, but when you start laying out all the answers, you rob them of the chance to grow their awareness and sharpen their own skills. A client who relies on you for everything doesn't make you a better coach; it limits both their development and yours. That's why boundaries are not optional—they're essential. True empathy means supporting without enabling, guiding without taking over.

GENERAL DOS AND DON'TS FOR PRACTICING EMPATHY

What I share here comes directly from my work as an ICF Master Certified Coach, a National Board Certified Health and Wellness Coach, a Certified Professional Diversity Coach, a Master NLP Practitioner, and a Master MBTI Practitioner. These recommendations aren't theory—they're evidence-based, rooted in positive psychology, and proven through years of practice. I've used these methods with hundreds of clients, trained life coaches on how to apply them in their own work, and taught them in lectures to graduate and medical students, as well as in Master Classes I deliver globally. Why? Because empathy isn't a soft skill—it's the backbone of lasting success and authentic connection.

And while these dos and don'ts are indispensable for coaches, healthcare professionals, and leaders working with clients, patients, and teams, their value extends far beyond the professional sphere. They're just as powerful in everyday life—helping you prevent misunderstandings, resolve conflicts, and strengthen the bonds that matter most, whether with your partner, your family, or your friends.

Some of these might sound repetitive after the last few chapters, but they're crucial for establishing a foundation you can rely upon in any situation that could benefit from empathy.

WHAT YOU SHOULD DO

Start by looking inward to understand how you show up for every conversation.

How are you coming to the table? What is happening beneath the surface that might influence how you open up to and present yourself to another person? If you don't understand all these things about yourself, how can you focus on someone else? How much of you is available to give you your attention to how they're feeling, and where they're coming from?

You might not even realize that your feelings and beliefs are being pushed to the forefront and consuming the session. It's crucial to cultivate and practice self-awareness before, during, and after sessions to prevent our own emotions and beliefs from overshadowing our clients' priorities.

To develop self-awareness, we must first recognize that our emotions and beliefs are powerful forces that can significantly impact our thoughts, actions, and interactions. They can cloud our judgment, making it difficult to remain objective and present during sessions. For example, if we are feeling anxious or stressed, we may be more likely to react defensively or withdraw from the conversation altogether. Similarly, if we hold strong beliefs about a particular topic, we may be less open to hearing alternative perspectives or considering new information.

Practicing self-awareness involves observing our thoughts, feelings, and bodily sensations without judgment. This can be challenging, as we often become so caught up in the moment that we fail to notice our internal state. However, by regularly taking a step back and observing ourselves, we can begin to identify patterns and triggers that influence our behavior.

Once we become more aware of our emotions and beliefs, we can start to take steps to manage them in a more client-centered way. This may involve challenging our negative thoughts, practicing relaxation techniques, or seeking support from others. By developing greater self-awareness, we can become more mindful of our impact on others and create a more positive and productive environment for client success and personal growth.

Here are some tips for cultivating and practicing self-awareness:

1. Pay attention to your physical sensations. What are you feeling in your body? Are you tense, relaxed, or somewhere in between?
2. Identify your emotions. What emotions are you experiencing? Are you feeling happy, sad, angry, or something else?
3. Observe your thoughts. What are you thinking about? Are your thoughts positive, negative, or neutral?
4. Consider your motivations. Why are you doing what you're doing? What are your goals and intentions?

Reflect on your interactions with your clients and others. How are you interacting with others? Are you being respectful, kind, and supportive? If not, you have more work to do.

With that said, let's consider another "do" for accurate empathy.

5. Do listen actively and nonjudgmentally.

Don't just wait for your turn to talk. If you're focused on what you'll say while someone's still talking, you won't be able to fully process and understand what they're saying and how and why they're saying it.

Whether you're in session or simply engaging with friends, family, and those who are near and dear to you, think about creating a safe space for the other person to speak honestly. Pay close attention to what they're telling you with their words and nonverbal cues.

Are you reflecting what they're saying back to them with your own insights, gestures, and facial expressions?

It's ideal to take some time after fully listening to them to think about your response, so you can respond with empathy. Don't make the mistake of trying to multitask. You'll miss out on what they mean, even if you don't miss out on the words they say.

6. Do build on what they're saying, so you can move toward greater understanding and connection.

When it's your turn to respond, don't just glaze over everything they told you. Ask clarifying questions. Repeat what they said so you can make sure you understand them. Validate their feelings. Then you can add your insights and experiences. It's essential that you *both* feel heard and understood, but that can't happen if one or both of you are simply waiting to interject your opinion or prematurely offer your support.

Yes, as a coach, you're supposed to help your clients based on what you know. However, what you know to be true for you or someone else might not be particularly helpful or true for another client.

You expect the human being behind the story to be open to learning, and you must expect the same from yourself.

7. Do revisit and reflect.

Regular introspection and reflection are critical on your journey of growth and self-actualization. If you can acknowledge that there's always room to improve, and you're willing to do the work to figure out how, then your outcomes will mirror your efforts.

Our experiences serve as data points that we can use to better understand ourselves and others. As we are now aware, this deep understanding is a crucial element of accurate empathy.

Now that we have the basic "dos" down, let's talk about actions that hinder the establishment and use of accurate empathy.

WHAT YOU SHOULDN'T DO

1. Don't ignore or downplay your own biases.

Be honest about where you're coming from and unpack your own baggage before you try to listen and engage in conversation. What are your personal triggers? Are there certain factors at play, like your age, race, gender, culture, personality type, or background that might be potential barriers to understanding?

Some limiting beliefs are more deeply rooted than others. However, being aware of them is a step in the right direction.

It's impossible to eliminate all biases, but it's entirely possible to choose whether they'll help or hinder you from properly showing empathy. You're teaching your clients to take a more objective and nonjudgmental viewpoint of themselves and their lives, so it only makes sense to do the same for yourself.

2. Don't overlook indicators of misplaced empathy.

Learn to recognize the early warning signs before getting into dangerous territory. Are you feeling excessive empathy that might lead to unwelcome outcomes such as exhaustion, apathy, or transference? Are you too emotionally involved, or not involved enough? Are you at risk of enabling instead of empowering?

The answers to these questions will always depend on the situation and on your relationship with the other person. A key part of *accurate empathy* is knowing when and how to apply it in ways that serve both you and them.

That said, there are moments when what's really needed isn't empathy, but sympathy—and it's important to know the difference. *Empathy* is about stepping into another person's experience, seeing the world through their eyes, and connecting with their feelings. *Sympathy*, on the other hand, means recognizing their pain from the outside and offering compassion without fully entering into their emotional space.

Most situations call for empathy because it builds a deeper connection and understanding. In some cases, such as when someone simply needs comfort or acknowledgment rather than exploration, sympathy may be more appropriate. While this distinction may seem subtle, understanding it helps you respond in a way that actually supports the other person, rather than overwhelming them or yourself.

3. Don't assume that you've mastered empathy and have no more work to do.

Learning accurate empathy is a lifelong process. As we've established, every person and situation is different. You'll also change a lot throughout your life. It might be easier to show empathy in one season of your life and more difficult in another.

If you adopt a learning mindset and get curious about yourself and others, you'll constantly improve your ability to show accurate empathy.

As I said before, you can apply these dos and don'ts to coaching, as well as any other situation. While most of this chapter is geared more toward coaches and clinicians, reading on will still benefit you and the people in your life.

THE COMPOUNDING EFFECTS OF MISUSING EMPATHY

In Chapter Two, we talked about the potential consequences of misusing empathy. There are many pitfalls we have to avoid as professionals, not only for legal and ethical reasons, but also for our own well-being.

We haven't necessarily discussed the detrimental effects of misusing or neglecting empathy over time. I don't want to scare you, especially because you're here putting in the work. You're already doing what you need to do to strengthen your relationships with others, as well as your relationship with yourself. However, I want to raise awareness about what can happen when a lack of or misuse of empathy chips away at our happiness, health, and success.

Knowing what this looks like may help you guide others toward a better life.

In both your personal and professional life, neglecting to show empathy and/or not receiving empathy often leads to the deterioration of:

1. Trust.
2. Respect.
3. Compassion.
4. Commitment.

The erosion of these key aspects of healthy relationships frequently leads to resentment. Once resentment is involved, showing empathy becomes even more challenging. However, it's not impossible. I've worked with couples who come into coaching with resentment existing between them. In any situation like this, empathy is crucial for helping them overcome their challenges and thrive, whether they decide to separate or stay together.

Many say love, trust, or respect is the glue that holds our relationships together. However, you can't sustain any of those things without empathy. While these things are important in any relationship, empathy is the true adhesive that helps us understand, forgive, and connect with others and ourselves. If you want to be heard and understood, make sure you're not holding the important people in your life to a double standard.

Now, I want to talk more about the importance of compassion when finding your way on your journey to accurate empathy in both a professional and personal context.

COMPASSION IN COACHING AND BEYOND

To use accurate empathy, I like to start with compassion. The word compassion means "to suffer with." As we've discussed in other chapters, accurate empathy shouldn't drain or destroy you, but it does require feeling with someone.

So, what does sitting with our clients in their pain and joy look like?

1. Listen instead of taking over the conversation.
2. Be present and ask them follow-up questions to truly understand them. You must demonstrate that you're fully present in the moment and genuinely invested in their growth. This is a good time to use reflections.
3. Validate how they feel, but also help them figure out why they feel that way without any judgment.
4. Help them find their way and make their own choices by guiding them to discover the answers and solutions, rather than simply telling them.

Notice how we're focused on understanding, validating, being present, and supporting them. It's not about pitying them, telling them what they should do, or getting so emotionally involved that we're showing them we're angry or sad on their behalf.

You may feel sad or angry on their behalf, so it's essential to check in with yourself to ensure you're not exacerbating their emotions or letting your own emotions take over their experiences. This is precisely why compassion is only one aspect of empathy.

LET'S CONSIDER COMPASSION AND EMPATHY IN OUR PERSONAL LIVES

Have you ever made a mistake and begged someone for forgiveness? Have you ever felt ashamed of yourself for not being more intentional, thoughtful, or considerate? What effects did this self-hatred have on the way you carried yourself and saw yourself moving forward? It likely left you jaded and guarded. Perhaps you don't trust yourself to treat others better or avoid similar mistakes in the future. So you have your walls up in future relationships, and you trust others less as well. A lack of self-compassion and empathy in these cases prevents you from showing these things toward others who are important to you.

What about the other way around? When someone betrays your trust or makes a mistake that affects you, are you willing to hear them out and try to understand where they're coming from? This isn't to say everyone deserves a second or third chance. You have to believe some people when they show you who they truly are. However, what about when someone realizes their mistake and is willing to do better going forward? You don't necessarily have to let them back into your life (showing yourself empathy might dictate that you let them go), but you *can* empathize and show compassion toward them and not let the experience affect your future relationships in a negative way.

I've mentioned how you have to show yourself compassion and empathy first. However, it's also possible to have empathy for yourself and either knowingly or unknowingly withhold it from others. Listening to understand someone is a crucial element of accurate empathy. Even if the other person doesn't necessarily deserve it, knowing how to give it while still maintaining boundaries will benefit you in the short and long run.

We often discuss the importance of listening and responding with empathy, but what does effective listening entail? Hint: it's not just hearing their words.

PICKING UP ON VERBAL AND NONVERBAL CUES

Whether you're in a coaching session, talking to a friend, or in a work meeting, there are different things you need to pay attention to.

It's not always about what the other person says, but *how* they say it, which will tell you what you need to know to apply empathy appropriately. If they say something that's not funny, especially if it's quite a serious topic, and it's followed by a laugh, you shouldn't ignore it. A client demonstrating inappropriate affect is certainly not something to ignore. Similarly, if they're discussing an emotional topic and their external composure suggests they're unaffected by it, you can assume there's more going on beneath the surface.

It's imperative to learn how to actively listen and respond in any situation, especially if you're a coach or leader in your organization. The person you're guiding—or your team member—is looking to you for support. Your presence and responses may influence how they share their feelings with you, and your demeanor can significantly affect how much they trust you. Remember: No trust—no relationship.

Set aside your ego and focus on the individual you're supporting during brainstorming sessions. Look for indicators in their tone, inflection, posture, breathing, hand movements, and body language. By observing these cues, you can better understand how they're feeling and tailor your approach accordingly.

Accurate empathy dictates that we don't simply observe and ignore nonverbal cues. In these cases, ask the person you're working with if you can point something out to them.

By asking your client's permission:

1. You create a pause that allows them to step back from being fully absorbed in their story. This small interruption helps them reintegrate, regain perspective, and see what's happening more clearly.
2. You gently bring attention to how the subject is affecting them emotionally, without forcing or overwhelming them. The act of asking permission fosters trust, demon-

strates respect, and maintains a collaborative coaching process. In doing so, you're not only protecting their emotional safety but also helping them develop the self-awareness necessary for genuine growth.

Once you have their permission, follow-up questions will enhance your understanding of their perspective and allow you to respond appropriately.

You might say something like, "When you just said that, I noticed that you laughed. What's funny about what you said?"

They might squeeze the arms of the chair they're sitting in, roll their eyes, or cross their arms instead of laughing, but the required follow-up is the same. While it might seem confrontational to make them address their subconscious responses, they must be aware and work toward resolving their feelings out in the open.

A good clinician recognizes an opportunity to explore why and how the subject is affecting their client, and the same holds true for an effective leader. By empathizing with them at that moment and affirming their emotional state, you're setting them up for introspection.

If the person you're working with is struggling, observe when they use extremes to describe their situation. Something I often hear is, "Nobody likes me." All that's needed here is reflection. You can encourage them to think about this more by asking, "Nobody? You're saying *nobody* likes you?" When they think about it more, they'll likely come to realize that their heightened emotions are leading them to amplify the severity of their situation.

When they express anger or sadness, accurate empathy is essential. For example, if someone is going through a really difficult time, such as losing a loved one to a terminal disease, and they start crying during the session, it's important to validate their feelings and acknowledge the difficulty of their situation. Instead of just giving them comfort and moving on, it's also an opportunity for a genuine connection. You can ask them to sit with their feelings and figure out what their emotions are telling them. This might seem obvious, but asking these questions can help them reflect and gain insight, rather than sending them further down the rabbit hole of despair. Accurate empathy won't eliminate their pain, but your presence can help them feel supported as they explore their feelings, gain insight, and discover new and better ways to cope.

WHAT YOUR CLIENTS (OR THE OTHER PERSON IN THE CONVERSATION) NEED FROM YOU

We've already fleshed out the differences between empathy and sympathy. However, knowing these differences doesn't make you immune to the sympathy trap.

While sympathy isn't always a bad thing, it leaves more to be desired in most situations. It also presents a unique problem for coaches. If we feel sympathy instead of empathy, it can come across as saying to the person we're supporting, "You poor thing." This labels them as a victim. That mentality will stifle their progress if they adopt it.

Alternatively, empathy encourages the individual to take ownership of their life. The people you're guiding don't need your pity—they likely pity themselves enough for both of you. For someone to truly grow from the coaching experience, they need your empathetic presence. It's not your job to make meaning of their feelings and thoughts. That's up to them, but you can guide the process by stimulating awareness and reflection. This requires you to be completely present and engage in active listening as long as you're with the person in front of you.

This brings us back to what coaching is all about. You want the individual to tap into their internal resources so they can rely on themselves for their health, success, and happiness. You don't want them to become stuck thinking you're the only one who can help them make sense of their life. That's unethical and goes against our purpose as coaches.

I always tell the people I coach, "You are so much stronger than you think." Through suffering and turmoil, we can tap into the better parts of ourselves. If a movie showed the primary character easily overcoming every challenge that came their way, that would be one boring movie. What puts us at the edge of our seats is that the hero needs to have hope, faith, and strength to overcome what's put before them. The same is true for those we support in this work.

Accurate empathy in coaching is essential to illuminate the rabbit holes people find themselves in. When properly utilized, accurate empathy shines a light on the untapped cognitive and emotional resources they possess.

Your empathy and compassion are the tools that give the individuals you serve the little nudges they need to take another step.

HOW A DISPLAY OF EMPATHY CHANGED THE TRAJECTORY OF MY COACHING PRACTICE

I have many experiences with my own clients that demonstrate the power of accurate empathy, but I also want to discuss being on the receiving end. Learning to receive empathy is just as important as giving it.

I had reached a point in my practice where I was comfortable, but I knew I was capable of much more. This comfort led me to work with high-profile clients whom I felt were more intelligent and more astute than I was. However, that sense of ease was short-lived because these clients were doctors, lawyers, and other professionals who had already achieved a great deal and were seeking someone to help them reach the next level. I remember feeling worried that they would present a situation I couldn't fathom or ask me questions I couldn't answer.

I thought to myself: *Am I really as good as I think? I hope I don't say or do anything to make a fool of myself.*

I recall calling my mentor, Margaret Moore, from the Institute of Coaching, an affiliate of Harvard Medical School, and sharing all this with her. I told her I felt stuck. She could have given me some generic advice and sent me on my way. Instead, she demonstrated accurate empathy.

She didn't answer any questions for me. Instead, she listened to my worst fears and responded with empathy and compassion so I could use what I had within me to move forward. That's what a great coach and mentor does.

She helped me look at my dilemma from the other side of the room—a new perspective. An hour later, I realized that my takeaway from our conversation was that I could focus on what I have control over and what I could do to ensure things go right, rather than dwell on what could go wrong. This doesn't mean I was delusional or relying on things to happen for me. I knew I would do whatever it took to move forward, one step at a time. She asked me, "What do you feel you're lacking?" She reflected my thoughts back to me, helping me shift from a mindset of "I'm stuck" to one of "I'm in a place where I have the chance to explore new approaches and strategies." It's all about recognizing that you're not stuck; you're simply paused in a positive way. That pause allowed me to engage in deep introspection and discover the "purpose" behind my circumstances. It certainly made a difference.

Accurate empathy set me on a trajectory of increased competence and awareness in my coaching role. The same can be true for you in your life, whether you're trying to improve your personal relationships or your leadership skills. When you choose empathy over sympathy for yourself and others, you choose how you're affected by challenges and setbacks. If you're a coach, you're helping your clients choose how they respond to situations in their lives.

Accurate empathy and positive psychology overlap in this way. You want to understand emotions and how to embrace them for all they have to offer so you can thrive individually and with others. Empathy is a major part of the pursuit of fulfillment and meaning. Embracing positive psychology and accurate empathy doesn't mean you're not allowed to have negative feelings toward yourself or others. It also doesn't mean you'll have the perfect empathetic response every time. However, once you have the tools to strengthen your personal and professional relationships with accurate empathy, it becomes a lot easier to get it right in various situations.

HOW TO APPLY ALL THIS TO YOUR LIFE (EVEN IF YOU'RE NOT A COACH)

I'll reiterate that even though much of this book, and this chapter in particular, is geared toward coaches, leaders, and clinicians, it still applies to everyone. These techniques aren't limited to a coaching or therapy environment. You can and should use accurate empathy with your friends, coworkers, clients, children, and other loved ones.

The approaches in this book share one core element. They help foster an environment where the person you're talking to feels seen and heard. It's not always easy to find the right approach that makes someone feel this way. As we've learned, even good intentions can result in an inaccurate use of empathy. It's crucial to shift the way we view our problems, as well as the problems of others, before we try to help.

Oftentimes, we're so desperate to solve a problem that we don't learn from the experience. Problems are learning opportunities. They give us the chance to tap into our own unearthed wisdom, tenacity, and courage. Without turmoil, our most potent gifts otherwise would remain untapped. You can see this when your child is learning to walk. As a parent, you must learn to strike a balance between not saying anything and encouraging them. Simply being there and being patient shows your child that you're there for them. You must let them learn and solve their problems while showing them your care. In a business setting, maybe you approach a team member with a tough task and tell them, "This isn't going to be easy, but you solved the last problem we had, so what can you take from that situation?" You're not telling them how to solve the problem, but you are telling them you trust them and have faith that they can succeed.

We've used a lot of examples of the power of empathy in many different situations and settings. You might be in a unique situation and feel desperate for answers. Just remember, accurate empathy has the answer in its title—"accurate." Be aware and mindfully present of where you are and where the other person is coming from so you can do what's accurate and appropriate for the circumstances.

THE BIG PICTURE

While accurate empathy requires adjusting your approach based on the person and situation, it's also necessary for us to zoom out and see the big picture.

Once again, I'm not excusing bad behavior, but I am advocating for grace as you work toward accurate empathy. When we use empathy accurately, grace is a by-product of trying to understand and feel with others. However, sometimes grace must come before we fully understand someone.

If the person you need to show empathy to right now is someone you've known for a long time, this can either help or hurt your ability to understand them. You might give them the benefit of the doubt if there are issues to resolve with them because you're aware of their character, and you know there's mutual respect. Unfortunately, being in a long-term relationship, romantic or otherwise, can also lead you to making unintentional assumptions. When this happens, you need to try to understand who they are and what they're feeling *now*. People change, and accurate empathy means being fully present *and* focusing on the present.

Here are some steps you can take to bring yourself back to the present when you're struggling to show accurate empathy.

1. Accept that the people in your life will have good times and bad.

Acceptance is the first step toward healing in any situation. You'll go through light, dark, and in-between periods. You'll change, even if it's only slightly, in all these seasons. The same is true for everyone else.

2. Check in with yourself. (Are you getting tired of hearing this yet?)

It's *always* essential to know where you are mentally and emotionally whenever you enter a conversation or conflict. Of course, you can't know how a conversation will go before it begins. However, this book is geared toward helping you do the work beforehand to develop the tools you need for accurate empathy and compassionate communication.

It's also okay to pause a conversation if you're not in the right headspace or you need some time to cool off and/or think.

3. Listen, observe, absorb, and respond. (Are you sensing a theme?)

We come to every conversation with preexisting beliefs and biases. The only way to overcome these and ensure they don't prevent us from showing and receiving empathy is to engage in active listening, which we've covered extensively in this chapter.

While you may know some things about yourself and others, you don't know all. Keep an open mind and be willing to learn something new with every interaction.

You can't have accurate empathy without openness.

4. Take care of yourself at all times.

If you prioritize your health and well-being, staying present and focusing on the person in front of you will be much easier. Commit to nurturing your body and mind daily, as you're doing now by reading this book and working on your ability to understand yourself and others.

I'll discuss self-care more later. It isn't selfish or self-indulgent. It's an absolute necessity if you want to thrive in life and business. Caring for yourself is a prerequisite for caring for others.

5. Acknowledge your limits.

We discussed acknowledging your limits in the context of coaching and being selective about who you work with and when you work. This is also crucial in your personal life. If you don't have the emotional capacity, or what someone needs is outside of your area of expertise, be honest about these barriers. It doesn't mean you can't show them empathy, but it does mean they might need help and understanding beyond your capabilities.

As I've said before, hurting people hurt people, so make sure you're able to handle taking on what's before you. This might mean taking some extra time to think and process your own feelings, as we discussed, or it might mean that you need to take a break from your relationship for a while. You can still show empathy even if you need to set some firm boundaries.

MAIN TAKEAWAYS FROM THIS CHAPTER

⇒ Using empathy in coaching and any other situation requires awareness and caution.

We know empathy can be dangerous if used incorrectly or carelessly. This is even more of a concern for coaches and clinicians, who are at an increased risk for burnout or jeopardizing the coach-client (or clinician-client) relationship.

Utilizing empathy in coaching has to be done with care so the person you're supporting can make their own decisions and create their own outcomes. You're there to empathize with them and guide them so *they* can learn to rely on themselves in the future.

⇒ Each situation and person is different, but the dos and don'ts in this chapter are the baseline requirements for employing accurate empathy.

If you follow these guidelines in your personal and professional interactions, you'll have a foundation you can build upon. You'll also have a greater understanding of yourself and others, which will improve your life in so many ways.

⇒ Listening, when the purpose is to engage in accurate empathy, doesn't only mean listening to what the other person says.

Listen to how they're saying it. Take notice of the situation and their nonverbal responses. There's always much more beneath the surface, and if you truly want to establish trust and deepen your relationship, you must be willing to look for it yourself instead of waiting for them to reveal it all to you.

Accurate empathy is easier to display when you have as much information as possible.

⇒ Brainstorming can be an effective tool in coaching, or even in a more personal context, like talking with a friend.

It allows the other person to find out more about how they're feeling and why on their own, but it also helps you further understand their perspective and position. They might realize something about themselves or the situation that they couldn't see before because they were so enmeshed in the same thoughts.

Offering a co-brainstorming session in coaching can be particularly helpful because it shows the individual navigating change that they're capable of figuring things out and taking the appropriate actions instead of making them feel reliant on you or others.

⇒ Sympathy is not more appropriate than empathy in most situations.

Think about a time when someone showed sympathy for you. Odds are you didn't feel seen and heard. You probably felt:

- Pitied
- Dismissed
- Like you should feel sorry for yourself
- Unmotivated to take action to change your situation

These are all results of giving or receiving sympathy when empathy should be present.

Sometimes we experience something horrible, and it's okay to feel sorry for ourselves for a time. These are the moments we need to show ourselves empathy.

⇒ I've experienced the power of receiving empathy, and it helped me change my path for the better.

I subscribe to everything I teach you in this book because I've lived these experiences.

My mentor, Margaret Moore, showed me what's possible when accurate empathy is used. She listened to me, assisted me with reflecting, and helped me figure out the problem and solution for myself. Because of her and many others who helped me realize what I was capable of, I'm writing this book for you now so you can improve your life and attain health, wealth, and happiness.

⇒ We all want to be seen and heard.

Even those who claim they want to be left alone or ignored have these base desires. I've said many times that if you don't see and understand yourself, nobody else will see or hear you in the way you wish to be seen and heard. Lead by example and show others what you want and need. Show yourself empathy and recognize it when others show it to you.

⇒ Show yourself and others grace.

As you work on refining your approach to empathy, you'll realize that giving yourself and others grace is a major part of the process.

Accurate empathy involves dealing with the situation in front of you and getting curious about the other person. Sometimes, having a long-standing relationship with someone can help you show empathy more easily, but there are other times when you're probably inhibited by biases you've developed throughout the relationship. It's helpful to be aware of these potential biases and beliefs toward the other person or the relationship in general so you can set them aside and focus on the current situation.

Chapter Five

THIS IS YOUR BRAIN ON EMPATHY

SO FAR, WE'VE ESTABLISHED EMPATHY as an essential skill for coaches, leaders, clinicians, and mental health professionals. However, we have yet to explore the scientific aspects of compassion and empathy. Comprehending the psychological and scientific dynamics behind empathy is crucial if we are to fully understand its potential to transform not only our lives but also the lives of our clients. As leaders, coaches, clinicians, and just ethical human beings, we must highlight that our assertions are not just personal beliefs or hypotheses but are backed by substantial evidence and research.

Emotions don't just happen to us, even though they may feel that way sometimes. We have more control than we realize over how we regulate and respond to our emotions. In this chapter, we'll discuss the neuroscience of empathy. Rest assured that it won't be boring or technical, and there won't be a quiz.

There are so many distractions throughout our day. Being empathetic is probably the last thing on your mind when facing everyday stressors like paying bills and putting out fires at work and at home. As our lives are filled with too many distractions, we tend to focus on cleaning up messes and solving problems instead of being proactive and intentional in our interactions and behaviors.

All of us want a better life. Nobody wants to wake up anxious, distracted, or distressed. It's not always possible to act with foresight rather than hindsight, but isn't it better when you can?

Who wants to be in problematic relationships? Who wants to recycle through the same thoughts, especially the debilitating type? The good news is, if those last few sentences describe your current situation, you can do something significant to counteract all the negative forces that are disrupting your life. Fact: the world will treat you how you treat yourself!

If you possess a strong sense of self-worth, and despite your healthy sense of self, you find yourself dealing with challenges in your relationships or still struggle to keep your focus while attempting to stay on track with achieving your goals, fear not. It's likely that adjusting your approach to empathy could be the key to unlocking its rewards for both you and those around you.

THE BRAIN AND EMPATHY

The prefrontal cortex (PFC) is the part of your brain that's involved in higher-level emotional and cognitive processes like abstract thinking, planning, foresight, decision-making, social functioning, altering emotion, and, you guessed it, empathy. Emotion and behavior are connected by a pathway from the orbito-ventromedial PFC (emotional control) to the dorsolateral PFC (cognitive control).

Before you become disinterested or overwhelmed by this technical language, it's important to understand that it highlights the correlation between emotions and behavior. This awareness is crucial as you embark on your journey to fully comprehend and apply accurate empathy while increasing your capacity to better regulate your own emotions and behaviors.

Some of what we know about the prefrontal cortex came from the experience of Phineas Gage, a railroad foreman who suffered a brain injury where an iron rod pierced his brain (Teles-Filho et al. 2020). While the injury wasn't life-threatening, his frontal lobes were damaged, and his personality was altered forever. Studies have shown that injury to the prefrontal cortex (PFC) can lead to difficulties with planning, decision-making, and impulse control. Of these difficulties, the loss of impulse control is particularly influential in various negative thought patterns and behaviors.

Your PFC develops throughout adolescence and continues to develop during the first stage of early adult life. Your experiences contribute to the learning and solidifying of skills like emotional regulation, planning, making judgments, and reasoning. We continue developing these executive functions as we age, but start losing them due to aging, neurological disease, and prolonged stress and anxiety.

While our experiences significantly influence our emotional and behavioral patterns during adolescence, the good news is that we can modify our neural networks and behavior. This is known as neuroplasticity, which we'll discuss in more detail later.

Now, we're going to talk about using the neuroscience top-down approach to master accurate empathy.

WHY THE TOP-DOWN APPROACH IS NECESSARY FOR ACCURATE EMPATHY

In my approach to behavioral neuroscience, I combine the most effective evidence and research-based practices from coaching and positive psychology. This holistic method for promoting well-being is both practical and enduring, as it encompasses both bottom-up and top-down processing and takes into strong consideration the various components of one's surroundings. My coaching methodology involves recognizing and being mindful of how these components interact with each other and impact our physical, emotional, cognitive, spiritual, and social well-being.

Bottom-up elements include biological or physiological components of brain health, such as:

- Genetics
- Nutrition
- Exercise
- Hormones
- The immune system
- Other lifestyle choices

Top-down elements involve our:

- Beliefs
- Mindset
- Thoughts
- Emotions
- Core values

Finally, outside-in covers:

- Stress
- Education
- Life events
- Family background
- Traumatic experiences
- Current circumstances
- Other social and environmental factors

All these elements contribute to our overall health, success, and well-being. Since empathy is rooted in thoughts and emotions, a top-down approach is essential for its effective application.

The brain works to provoke empathic responses in two different ways:

1. Bottom-up processing.
2. Top-down processing.

Bottom-up processing is immediate and involuntary, enabling us to detect others' emotional states through mechanisms such as emotional contagion and facial mimicry. These presentations are primal, overt, and reactive. Put simply, they're instinctive with one goal in mind—survival. An example of this is how our mirror neurons drive us to assimilate with who and what's in our environment. If someone smiles at us, we feel the need to smile back. If people appear distressed or sad, we instinctively know not to smile or appear jovial. However, matching others' facial expressions doesn't mean we're actually empathizing with them. The same is true for other responses under bottom-up processing. We're not necessarily feeling their suffering just because we mirror the grimace that reflects their pain.

Top-down processing is a conscious and flexible approach that enables us to regulate our empathic responses by considering factors such as perspective-taking, core values, and intention. This method involves actively imagining and trying to understand how an individual, including ourselves, might experience certain emotions before reacting impulsively. Another method is contextual appraisal, which entails adjusting an automatic response based on the specific context of a situation. By combining contextual appraisal and top-down processing, we empower ourselves to influence our outcomes deliberately. It's not surprising that proactive thinking leads to more favorable results compared to realizing things in hindsight.

To develop a well-rounded understanding of empathy, it's essential to consider both internal and external factors. While some internal elements may be difficult or impossible to change, they tend to be more adaptable than external factors. It's crucial to focus on these internal components consciously. Additionally, it's essential to recognize that intentional effort is required for top-down processing, as highlighted in the previous chapter. Building accurate empathy necessitates thoughtful and purposeful engagement. Without this intentionality and mindfulness, there is a heightened risk of misunderstanding or misusing empathy, which can be detrimental to both yourself and others.

Intention and self-empathy have saved me in my personal life and my practice time and time again.

THE REALIZATION THAT MADE ME SHIFT MY APPROACH...AGAIN

Every day, people walk into my office feeling exploited, overlooked, or underappreciated. These emotions often grow out of two sources: mistakes from the past they can't undo, or an inability to forgive themselves or others for things beyond their control. What I've learned from listening to their stories is this: their struggles mirror my own. The challenges they face in their relationships and responsibilities aren't so different from the ones I've wrestled with personally and professionally.

The truth is, we teach others how to treat us by the way we treat ourselves. Our thoughts, habits, and daily choices shape not only our careers and relationships but also our overall well-being. For years, I didn't realize how dissatisfied I was with the way I treated myself—until the disappointment I felt in how others treated me forced me to see it. That revelation led to a hard but obvious conclusion: the first step in gaining the respect of others is recognizing the need to respect yourself. When you raise the standard for how you treat and view yourself, you set the bar for how the world engages with you.

Think about it like this: How can you get a desirable outcome with a tainted thought process? You can't change your actions and create healthy, sustainable approaches to improving your health and happiness without adjusting or completely changing your mindset. Put another way, "Reality is perception. To change your reality, you must change your perception."

Many of us tend to default to a negative mindset. This can be due to a variety of factors, including our experiences, our environment, and our biology. For example, people who belong to marginalized groups or who have been in survival mode for a long time may be more likely to have a negative mindset. This is because they have often been exposed to trauma, discrimination, and other stressors that can lead to negative thoughts and emotions.

In the bigger picture, this predisposition toward being prone to stress and anxiety has been part of the human condition since early times. In prehistoric eras, being hypervigilant was crucial for survival. Being alert to a moving shadow in the night or a suspicious stare from a member of an unfamiliar tribe could mean the difference between life and death. So, it's not surprising that we are still prewired to be hypervigilant today; it's in our genes. However, with awareness and self-compassion, we can learn to manage these instincts in a way that serves our well-being.

Being on social media and watching TV puts us on a path of comparing ourselves and our lives to others and what we see of their lives. We tend to view what's wrong with ourselves more often than what's right. We compare our appearance, lifestyle, and other aspects of our lives to those of people we don't even know. What makes this more concerning is that much of what we see is a lie, or a small part of the truth. Now, it's more crucial than ever to put things in perspective. It's up to you to intentionally make the choice to care about yourself and your emotional health more than concerning yourself with keeping up appearances.

In some cases, a negative mindset can become chronic or even generational. This means that it can be passed down from parents to children through various mechanisms, such as modeling, parenting style, and genetic factors. For example, children who grow up in homes where their parents are constantly negative are more likely to develop a negative mindset themselves.

The good news is that it is possible to shift our perspective and break free from negative patterns. This takes time and effort, but it's possible. One way to do this is to challenge our negative thoughts and beliefs. When we catch ourselves thinking negatively, we can ask ourselves if there is any evidence to support our thoughts. We can also try to come up with alternative, more positive thoughts.

Another way to shift our perspective is to focus on gratitude. When we focus on the things we're grateful for, it's harder to dwell on the negatives. We can practice gratitude by keeping a gratitude journal, saying thank you to people who have helped us, or simply taking time each day to appreciate the good things in our lives.

Even if you're a credentialed coach or clinician, it's crucial to seek professional help if you're struggling with a negative mindset. A Master-Certified Coach or licensed therapist can help you identify the root of your negative thoughts and help you develop more effective coping mechanisms while increasing your self-efficacy and resilience.

In the early years of my practice, I would often become too immersed in my clients' problems. As a young, struggling clinician, I wasn't taking any days off. I took phone calls at inconvenient times, even on the weekends and in the wee hours of the night, because I wanted to accomplish two goals: help my clients and pay my bills.

To achieve both objectives, I thought I had to be everything for everyone all at once. Little did I realize the toll it was taking on my emotional and mental well-being. I was stressing myself the hell out.

> "Burned out from blurred boundaries, I asked myself a hard question: *How can I empower others so well, yet fail to protect my own well-being?* That moment changed everything—it taught me that real empowerment begins with the boundaries I set for myself."
>
> —Dr. D Ivan Young, MCC, NBC-HWC

I had to stop and ask myself what I could actually do to help myself. For years, I'd been exceptional at coaching others—teaching them how to build self-efficacy, resilience, faith, and confidence. Yet when it came to applying those same principles to my own life, I realized I was falling short. Coming from a challenging background as a minority in a predominantly Anglo-centric environment, I know all too well the struggle of living without the privilege of self-actualization. For me, the goal was simple: just get through the day. Over time, I've seen that many people in similar circumstances are so consumed with survival that they never truly learn how to live—productively, joyfully, or in a way that nurtures their health. I have to be honest: I'm no exception. Even now, the constant code-switching wears on me. It gets old. It takes a toll.

For many of my clients, myself included, failing to empathize with oneself creates an unstable mental and emotional environment. What do you do when you haven't been equipped with the tools to create an equal playing field for yourself and your loved ones? How can you improve if you lack the knowledge to do so? Even after overcoming numerous physical obstacles, there are still mental barriers that limit our perceptions of what we deserve and what we're capable of achieving. This realization necessitates a thorough examination of our self-perception and the reality we have embraced.

Limiting beliefs are often so deeply ingrained in your subconscious that it takes cultivating self-awareness and intentional action to escape their grasp. For example, if you come from a background of poverty and struggle, you might have trouble appreciating your success when you finally attain it. You may feel guilty for not struggling when your family did for so long, or maybe you think you need to continue working your butt off to an unnecessary degree to deserve your success. Cultivating self-empathy is the first step in changing your mindset and allowing yourself happiness and success. Once you do it for yourself, you can do it for others. Spreading this outlook can only positively impact those in your life.

By the end of this chapter, I hope that you'll finally be able to give yourself accurate empathy. Only then can you change your life and the lives of those around you for the better.

GRAB YOUR PEN AND PAPER: IT'S TIME FOR MORE INTROSPECTION

Remember, be honest with yourself.

1. Write down the current status of your life.

I don't mean just your credit score or what's in your savings account. Yes, those things matter, but I want you to look deeper. Focus on the *intangibles*, the quiet forces that either contribute to your happiness or quietly drain it away.

How happy are you—really?

You're the only one who will see this unless you decide to share it, so be brutally honest. Are you truly happy right now? If yes, that's something to be grateful for. If not, let that honesty become your starting point.

From there, go deeper: *why aren't you happy?*

We all have rough days and seasons of struggle. However, if most mornings you wake up feeling out of sync with the life you want, that's not just fatigue—it's a signal. Signals are meant to be acted on. There's no better time than the present to start making those changes.

Ask yourself:

- Do you have relationships that feel more draining than supportive?
- Do you run out of money before the month runs out?
- Are you or someone you love carrying the weight of a chronic or serious health issue?
- Are you in the middle of a breakup or bracing yourself for one?

This is real life, and the truth is, you can't escape it. No amount of money or resources will erase these realities. Only you can decide your next move.

You have two options:

- You can take responsibility, extend grace to yourself, and keep moving forward.
- You can slip into self-pity—confusing self-sympathy with self-empathy—and remain stuck, overwhelmed, and maybe even miserable.

One path leads to growth and resilience. The other keeps you trapped. The choice is yours.

2. Let's go deeper—pause and reflect on what you've experienced over the last five to ten years.
   - Have you lost someone close to you or even a beloved pet who was like family?
   - Have you faced a major financial shift that shook your sense of stability?
   - Have you struggled with your body image or felt dissatisfied with your physical appearance?
   - Have you battled serious health challenges or lived with ongoing issues that drain your energy?
   - Has your marriage or relationship lost its spark, or become a source of strain rather than strength?

These aren't just surface-level questions. They point to the real transitions that shape how we see ourselves and the world. It's normal to go through seasons of turbulence, where change feels heavier and the struggle sharper. What makes the difference isn't avoiding those experiences—it's how you meet them.

This is where empathy, especially self-empathy, becomes vital. Your experiences shape your mental and physical state, but they don't get the final word. You still have power in how you respond. You can stay stuck, replaying the pain and feeding negativity, or you can choose to move forward, using empathy and a growth mindset to turn those very struggles into fuel for your resilience.

> "Life may hand you struggle, but empathy and perspective decide whether you stay stuck in it or rise because of it."
>
> —Dr. D Ivan Young, MCC, NBC-HWC

3. Let's think about what you can't (or couldn't) control.
   - Did you grow up in a dysfunctional family that shaped how you see yourself and others?
   - Are your coworkers less determined or focused than you are?
   - Do you find yourself code-switching just to be accepted or fit in?
   - Have you battled health issues despite doing everything in your power to stay healthy?

The truth is, sometimes life happens, and there's no clear reason for it. When you find yourself in one of those seasons, the best thing you can do is give yourself grace. Accept that not everything is within your control—some things are in God's hands, or in the hands of whatever higher power or universal order you believe in.

Now, don't misunderstand me: I believe in taking responsibility for our thoughts, choices, and actions. However, responsibility is not the same as blame. Don't make something your fault if it isn't. The real wisdom lies in learning to tell the difference between what requires your accountability and what requires your release. That discernment is where peace begins.

This brings us to one of the most important aspects of accurate empathy: humility. Being humble means acknowledging your limits—recognizing that you can only give so much of yourself and do so much for others before it becomes damaging to you, to them, or to both. Boundaries don't weaken empathy; they protect it. Without them, compassion becomes unsustainable, and what once felt like care can quickly turn into self-destruction.

Consider what you can control.

Are the people in your inner circle building you up or quietly tearing you down?

If you're the one everyone relies on—the "alpha" in your family—are you tired of being asked for help without anyone stopping to ask how *you're* really doing? Is the only time your phone rings when someone needs something from you?

Do you recognize that some of your own habits may be holding you back—keeping you from feeling energized, fulfilled, and motivated?

Are you struggling with patterns of addiction, dependency, or unhealthy escapes—whether that's through substances, food, sex, religion, work, or anything else that numbs more than it heals?

Pause and reflect on these questions. If you can see yourself in them, it's no wonder you wish things were different. But here's the good news: awareness is the first step toward freedom. If your answers reveal disruption, turmoil, or stress, this is your invitation to turn that awareness inward. It's time to begin applying empathy and compassion toward yourself.

Self-empathy isn't about letting yourself off the hook. It's about holding yourself accountable in a way that is constructive, caring, and sustainable. Instead of shaming yourself when it gets hard, you learn to stand beside yourself.

Here's a practical way to try it: imagine you are your own older sibling, your own parent, or even your own guardian angel. What would you say to yourself right now? What would you do for yourself, given everything you just admitted? Write it down, or if that feels like too much, record it into your phone and listen back.

Then, take a moment to visualize a physical act of comfort that feels real to you. Maybe it's your guardian angel wrapping you in a hug. Maybe it's sitting in a park, walking along the ocean, or spending quiet time with a pet. It could even be something simple—reading a book, watching a favorite show, or just sitting in nature without doing anything at all.

Now ask yourself: if someone you loved needed comfort, wouldn't you encourage them to find it in their own way? Of course you would. So why not give yourself the same permission?

How does it feel to think about showing yourself compassion? Does it make you feel seen, heard, valued, or respected? The truth is, many of us rarely experience those feelings—or we push them away because they're unfamiliar. We've been trained to dismiss healthy attention and equate worth with productivity.

It's normal to feel guilty when you're not "doing enough," even when your body and mind desperately need a break. Maybe you've even felt shame when certain emotions surface, leading you to push yourself harder instead of extending compassion. And if you grew up hearing phrases like "man up" or "stop acting like a little b*tch," those messages may still echo inside you. Too often, the most critical voices in our heads belong to authority figures from our past. Here's the truth: you don't need their approval anymore.

You get to write your own story of worth, resilience, and self-respect, and it starts with how you choose to treat yourself right now.

What if now is the time to accept that the only person you truly need approval from is yourself?

If you don't heal your inner child, every relationship you have, whether it's romantic or platonic, will be tainted by your disdain for yourself and your experiences. How you feel and treat yourself heavily influences the relationships you attract and allow into your life.

BEING SELECTIVE

When it comes to choosing a pet, I'm a firm advocate for making wise decisions. It's imperative to conduct thorough research and select a furry companion that seamlessly fits into your lifestyle. Have you ever considered applying the same principle to the people you surround yourself with? Each individual and event in our lives holds the power to either hinder us or propel us forward, ultimately affecting not only ourselves but also everything we hold dear.

> "I often tell my clients that because you can't choose your relatives, God allows us to choose our friends and pets to compensate for the people you ended up stuck with."
>
> —Dr. D Ivan Young, MCC, NBC-HWC

It's important to get to know people to ensure that you share common values and beliefs, which are aligned with your expectations, like how you want to be treated. This doesn't mean you should interrogate them. It's best to give people the benefit of the doubt and let them earn your trust over time. However, pay attention to how they treat you. Are they honest? Do they keep their promises? Can you rely on them as much as they can rely on you? How do they speak about others, especially their exes and relatives? Keep in mind that's how they'll talk about you if you become an ex or if they have an issue with you. Also, observe how they treat others, such as service industry employees and those to whom they technically don't owe anything. The way people treat those who don't "matter" to them indicates how they'll treat people who do.

Now, hold the mirror up to yourself. Are you kind to those people? If not, it's a sign that you need to work on your self-empathy. As we've discussed, those who lack empathy and compassion often don't give it to other people.

To make a shift toward being more appreciated and respected, you must value yourself and others. Love is free, but taking it for granted or not giving it can have severe costs.

So, if you want to use empathy in an impactful and sustainable way, you have to get your gratitude practice down and leave no room for taking who and what you have now and in the future for granted.

THE ROLE OF GRATITUDE

Being grateful goes a long way. Make it your mission to not lose sight of what's going well when it seems like everything is falling apart. Be grateful that you can stand up on your own. Be happy you can feed yourself. Maybe your house payment is late, but you still have a house. Maybe your car is banged up, but you still have transportation.

Until you're thankful for the few things you have, why would God or the universe give you more?

Gratitude must be a part of your approach to empathy. If it's not, it'll be difficult to show empathy to yourself when it feels like life is against you and favoring others. Comparing yourself to others and envying them will lead to being desensitized to their struggles. Gratitude, like empathy, is one of those concepts that sounds a little woo-woo until you start applying it to your own life. There are a lot of cold, hard facts to vouch for these practices and their benefits.

Both gratitude and empathy involve shifting your perspective and opening yourself up to learning. Changing your actions without first addressing and strengthening your beliefs, values, and thoughts usually leads to relapses and eventually, a permanent return to your old habits and ways of thinking. This is why accurate empathy requires a top-down approach that begins with your thoughts and emotions.

So, what can you do to shift your perspective and improve your ability to show empathy?

COGNITIVE, PHYSIOLOGICAL, AND EMOTIONAL CUES FOR EMPLOYING ACCURATE EMPATHY

As with everything else in nature, there's a cause-and-effect relationship between the cues in our environment and our reactions, as well as between our reactions and others' responses to them. An effective clinician knows the importance of observing their client's responses without judgment and in a way that allows the client to make observations and conclusions of their own. During client sessions and other personal interactions, regulating your emotions is the best way to avoid misunderstandings and properly use accurate empathy.

We often ignore warning signs from those we support, and even within ourselves, because we're not fully present. A person's transformation depends on several factors, but your ability to give them your undivided attention is one of the most important. This allows us to notice cues like facial expressions, posture, tone, and more.

No matter what language you speak, even if you're hard of hearing or can't speak, facial expressions are universally understood. We're often able to accurately detect emotions like sadness, shock, and fear simply by observing someone's expressions, posture, or breathing.

We know communication is far more than just words. Someone can say, "Good morning," and end it with a high-pitched or low-pitched voice. We intuitively recognize that the message changes depending on the tone.

You don't always know how someone is feeling based on somatic responses alone, and if you're a coach or clinician, you shouldn't make assumptions about the individual's facial expressions or tone. However, observing these responses can lead to powerful revelations if you know how to address them skillfully. By being mindfully present, we can help the person in front of us become more self-aware of their inner experiences simply by stating what we observe. Yet this isn't as simple as it sounds.

As a clinician, you can become an accomplished observer, but it takes intention and self-awareness to channel those observations into accurate empathy. A lack of presence or emotional awareness on your part can have a detrimental impact on the outcomes of the person you're working with.

They might make assumptions if you visibly react to their expressions or body language. For example, if someone tells you something you personally find offensive, it's important not to respond with an open mouth or a raised eyebrow. Even a head nod when mistimed can unintentionally damage rapport or derail the session.

You should acknowledge the individual and what they're sharing, but avoid giving any indication that you're judging them, whether positively or negatively. I learned early on that it's crucial to keep my personal reactions and assessments as a coach in check. It might seem counterintuitive in this profession, but ultimately, a coaching session isn't about me or my interpretation. It's about the person in the chair building awareness about how they're affected and how they respond to their circumstances.

Your self-awareness can protect both you and the people you support from unnecessary missteps.

If you affirm someone's feelings or behavior and it later leads to an unfavorable outcome, they may—whether consciously or subconsciously—associate that outcome with you. That's one reason it's often safer and more effective to let your words carry your observations rather than allowing your facial expressions or body language to speak for you. When you thoughtfully verbalize what you're noticing about the individual in front of you, you offer them an opportunity to view themselves from a new angle—one they may not have considered before.

A good example of this is if a client is having horrible separation anxiety because of death or divorce, you should try to maintain a demeanor that shows you're present but not embedded in their emotions. You want to show accurate empathy by helping them cultivate self-awareness and self-empathy. You can only do so if you're present and mindful enough to observe and communicate in an intentional, controlled way.

With all that said, there are three steps you can take to deepen your understanding of yourself and others to properly engage in accurate empathy.

1. Observe your initial reactions and thoughts to your own emotions, as well as others' emotions.

This practice allows you to do three powerful things:

- *Check in with yourself.* By noticing how you feel in the moment, you give yourself the chance to regulate your responses and adjust your thoughts—especially if they're harmful to you or getting in the way of showing empathy to yourself and others.
- *Identify the root cause.* Instead of just reacting, you can ask, "Where is this feeling coming from?" Tracing it back to its source helps you process the experience so it doesn't keep resurfacing as a problem in the future.
- *Validate your emotions.* Acknowledging that your feelings are real—and that they exist for a reason—helps you extend grace to yourself. This kind of self-validation builds stronger self-understanding and makes it easier to move forward with clarity.

Your feelings exist for a reason, so give them the attention they deserve. Negative feelings are not your enemy; they are messengers.

Just like positive emotions, they can guide you toward greater clarity, balance, and growth if you're willing to listen.

The real danger comes when we fall into toxic positivity, the habit of dismissing or suppressing negative emotions in an attempt to replace them immediately with something cheerful. This short-circuits the healing process, and when you skip over your pain, you rob yourself of the chance to learn from it.

Instead, lean in. Listen. Understand what your emotions are trying to tell you. Processing negative feelings doesn't mean wallowing in them; it means giving them space long enough to uncover the lesson, and then choosing to move forward without letting them chain you to the past.

Take jealousy, for example. A friend shares their success, and your gut reaction is envy. Don't condemn yourself for it. You can love your friend and still feel envy at the same time. The key is to use that feeling as a signal: Am I feeling stuck? Did I suffer a recent setback? Am I afraid I'll never get there myself? Once you uncover the reason, you can redirect that energy into making positive changes in your own life. That's self-empathy in action, choosing growth instead of self-criticism.

Think of it this way: your emotions are like dashboard lights in a car. Ignoring them won't make the problem disappear; it only increases the risk of a breakdown. Paying attention, on the other hand, gives you the power to take corrective action before things spiral out of control.

2. Commit to learning how to communicate properly.

We've talked a lot about active listening in the last few chapters, and we know there's much more to listening than hearing the other person's words.

Empathy requires listening, absorbing, and trying to understand where the other person is coming from, even if you don't get it right away.

If your friend tells you they're sad about a recent breakup, don't tell them it's for the best and send them on their way. Let them talk, cry, or do whatever they need to do. Let them know it's okay to feel sad, angry, or have mixed feelings. Ask them what they need. Be active in your support by checking on them or sending a thoughtful text.

Similarly, if your child is upset about something that seems trivial to you, don't try to convince them they're overreacting. Validate their feelings and try to understand why it's a big deal to them. This process is crucial when you're trying to show empathy to anyone, but especially to your children. They may not be fully aware of their emotions and might struggle to express them, so it's important to be patient and help them learn to not ignore their feelings.

When we urge someone to "get over" their negative feelings, it's usually a sign that we're uncomfortable with our own. This is a telltale sign that you need to check in with yourself and give yourself empathy and permission to feel and understand all your emotions.

3. Pay attention to someone's physiological cues, as well as yours.

When someone tells you how they feel, notice their nonverbal signals. You can often glean more information from what they're not saying than from what they're saying if you know what to look for.

It's also crucial to recognize cues from your own body that come up either at the start of a situation or as you go through the process of showing accurate empathy.

An example is if your partner tells you they're upset about something you did. Your heart starts racing, and you feel anger rising in your chest. While you may need to correct whatever made your partner feel this way, it makes sense that your automatic response would be to defend yourself. However, while this response may be involuntary, you still have control over how you respond.

It's essential to notice your body's cues and do some introspection when they come up, especially in situations where you need to show yourself and others empathy.

RECOGNIZING AND ACTING UPON INAPPROPRIATE AFFECT AND FLAT AFFECT

We have already gone over examples of inappropriate affect, but we have not called it out by name or explored it in depth. The textbook definition is when physical responses such as facial expressions, posture, or vocal tone do not match the situation or the person's true feelings.

When I was younger, I often got into trouble. I remember being at a social gathering with my parents, doing things that might have made for entertaining television but were embarrassing for parents as conservative as mine. My mother pulled me aside, smiled, and said, "I'm going to kill you if you keep doing that." I knew she did not mean it literally, but I also knew she was far from pleased. Her words carried the real message, not the smile on her face.

That experience taught me something important. The words coming out of her mouth were what I had to pay attention to, not her expression. This kind of analysis is critical in any interaction that requires accurate empathy. Never take what someone says at face value while ignoring their other signals. Never do the opposite either. Pay attention to as many cues as possible and ask clarifying questions to understand the other person better.

Inappropriate affect should be seen as a red flag, or at least a yellow one, in any context, but especially for clinicians. If a client says, "My life sucks, I want to off myself," and then laughs, that is not a joke. We know there is nothing funny about such a statement. In that moment, it is the clinician's responsibility to call attention to the mismatch, help the client explore it, and guide them inward. Doing so may feel uncomfortable, especially early in your career or relationship with that client, but it is essential for their development of self-awareness and self-empathy.

Flat affect requires a similar sensitivity. This occurs when someone shows little or no outward emotion in situations where strong emotions would normally be expected. For example, someone who does not cry or appear upset at a funeral may be experiencing flat affect. Everyone has a right to their emotions, both positive and negative, but there are healthy ways to process them. You can support someone in this state by showing accurate empathy, giving them space to process over time, trying to understand their experience as fully as possible, and gently encouraging inward reflection.

These kinds of responses are among the most important signals to pay attention to when you are trying to show accurate empathy, whether with a client or a loved one. You may not fully understand what they mean at first, but that is why asking thoughtful questions and listening carefully are crucial. Without that effort, you risk making assumptions, misunderstanding the other person, or missing an opportunity to connect

MAIN TAKEAWAYS FROM THIS CHAPTER

⇒ Positive outcomes are impossible if you have a negative mindset.

Stress, a lack of boundaries, and being fed constant negativity are common issues most of us deal with, but that doesn't mean we have no control over them.

When you give yourself empathy, keeping these problems at bay becomes much easier.

⇒ Having a positive mindset doesn't mean suppressing or neglecting your negative emotions.

Your emotions are real and valid.

Embracing a positive mindset does not mean forcing yourself to feel positive all the time. Negative emotions have value, too. They can act as a compass, pointing you toward what needs attention, if you are willing to sit with them, explore where they come from, and show yourself empathy, no matter the outcome.

⇒ Consider where you are right now in terms of happiness, success, and health.

Are you where you want to be?

Think about what you have experienced over the last few years. Assess your current environment and the people who surround you. Then consider what you can and cannot control. Too often, we focus on what lies outside our control and end up feeling overwhelmed. As a result, we neglect the areas where we actually have power to create change.

Once you have done this reflection, write down what you would want to tell yourself based on your answers. Here is the key: frame it as if you were speaking to someone you love who was in your exact position. This perspective helps you avoid the bias of being overly harsh or unkind toward yourself and allows you to respond with the same empathy and compassion you would naturally offer to others.

Give yourself empathy as you would a loved one.

⇒ Gratitude is a necessary part of empathy.

Do you know how hard it is to show yourself and others empathy if you think the world is out to get you?

Do you think that everyone around you doesn't deserve what they have as much as *you* deserve what they have?

What about feeling entitled to what you have?

I'll just tell you, it's nearly impossible.

Gratitude practices are proven to improve health and happiness. There's not a person alive who doesn't want those two things. Before you're ready to receive more in your life, whether it's more money, love, or acceptance, you have to be grateful for what you have now.

⇒ Using a top-down approach is essential for accurately showing empathy.

Top-down processing is intentional and flexible. It embraces listening, learning, and adjusting your empathic responses for every situation. Top-down elements include our thoughts, mindset, emotions, and beliefs, all of which can be changed.

Bottom-up processing is automatic and doesn't guarantee accurate empathy. It consists of your body's natural and learned responses, like facial mimicry.

⇒ Being in tune with your emotional and physiological responses can help you determine and understand their roots.

Once you learn how and why you respond the way you do, you can start applying that same process of observing, analyzing, and understanding with others to display accurate empathy.

Knowing why you're feeling a certain way should help you practice having grace for yourself. It's not an easy process, but doing so will greatly benefit you and your relationships. While the display of empathy is subjective and dependent on each unique situation, taking a more objective view of yourself and your feelings can prevent unwanted responses like self-pity, self-loathing, and codependent behavior.

⇒ Don't miss the somatic cues your client or the person across from you is giving you.

What's left unsaid often says more than what's actually said. Read that again.

We tend to suppress or downplay our emotions, especially when our system senses they'll be too overwhelming to manage. This leads to displays like flat affect or inappropriate affect. If you notice these cues or displays, don't brush them off. Bring attention to them in a gentle and productive way so that the person who's using them can reflect and direct their attention inward. This will help them understand themselves, so you can understand them better as well.

⇒ Showing accurate empathy to yourself and others will sometimes feel uncomfortable. Confronting difficult emotions and situations always does.

Life is not about being happy and positive all the time. The real growth comes when you learn to sit with your negative emotions, process them, and try to understand the complicated emotions of others. The more comfortable you become with this, the stronger and more resilient you become in facing whatever life brings.

Acknowledging your own struggles and extending empathy to yourself in spite of them sets a powerful example. If you are a parent, you are teaching your children how to treat themselves with dignity and care. If you are a leader, you are showing your team that it is human to struggle and still move forward. Leading by example is always the most impactful path, and when it comes to empathy, it may be the most important lesson you can teach.

Chapter Six

START WITH YOURSELF

AS YOU MOVE THROUGH THIS book, you may be tempted to focus only on the parts that confirm what you already believe. That's human nature, but I challenge you to resist that urge. Growth comes not from what feels familiar, but from what stretches you.

In this chapter, we will talk about letting go of the "superhero" image you may be clinging to and embracing something far more powerful—your humanity. Here you'll encounter the first step of the accurate empathy process. On the surface, it may look like common sense, and that is why so many people underestimate it. Make no mistake, this step is anything but ordinary. Within it lies content that can reshape not only how you see yourself, but how you connect with everyone around you.

I have two goals for this book.

1. Help you form deeper, more meaningful connections with yourself and others in and outside of your professional life.
2. Support clinicians and leaders in enhancing their ability to demonstrate and practice self-compassion and empa-

thy toward their clients, team members, and themselves in an authentic, meaningful way.

As you progress through this section of the book, you may ponder the relevance of combining interconnectedness, self-awareness, self-compassion, and accurate empathy. What is the significance of aligning these concepts with one another? Moreover, what makes combining them so powerful?

THE SECRET SAUCE FOR SELF-ACTUALIZATION

What follows may feel familiar, but remember this: common sense is rarely common practice. Seasoned coaches, clinicians, and leaders alike often take these basics for granted, which is why they stumble when challenges arise. My experience at the master's level of coaching has taught me a lesson I return to daily: never overestimate your competence, and never stop refining your self-awareness. I strongly encourage you to approach this material with that same humility.

These core elements are not optional; they are essential for personal growth, self-acceptance, and overall well-being. They also provide the foundation for building influence that lasts, whether you are leading teams, clients, patients, or entire organizations. A clinical practice, a coaching career, or a leadership role can only create lasting impact if it rests on the bedrock of these principles.

If you are new to coaching, stepping into a leadership role, or simply reassessing your direction, the insights here are essential for your growth. The first step is enhancing your self-awareness. This means recognizing the power of self-awareness and self-compassion, and learning to cultivate accurate empathy. These qualities are the building blocks of self-actualization. Without them, success remains unstable, and fulfillment always feels just out of reach.

Self-awareness is more than noticing your thoughts or emotions; it is the ability to understand your patterns and motivations, and how they affect those around you. It drives personal growth because it reveals where you need to change and where you need to improve. Just as important, it strengthens your relationships. When you know yourself more clearly, you can see others more clearly too. Whether you are a coach, a clinician, or a leader, the ability to understand perspectives beyond your own is what sets you apart.

Self-compassion is the ability to treat yourself with kindness and understanding, even when you make mistakes. It's essential for personal growth because it allows you to learn from your mistakes and keep moving forward. Doing so not only supports resilience in the face of challenges but also strengthens your capacity for healthy self-esteem.

Accurate empathy is the ability to truly understand and share the feelings of others, and it's foundational to personal growth. It enables you to build strong, trusting relationships and communicate with greater effectiveness. It also fosters deeper compassion and helps you develop a more nuanced understanding of the world around you.

When you increase self-awareness, embrace the power of self-compassion, and refine your ability to practice accurate empathy, you'll lay the foundation for thriving; one that transforms not only your life, but the lives of the individuals you serve. Here's why:

You'll enhance your relatability when you deeply understand yourself. Authenticity builds trust and rapport, empowering leaders and practitioners to deliver tailored support that meets each person's unique needs. Transparent, relatable communication creates a solid foundation for mutual understanding, allowing those on your team or in your care to feel truly seen, heard, and supported.

You'll also build stronger, more meaningful connections. When you can empathize with others and genuinely understand their perspectives, the work becomes more engaging and fulfilling.

Perhaps most importantly, you'll be better equipped to help people achieve their goals. A deep understanding of yourself and those you support allows you to foster greater self-efficacy and resilience in them, ultimately amplifying the impact of your work.

The fact that you're reading or listening to this book is evidence that you're already an excellent practitioner. If you're not a clinician or coach by title, it's likely that you're someone with a high degree of emotional intelligence or someone who simply wants to show up better for yourself and for others. Either way, you're doing the work. You're choosing to evolve, and that, in itself, is something to celebrate.

> "It's not about being perfect; it's about perfecting."
>
> —Dr. D Ivan Young, MCC, NBC-HWC

You're only human if the weight of your life and the emotional energy you hold for others feels heavy sometimes. That's not a flaw; that's a sign that you care deeply. The only reason it affects you so much is because you're fully invested. If you didn't care, none of it would touch you.

You're a powerful coach or leader because you *do* take it personally. The real challenge is learning when and how to lovingly detach.

Remember the following:

Trying to please everyone is not only exhausting, it is impossible. One of the greatest lessons I have learned is the power of self-forgiveness. Mistakes, whether mine or those of my clients, are not failures; they are an essential part of the learning process. This truth applies even more to masterful coaches, seasoned clinicians, and leaders at the highest levels.

The best leaders and practitioners know how to admit their mistakes and extract the lessons within them. The challenge is that they often do this at the expense of their own emotional and mental well-being. This is where self-empathy and self-compassion become non-negotiable. Practicing both and weaving them into your coaching or leadership style protects you from burnout and keeps your influence sustainable.

If you neglect these qualities, you will struggle to model them for the very people you are guiding, whether they are your clients, team, or organization. When you over-identify with their struggles and fail to care for your own needs, you create the conditions for stress, fatigue, and disconnection. When you lead with empathy for yourself first, you demonstrate strength, resilience, and a healthier way forward for everyone who looks to you as an example.

Some Encouragement:

> "Holding someone accountable may create tension at first, but it unlocks their potential. To do the same for others, you must stay authentic and grounded, which means having your own coach or accountability partner. You cannot serve others well if you neglect your own well-being."
>
> —Dr. D Ivan Young, MCC, NBC-HWC

I have preached hope with a microphone in my hand while my own soul whispered, help. I have taken the stage smiling, said profound things, and walked off carrying a storm no one could see. If you show up for people every day, you know that mask. It fits, and it burns.

Care makes us great, and care is how we crack. I have watched dawn arrive after sleepless nights, mind racing through clients and crises. I have sat in sessions and heard words I could not fully absorb, because my life was loud and contained health concerns, money stress, and family fracture. The body was present, the mind was somewhere else.

Here is the peril. When you ignore your limits, compassion curdles into resentment, presence thins into performance, and service becomes a slow erosion of the self. The bill comes due with interest. Reputations fray. Credentials mean less. The work you love begins to steal from you.

Here is the promise. When you practice self-empathy and self-compassion, you recover the one advantage that changes everything, your full presence. You think more clearly, you hear what is not being said, you make better calls, and you create outcomes that last. Protecting your well-being does not weaken your service; it strengthens your impact and extends your reach.

Do not wait for a breakdown to become your teacher. Make yourself a priority before life forces you to. Respect the fragility of your sanity, because it is the ground your purpose stands on. Whether you lead a team, a practice, a family, or a room full of strangers, the people you serve are safest when you are healthy.

If you burn out, your gifts go dark. If you stay whole, your gifts turn the lights on for everyone in the room.

YOUR INTERNAL EMPATHY

Think back to the last terrible, screwed up day you had. You know, the kind where it felt like nothing was going your way and you were being punished for some unknown reason.

Maybe the day started off wrong when you got out of bed. You spilled your morning beverage on your clothes. Next, you ended up bickering with your partner over something stupid. Then the traffic gods ensured that you were late for your first meeting, and to top it off, you forgot all about an appointment with a new client. By lunchtime, you were ready to cash it in, crawl back into bed, and just fast-forward to tomorrow.

Believe it or not, all of that has happened to me more than once. If it hasn't happened to you, pretend that it did for the sake of this illustration.

- What emotions were swirling around inside of you that day?
- How did you respond or react to them?
- How did your emotions affect your thoughts and actions?
- How did your emotions, thoughts, and actions influence your interactions with other people throughout the day?

Of these three scenarios, which one did you find yourself in?

1. You tried to power through the awful day. You thought, *I don't have time to deal with this right now*, and you did your best to bottle up all the unpleasant emotions and keep barreling ahead; feelings be damned.

There are several obvious issues with this response. Even the most self-aware person who knows how to practice accurate empathy will still respond in this way from time to time.

Your emotions are there for a reason. You can either view them as inconveniences you have to avoid or hide from, or you can take them for what they are, which is data. Data that you can use to analyze your circumstances and figure out a better way forward.

Here's the second scenario.

2. You let your emotions take the wheel. Frustration, annoyance, and criticism were in the driver's seat all day. By the end of the day, they had left their mark on every action you took or every conversation you had.

Once again, this response is only human. While you'll never completely avoid this type of reaction, it's important to recognize its impact on yourself and others. It can make a bad day much worse.

Have you ever noticed how one small thing can throw off your whole day? You spill your coffee, misplace your keys, or trip over your shoes on the way out, and suddenly it feels like mistake after mistake follows. By noon, you are convinced the entire day is doomed.

The next time this happens, pause and check in with yourself. Ask, *What am I feeling right now? Am I slowing down and choosing to reset so the rest of my day improves, or am I deciding that I woke up on the wrong side of the bed and letting that belief ruin everything?*

Maybe you're thinking that, *of course, you aren't deciding to be in a sour mood.* Bad things just keep happening to you throughout the day.

Trust me, you have far more control over the course of your day than you realize. Yet when things go wrong, our first instinct is often to sigh, *Why me?* or to shrug it off as *This just isn't my day.* What seems like harmless self-talk is actually training your mind to expect more negativity—and once you expect it, you usually find it.

If you fall into this pattern often, it not just shapes your day; it reshapes your life. Left unchecked, a string of small frustrations can snowball into chronic stress, resentment, and a sense of powerlessness. Dwelling on negative thoughts without addressing them can turn a rough morning into a wasted day, a wasted week, or worse, a habit of defeat.

The good news is that you can break this cycle. You may not be able to control what happens to you, but you can absolutely control how you respond. By paying attention to your reactions and choosing to reset instead of spiral, you redirect your energy and reclaim your influence over the day. Do this consistently, and it does more than save your week—it rewires the way you approach your entire life.

Nobody likes to hear that they are the ones sabotaging their own peace, but it has to be said. Growth demands honesty. You cannot control every event, but you can control the meaning you assign to it and how you respond. That is where your real power begins.

Here's the last scenario.

3. You paused to observe, experience, and feel your emotions. You got curious instead of judgmental, paying attention to what was happening inside you and how it was affecting you. You acknowledged your experience before moving forward. It wasn't the best day, but you were able to check your mood before it soured every interaction.

If you recognize yourself in scenario one or two, don't feel bad. You're human. We've all had more of those days than we'd like to admit.

Scenario three is the one I want you to take a closer look at. That process of noticing, recognizing, experiencing, and feeling what is going on in your inner world, with openness and not judgment, is self-empathy. Learning how to give yourself empathy is the first and most important step in empathizing with others. This response will become more instinctive as you practice self-empathy and cultivate a deeper connection with yourself.

SELF-EMPATHY IS NOT SELF-INDULGENT

Many people, especially those who are used to putting others before themselves, have a difficult time with the idea of putting themselves first. You might feel selfish or guilty taking care of yourself because you grew up trying to be everything for everyone, but nobody validated your feelings or offered you support. Maybe you were in a toxic relationship in which your partner made you feel responsible for them and their feelings, and they never reciprocated by validating yours. If you've experienced either of these situations or something similar, I know it can take some time to trust that putting yourself first is ultimately more of a selfless endeavor than a selfish one. I promise you that you and everyone else around you will be better off if you take care of your physical, emotional, and spiritual health.

If you are not tuned in to your own inner world, how can you possibly hope to understand someone else's? If you are unaware of how your thoughts and emotions are shaping you, how can you be sure they are not clouding your judgment or weakening your ability to connect with yourself and with others?

Empathy always begins within. Before it can be offered outward, it must be cultivated inward. Consider how you want to show up for people in every corner of your life—at work, at home, and in your closest relationships. Picture the kind of presence and support you want to extend to your clients, patients, students, or team members. Imagine how you want to stand beside your partner, your children, or your friends.

You cannot pour from an empty vessel. To lead, to guide, or to love with authenticity, you must first fill your own empathy tank. Only then can you give to others in a way that is sustainable, genuine, and transformative.

Self-empathy isn't selfish or self-indulgent; it's essential. If you skip this first step, you are in no position to empathize with anyone else.

Even if you're able to be kind and compassionate toward others, your lack of self-empathy will soon catch up to you in more ways than one. Then, it will infect your relationships, both personal and professional.

As we've discussed in previous chapters, a lack of self-empathy can lead to burnout, resentment, apathy, and many other consequences that make it impossible to connect with yourself and others in a meaningful way.

So before you do anything else, go through the process of cultivating self-empathy. This isn't a step you can or should skip. Even if you believe you have a decent grip on self-empathy, use the exercises from this chapter and previous chapters to learn something new about yourself and see your approach to empathy in a different light.

Start at the beginning, even if you believe you're past it already.

WHAT'S YOUR STARTING POINT?

In the 1990s, before we all carried minicomputers in our pockets, handheld GPS devices were just entering the consumer market.

Now, you can open Google Maps or the Waze app on your smartphone, and it will quickly calculate your location. However, early GPS devices required manual setup. You had to enter your current position to initialize the GPS receiver, and then it could start tracking nearby satellites to determine your latitude, longitude, and altitude. You needed to know your starting point before you could think about navigating to your destination.

This is also how empathy works. Before you can empathize with someone else, you have to know where you're starting from. How are you coming to the table at this moment? What are you bringing with you? Get curious about your starting point.

We've gone over some of these questions already, but ultimately, you should be checking in with yourself about your answers regularly. While certain facts may not change, your perspective and circumstances certainly can.

Here's a self-awareness checklist:

- What are your triggers?
- What are your core values?
- What's your personality type?
- What are your belief systems?
- Which groups do you belong to?
- How do factors like your age, race, gender, sexual orientation, nationality, geography, culture, family dynamics, and socioeconomic background affect your perspective?
- How do you see yourself, and how does that influence how you see the world?
- What's going on in your life right now that is taking up mental or emotional space?
- Are those situations and events taking up space in a positive or negative way? How can you be more intentional about what's taking up space?

Answering and reflecting on all these questions will help you get to know yourself on a deeper level. They can provide insights into your background and how these different aspects can influence your relationships and interactions with others.

LEADING BY EXAMPLE—MY STORY

As I reflect on these questions, I realize that I cannot separate who I am from the environment that has shaped me. I was raised in the segregated South, a world designed to remind people of color their "place" in society. While the laws eventually changed, the reality is that microaggressions still persist, subtle yet persistent reminders that the playing field is not equal.

My family story carried its own complexity. I was adopted within my biological family and raised as an only child, even though I had siblings. The truth is, I barely knew them. I only saw one or two of them, never all of them together. That distance created a longing for connection and left me with a deep awareness of what it means to feel both part of a family and separate from it at the same time.

From my earliest years, I was reminded of another truth. My caregivers, especially my mother, told me over and over, *You are a Black child, and you will have to work twice as hard as your White peers just to be seen as equal.* That was not advice, it was a survival strategy. It was repeated so often that it became part of me, shaping how I approached every goal and every opportunity.

Racism, sometimes overt and brutal, other times quiet and subtle, has been a latent presence in my life. The sting of passive racism, the kind that hides in assumptions and backhanded comments, still lingers even now.

One of the realizations I came to much later was how deeply this fed my need to prove myself. As I built my reputation as a coach, I worked relentlessly to overachieve, collecting accolades, credentials, and recognition, almost as if I were shouting to the world, *See? I am worthy. I will prove myself to you.* That drive fueled me, but it also left me drained and, at times, disconnected from my own sense of worth.

That is why I came to see self-compassion and self-empathy not as luxuries, but as necessities. For me, checking in with myself is like checking vital signs. Doctors do it before they make any decision, and we need to do the same for our emotional and spiritual health. Sometimes I am simply tired from a restless night. Other times I realize I am distracted by a difficult conversation, or that hunger is affecting my focus more than I realized. These "emotional vitals" tell me where I need care and keep me grounded enough to serve others with strength instead of depletion.

The same is true for you. Just as a physician cannot diagnose without checking vitals, you cannot lead, coach, or even love fully without first checking your own. When you learn to pause and take stock of your energy, your emotions, and your needs, you protect yourself from burnout and create space to show up with clarity and authenticity. That is what makes empathy sustainable.

> "You cannot offer empathy to others until you first give it to yourself, and that begins with unpacking your own baggage every single day."
>
> —Dr. D Ivan Young, MCC, NBC-HWC

People can immediately tell when you aren't mindfully present with them. They can sense when your internal issues are becoming your external obstacles. You must adjust your perspective before you can effectively connect and empathize with others. Be honest about where you are and who you have become. If you can't be honest with yourself and address your issues, how are you supposed to be honest and open with others while helping them to confront theirs? The answer is you can't.

WHAT'S YOUR DESTINATION?

Once you determine your starting point, you can focus on your destination. Where are you trying to go? What are you hoping to accomplish? Our goals can flow and change all the time, but our values often keep us on track.

A big problem with early GPS devices was that they only navigated to destinations according to the most current version of maps they had uploaded. They weren't connected to data or Wi-Fi like smartphones, so unless you had intentionally updated the maps before setting out, you could be in for some unwelcome surprises.

The GPS says to take a left on First Street, but First Street is under construction. It then says to take Exit 25 and park at the Grand Hotel, but there's a detour at Exit 25, and the Grand Hotel has been renamed The Luxury Lodge. Suddenly, you're lost, frustrated, and unsure of how to proceed.

This same problem often shows up in interactions with other people. You know where you're starting from and where you want to end up, but you're using outdated maps that get you off track. Some of these outdated maps might look like:

- Biases, prejudices, or preconceptions
- Previous experiences with certain individuals
- Cultural, generational, or language differences
- Perspectives or beliefs that haven't been questioned or challenged

The maps you use affect how you perceive and process information and how you think about and interact with others. As a coach, using outdated maps can cause a disconnect with the person navigating change and sabotage the outcomes you both want to achieve in a coaching session. As an organizational leader, using outdated maps (assumptions and biases) can break trust within a team and interfere with your shared goals. As a parent or partner, using outdated maps can create misunderstandings and instigate fights with someone you love.

We often see this in long-term relationships when someone has put in the work to change, yet their partner still treats them like who they used to be and won't let go of their feelings toward the previous version of that individual.

It's critical that you take responsibility for identifying your biases and the obsolete, incorrect, or incomplete information you are carrying around with you so you can feel confident that you're taking steps forward to refresh it.

PUTTING SELF-EMPATHY INTO PRACTICE

Giving yourself empathy may not come easily at first. You might feel awkward or self-centered thinking so much about your inner world, but this isn't navel-gazing. Learning to be empathetic from the inside out will help you be the best version of yourself and fully show up for other people in your life. It's one of the least selfish things you can do.

Try these exercises to put self-empathy into practice. I suggest you do these weekly or monthly, not just when you need to.

1. Find your starting point.

Reread the questions in the "What's Your Starting Point?" section of this chapter. Get out your journal or notebook and answer each question in detail. This may be an exercise you complete in several sessions.

Take your time. Stay open and curious and notice (without judgment) if you have a hard time answering certain questions. Dig deeper when this happens. Ask yourself more follow-up questions. What's that about? What is it telling you?

Let your responses sit for a day or two, then come back and read them with fresh eyes. What insights can you draw from your answers? How can you use this self-awareness to improve your connections and conversations with other people?

Spending time alone with yourself is a much-needed part of this process. There's a quote in my book, *Break Up, Don't Break*

Down, that got picked up by a lot of media outlets. It was along the lines of:

"If you can't stand to be alone with you, why would anyone else want to be alone with you?"

Spending time alone with myself was a huge part of my healing process following my cancer diagnosis. I still spend time with myself weekly. I've even set aside time for introspection two to three times per day. This doesn't have to mean sitting alone in your house in silence. In fact, I encourage you to do things like take a walk near the water if you live anywhere near the ocean, lake, or even a small creek.

If you live by the mountains, take in the fresh air and enjoy the view.

If you're in the middle of the desert, you can enjoy the stillness and quiet.

I've even done a float tank to experience the silence and peace that it offers.

No matter where you live or what your schedule is like, you can take time to be present. Spending time with yourself in nature doesn't cost you anything, but it pays off big-time for your health and well-being.

During this time, nourish the spiritual part of you. I'm not necessarily talking about religious beliefs. I personally believe in God as my higher power, but even if you don't believe in a higher power, there are simple ways to connect with your spiritual side, such as painting, listening to music, gardening, or simply being out in nature.

If the idea of spirituality doesn't resonate with you at all, tap into your humanity by giving to others. That doesn't have to mean giving others money. You can give your time, energy, or even a listening ear. Whatever you can do to improve others' lives in a way that fills up your cup and theirs is a good idea.

Once you find out what brings you peace and joy and allows you time for introspection, do more of it. Get away from others' words and judgments and focus on the greater part of yourself. The part that allows you to broaden your capacity for happiness and success, so you can contribute to others' lives in a positive and meaningful way.

2. Update your maps.

Think about a recent interaction you had with a client, colleague, patient, or loved one that didn't go as you had intended. Use this as an opportunity to evaluate the maps you have uploaded to your internal GPS.

What went wrong in the conversation? What was the point of disconnection? Can you pinpoint a certain set of beliefs, ideas, or actions that triggered you or caused you to go off track? Why do you think that is?

In our daily interactions with others, we often make assumptions based on our past experiences. While we must remain open to the potential for change, it's equally important to establish and uphold personal boundaries. It's crucial to remember that while people have the potential to change, their actions and words may not always immediately reflect that. In such scenarios, it's vital to acknowledge our own fallibility. Rather than casting blame, it's beneficial to strive to serve as a model of personal growth. It's essential to not only track our own personal development but also to be attentive to the growth of those around us. Keep in mind that expecting a relationship to evolve without being willing to change ourselves is unrealistic.

When encountering new people, be mindful of your cognitive and emotional perception of others. Even in the absence of pri-

or interactions, superficial attributes such as appearance, ethnicity, nationality, gender, and even speech patterns can shape your perceptions and predispositions. Conscientiously acknowledge any preconceived notions you might hold about the other person. This self-awareness is instrumental in identifying and confronting these biases, thereby preventing them from undermining your capacity to relate to and connect with others genuinely.

> "Empathy begins where assumptions end."
>
> —Dr. D Ivan Young, MCC, NBC-HWC

3. Take a self-compassion break.

Showing yourself intentional kindness and care has myriad benefits, both for you and for others around you. Many studies show that:

- Self-compassion—treating yourself the way you would a good friend who is having a difficult time—has a significant positive association with measures of optimism, happiness, curiosity, initiative, agreeableness, and conscientiousness.
- Self-compassionate individuals are described by their partners as more caring in romantic relationships.
- Self-compassionate counselors and therapists are more satisfied with their careers and less likely to experience stress and burnout.

Kristin Neff, Ph.D., a psychologist and author who specializes in studying self-compassion, recommends taking a brief self-compassion break when you encounter a difficult situation (Gaiswinkler et al. 2019). Take the following steps to demonstrate the three components of self-compassion—self-kindness, common humanity, and mindfulness:

- Be mindful of what you are experiencing and acknowledge your emotions. Say something compassionate to yourself along the lines of, "This is hard," or "This is a moment of suffering."
- Recognize that you are not alone in what you are feeling. Say to yourself, "Everyone struggles sometimes," or "Other people feel this way, too."
- Put your hands over your heart and repeat a message of self-compassion, such as: "May I be kind to myself," or "May I give myself the care that I need."

If you can't figure out where you're coming from and learn to recognize where someone else is coming from, you'll experience a lot of disappointment due to unrealistic expectations.

Allowing yourself to be human and imperfect is one of the most important steps in showing empathy to yourself first, and then to others. That brings us to the fourth step.

4. Stop trying to be perfect and accept that you have issues, too.

I know this is easier said than done. Many of us carry the heavy habit of blaming ourselves for the actions of others. You may find yourself replaying conversations, asking what you did wrong, or wondering what you could have done differently to change the outcome.

Chances are, the pressure to be perfect was planted in you early. It takes time and courage to accept that perfection is not possible, and it was never required of you.

Taking responsibility can be admirable, and putting others first can feel virtuous, but there is a danger here. Some people will exploit your kindness and selflessness. The more you give without boundaries, the more they will take, until you are empty.

This is why you must sometimes step back and prioritize your well-being. One of the simplest but most powerful tools is to document what weighs on your mind. Writing things down strips away the distortions of memory and excuses. On paper, the truth takes shape, patterns emerge, and clarity rises.

Consider a difficult relationship. In your head, it is easy to justify, minimize, or even ignore the pain by focusing on isolated moments. Perhaps you overlook your own role in the dynamic. But when you write everything down, excuses lose their power, and reality becomes harder to deny.

Do not let your problems consume you. Name them, face them, and develop the skills that will allow you to rise above them. Ignoring your own needs is not an option if you want to deepen your empathy, strengthen your compassion, and remain genuine in your relationships—both personal and professional.

One of my favorite quotes is, "Yesterday is history, tomorrow is a mystery, but today is a gift. That is why it's called the present." This mindset fits with what I'm encouraging you to do. There's no point agonizing over your mistakes and beating yourself up for not being perfect. If you're here right now, you're willing to put in the work and better yourself. That's what's important—not that you're perfect or that you've always made the right decisions—just that you're *trying*.

So, forgive yourself, use the past as your guide to do better and be better. Start giving yourself empathy so you can give it to others. Trust me when I say that you and the world will be better for it.

If you neglect self-empathy, you'll always be lacking in your relationships.

THE CONSEQUENCES OF A LACK OF SELF-EMPATHY IN DIFFERENT CIRCUMSTANCES

How can you build a healthy relationship with someone else if you are at war with yourself?

The gap between how you see yourself and how you want others to see you can quietly sabotage your connections. It breeds unfair assumptions, creates ineffective communication, and fuels destructive coping strategies like self-sabotage or pushing people away. Many people chase happiness and fulfillment through others, but entering relationships with that mindset is a recipe for disappointment. No one wants to be tethered to someone who drains them emotionally or tries to control them.

Yes, you should expect support and growth from your partner, but you must also acknowledge and accept your weaknesses as much as your strengths. True love and acceptance begin when you can look yourself in the mirror, flaws and all, and say, *This is who I am, and I am still worthy of love.*

Does any of this sound familiar?

- You rely on your partner for constant validation, and if their reaction does not match your expectations, you take it personally.
- When your partner expresses a need you are not fulfilling, you interpret it as an attack.
- When they compliment you or show affection, you retreat, dismiss, or respond by putting yourself down.

Relationships are complicated because human beings are complicated. We all want to be unconditionally loved, yet struggle to extend that same acceptance to others, especially when they reveal imperfections that mirror our own insecurities. The truth is, the standards we set for ourselves often spill over into the expectations we place on others. When we demand perfection from ourselves, we end up demanding it from them.

Cultivating self-empathy and self-compassion breaks that cycle. It frees you from the need to perform and allows you to connect from a place of authenticity rather than fear. When you accept yourself, you make space to accept others. When you stop expecting flawlessness, you discover the real intimacy that comes from two imperfect people learning to love each other well.

"Even if we believe that our insecurities have no impact on our relationships, our subconscious tendencies can subtly affect our behavior in negative ways. This can manifest as underlying feelings of resentment, self-centeredness, and even passive-aggressive tendencies toward our partner. A prominent sign of this dynamic is when our partner communicates that they feel unappreciated, despite their consistent efforts to show care and understanding toward us."

—Dr. D Ivan Young, MCC, NBC-HWC

Often, our fears and insecurities are deeply ingrained and can be challenging to identify because they have been controlling our actions for a long time. Children who grow up in toxic relationships or witness them can struggle with forming and maintaining healthy relationships later in life. Their past experiences can have a significant impact on their ability to trust and connect with others.

In over twenty years of practice, I've seen a consistent pattern. When a young girl grows up witnessing her parents' toxic relationship, especially when it includes infidelity or abuse, it often shapes how she views men and love itself. The trauma doesn't just leave emotional scars, it rewires her understanding of intimacy. Even when she meets someone who is safe, kind, and emotionally available, those early experiences can still dictate her reactions. She might pull away, sabotage the relationship, or feel anxious for reasons that don't match her current reality. What appears irrational is often a learned survival strategy, rooted in a nervous system that was trained to expect chaos where there should be calm. Without healing, that early conditioning continues to echo through every adult connection, not because she is broken, but because the brain remembers what it had to in order to survive.

The other type of consequence that can result from a lack of self-empathy is settling for less than you deserve in your relationships and your career. This is also a result of the examples above. Those who don't know what empathy feels or looks like—because they've never received it from others, given it to themselves, or had it modeled for them—will unintentionally seek out similar relationships. It's difficult to look for something better when you don't know any better. Sometimes, you're at least partially aware that your relationship is unhealthy or they're not treating you properly, but you might still feel like you don't deserve better.

This often looks like:

1. Staying in abusive or manipulative relationships because you don't think anyone else will love you (maybe your partner has even told you that).
2. Being with someone who looks good on paper but with whom you have no real connection.
3. Entering codependent relationships with people who are as lost as you are and don't encourage or contribute to your growth.
4. Engaging in people-pleasing tendencies and not taking care of yourself because you want love and affection from others (as we all do).

You are responsible for you.

You must be willing to clean up your own inner world and make sure everything is working well before you can be there for

"Our insecurities do not stay hidden; they quietly shape the way we love and the way we are loved."

—Dr. D Ivan Young, MCC, NBC-HWC

someone else who's going through something similar. This doesn't mean you have to be the best you can be all the time. (Once again, you're human!) It also doesn't mean you can't grow as an individual while you're in a relationship. It just means you need to give yourself the love, grace, respect, and empathy you give to others, and you usually need to give these things to yourself before you can understand how to properly give them to others.

MAIN TAKEAWAYS FROM THIS CHAPTER

⇒ No matter what role you're playing, you need to have self-empathy before you can give it.

To be effective, successful, happy, or healthy, you need to fill your cup regularly.

If you're a dedicated clinician or coach who genuinely cares about the people you serve, chances are you've prioritized their well-being over your own more than once. If you're reading this book, it's safe to assume you've come to realize that this approach, though well-intentioned, isn't sustainable. The good news is, there's a more effective way forward—one that benefits both you *and* those you support: practicing self-empathy first, before extending it to others.

For many dedicated clinicians and coaches, the profound commitment to their clients' well-being often leads to a subtle, yet significant, personal sacrifice. Driven by a genuine desire to serve and heal, it's not uncommon for you to place the needs of others consistently above your own. This admirable dedication, while deeply rooted in compassion and professional ethics, can inadvertently lead to a state of depletion. If you find yourself holding this book, it's likely you've reached a pivotal realization: this well-intentioned, altruistic approach, despite its noble origins, is ultimately unsustainable in the long run.

The good news, however, is not just that there's a solution, but that this solution offers a far more effective and harmonious path forward. This alternative paradigm benefits not only you, the compassionate professional, but also, and paradoxically, those very individuals you are committed to supporting. The key lies in a fundamental shift in perspective and practice: prioritizing self-empathy as a foundational step, *before* extending that empathy outward to others.

This isn't a call for selfishness, but rather a profound recognition that a wellspring of compassion, deeply nourished from within, is far more potent and sustainable than one that is constantly drawn upon without replenishment. By cultivating a deep understanding and acceptance of your own needs, limitations, and emotional landscape, you build a reservoir of resilience and genuine care that can then flow more authentically and effectively to those you serve. This approach fosters a virtuous cycle, where your own well-being becomes the bedrock upon which truly impactful and enduring support for others can be built.

⇒ Accurate self-empathy requires curiosity rather than judgment, and feeling your emotions rather than suppressing them.

It's amazing what you can learn about yourself and others when you dig deep into your thoughts, feelings, and beliefs without criticizing them. If you treat yourself the same way you'd treat a friend who is having a bad day, there's much more room for growth and improvement.

⇒ There are four steps you can start taking today to put self-empathy into practice.

1. Find your starting point. Figure out where you're coming from and what you're bringing to the table.
2. Update your maps. Learn from previous experiences and think about how you can improve going forward.
3. Practice self-compassion. Try to understand your feelings and your circumstances from a nonjudgmental, curious perspective.
4. Accept that you aren't perfect and you never will be; it's impossible. However, you *can* be a better version of yourself who shines your inner light onto others.

⇒ A lack of self-empathy doesn't only affect you.

Often, we project our negative feelings about ourselves and the world onto others. If we don't take the time to show ourselves empathy and compassion, we'll get into trouble when interacting with others, whether they're close to us or not.

Being intentional about your relationship with yourself and carving out time to fill up your own cup is not selfish. When you look at your interactions based on how you're feeling, you'll likely realize that the better you feel about yourself, the better you treat others.

You may already have a decent relationship with yourself, but I encourage you to take the time to explore your beliefs, feelings, thoughts, and actions as you read through this book. It can only get better from here.

⇒ Spend time alone with yourself.

This is difficult for many people, especially those who have a lot of trauma to work through and overcome. However, it's a necessary part of your healing and an ingredient in the recipe for a healthy life.

If you don't want to be alone with you, nobody else will. Being out of touch with your emotions and thoughts will ensure you stay out of touch with others' feelings. This is a solid barrier to your ability to show accurate empathy toward yourself and others.

Chapter Seven

PUTTING ACCURATE EMPATHY INTO ACTION (THE CRUCIAL ROLE OF POSITIVE PSYCHOLOGY)

ONCE YOU'VE DEVELOPED THE PRACTICE of giving yourself empathy, you're much better equipped to offer it to and encourage it in others. The approaches to accurate empathy in this book will make you a better coach, clinician, leader, partner, parent, and friend.

Positive psychology highlights the importance of positive experiences, individual traits, and supportive institutions, shifting the focus from merely fixing problems to fostering flourishing and well-being (Seligman et al. 2005). Rather than put a sole spotlight on suffering and how to "fix" it, positive psychology is aimed at optimizing well-being and function. It's one of the evidence-based techniques that I use to help my clients go from simply surviving to thriving in their personal and professional lives.

Accurate empathy, when applied externally, involves the ability to understand and share the emotions of others while maintaining a balanced and objective perspective within yourself. For coaches, positive psychology serves as an essential instrument within the accurate empathy toolkit. By incorporating positive psychology principles, you can enhance your capacity for both compassion and accurate empathy, enabling you to better connect with your clients, patients, and team members, and provide them with far more effective support.

One key aspect of positive psychology is the focus on strengths, core values, and virtues. This approach encourages coaches and their clients to identify and cultivate their unique strengths, such as compassion, resilience, optimism, and gratitude. By recognizing and building upon these strengths, individuals can develop a stronger sense of self-worth and self-compassion. This, in turn, helps you to be more open and receptive to the emotions of others, fostering accurate empathy.

Another critical element of positive psychology is the practice of mindfulness. Mindfulness involves paying attention to the present moment without judgment. By cultivating mindfulness, you can become much more aware of your own thoughts, emotions, and sensations. This increased self-awareness allows you to better regulate your own emotions and respond to other people's needs with greater empathy and understanding.

Positive psychology also emphasizes the importance of positive emotions, such as joy, gratitude, and love. These emotions can serve as powerful catalysts for personal growth and transformation. When coaches, clinicians, and leaders help their clients or team members cultivate positive emotions, they create a more conducive environment for self-compassion and accurate empathy to flourish.

Positive psychology offers a wide array of practical techniques and activities aimed at strengthening self-compassion and empathetic understanding. For instance, the Loving-Kindness Meditation is a transformative practice designed to guide individuals in nurturing feelings of genuine love and empathy, both toward themselves and others. Another technique is the RAIN method (Recognize, Allow, Investigate, Nurture), which is a mindfulness-based approach that helps you respond to difficult emotions with greater kindness and acceptance. These are a couple of my favorites, but there are many more positive psychology tools and techniques that I strongly suggest you explore.

For years, Cognitive Behavioral Therapy (CBT) has been the go-to method for therapists and coaches. CBT is built on surveying the cognitive landscape, slowing things down, and reconstituting how we conceive thoughts. We adjust how we engage with a client based on this reconstitution of the psyche. That's an elaborate way of saying:

"I'm going to listen to what you say and amplify it with the intention of inspiring you to become more comprehensive in your approach to life's challenges."

Here's the problem. It's in our nature to focus more on the negative than the positive. We tend to consider all potential negative outcomes in an attempt to safeguard our mental, emotional, and physical well-being and comfort. As I mentioned in a previous chapter, this hypervigilance is indigenous to us, as it used to literally mean the difference between life and death, survival and extinction.

However, overthinking, especially the negative kind, which I like to call "stinking thinking," isn't as helpful today as it used to be. In fact, it's more detrimental than ever to our health, happiness, and success. While we've evolved with technology and science, our brains are still playing catch-up. We haven't moved much past our default survival mode.

When people come to work with you, it's usually because they're facing challenges. These psychological trip wires are often rooted in distressing thoughts, disruptive behaviors, or unresolved emotions. The encouraging news is that they're seeking change. The more sobering reality is that much of traditional coaching and psychology still relies on templated, cookie-cutter interactions. These surface-level exchanges often look like this:

Coach: What brought you in today?

Client: [Shares what they believe is the problem]

Coach: How has that affected your life?

Client: [Responds again]

Coach: What have you done about it? How have you tried to resolve this?

Client: [Another response]

Coach: How did that work for you?

Client: [Continues]

Coach: What do you think you can do to change that?

Client: [May or may not have ideas]

Coach: Let's try *X* and talk about how it goes next week.

This formulaic pattern is the equivalent of applying a bandage to a wound that actually requires surgery. It barely scratches the surface.

Positive psychology offers us an opportunity to go deeper and to be more curious, creative, and assertive. There is no one-size-fits-all solution, which is why I encourage practitioners to blend the principles of positive psychology with other evidence-based methods and areas of expertise, whether that's Cognitive Behavioral Therapy (CBT), Dialectical Behavior Therapy (DBT), Emotion-Focused Coaching, or another specialty. When used skillfully, this integrated approach gives the individuals you serve a far greater chance of identifying and taking control of the internal barriers that are stunting their growth.

Wouldn't it be far more meaningful to help others through a comprehensive, sustainable process instead of a rehearsed, short-term fix?

The answer is yes, and it's the same holistic approach you should be applying to your own life.

APPLYING POSITIVE PSYCHOLOGY TO *YOUR* LIFE

Like every other process outlined in this book, this one also begins with an honest inventory of your thoughts, patterns, and internal wiring.

In the preceding chapters, we explored the rich tapestry of your personal history, cultural background, and the many influences shaping your current self-perception. This journey has made one thing clear: the path to clarity and self-awareness is never linear, and it's certainly not universal.

As you reflect on your own story, I hope you're able to appreciate the people and experiences that shaped the person you've become. Just as importantly, I hope you come to recognize that those you support have been molded by their own unique influences, each one coloring how they see themselves, others, and the world at large.

The blind cannot lead the blind. Only someone who has regained their sight, who has faced the darkness and found their way through it, can lead others with real wisdom. Experience does more than inform us, it transforms us. You cannot guide someone through pain you have never had the courage to confront in yourself. You cannot teach what you are unwilling to practice. That is why I stand firmly on this truth. You are not ready to coach anyone until you have done your own work. Not just talked about it, but faced it, healed through it, and grown beyond it. Anything less is performance. The real power begins when you lead from the clarity of your own transformation.

Positive psychology offers you the opportunity to change your perception. I've heard many times that reality is perception, and I believe that to be true.

So, what happens if your perception is generally positive? I'm not asking you to be positive about everything. In fact, it's unhealthy to force positivity all the time and neglect your negative feelings. However, when you train your brain to look for the good, as well as properly process and overcome the bad, you're much more likely to have an overall positive reality.

You can help the people you're supporting do this as well, setting them up to create a beautiful, rich reality for themselves that will last long after your coaching sessions with them are over. This will prepare them to have empathy for themselves and others.

USING POSITIVE PSYCHOLOGY IN COACHING

Imagine being able to inspire the people you work with to question their beliefs and reconsider them. This would enable them to assess their situations effectively from a comprehensive and unbiased viewpoint, promoting a deeper self-awareness and a better understanding of their relationship with and contribution to their current circumstances.

Encouraging clients to view their dilemmas as signals rather than obstacles can help them move from a mindset rooted in hypervigilance to one focused on objectivity. To make this happen, as coaches and clinicians, we must first disconnect our hard wiring and be permeable to new perceptions and perspectives. By modeling these skills in our own behaviors, we can inspire our clients to become curious about the nature of what their circumstances have to offer.

In the early stages of my career, I distinctly remember feeling quite anxious when clients presented me with complex challenges that they had created themselves. My anxious feelings persisted even though I was becoming globally recognized for effectively guiding even the most challenging clients toward self-actualization and high functionality.

I often found myself grappling with overwhelming frustration and self-doubt due to my inner struggle. Very few people knew how frequently I battled my self-defeating thoughts while doing everything possible to help my clients meet their intricate needs. This emotional turmoil, commonly known as imposter syndrome, affected me deeply, illustrating how even the most experienced professionals can be impacted.

I questioned my commitment to excellence, wondering if I was truly living up to my own standards. I realized that I was too emotionally invested in my clients, which led to excessive attachment and a host of other challenges. This emotional entanglement made it difficult for me to maintain objectivity and effectively serve them.

Recognizing the need for change, I made a conscious effort to disengage. This involved temporarily stepping back to gain a fresh perspective. I forced myself to detach, creating a physical and emotional distance that allowed me to recharge and regain my composure. This act of detachment was crucial for my survival and the integrity of my brand.

I learned that detachment was not about abandoning my clients or neglecting their needs. Instead, it was about creating a healthy boundary that allowed me to provide the best possible care for them while also preserving my well-being. I was able to return ready to offer my clients the support and guidance they needed in an empathetic way.

The process of disengaging was not easy. It required discipline and a willingness to challenge my own assumptions and beliefs. Initially, I felt guilty and anxious about stepping back, worried that I was letting my clients down. However, as I practiced detachment, I began to recognize the benefits. I could approach my work with greater clarity and objectivity, making decisions based on reason rather than emotion. This shift in perspective not only improved the quality of my work but also allowed me to maintain a healthier work-life balance.

One of the biggest mistakes any clinician can make is to lose sight of the fact that challenges are opportunities to improve and opportunities to find alternative ways to do something. Having to consider a client's situation more deeply in between sessions isn't a bad thing unless you're misusing accurate empathy and allowing it to consume your life.

As we explore the way we interpret the stressors our clients present, it's our job to deconstruct these things and look at them comprehensively. We must do a few things to make this comprehensive view possible.

BREAK DOWN WHAT WE'VE OBSERVED INTO DIFFERENT HEMISPHERES OF A CLIENT'S LIFE

We must look at how it's affecting them personally and professionally in their day-to-day life.

How is their situation affecting their relationships with their partner, children, coworkers, friends, and themselves?

How is all of this detrimental to their ability to function and thrive in their day-to-day activities?

Is this issue getting far too much negative attention rather than being seen as a potential point for positive redirection?

Focusing solely on the big picture or getting lost in the fine details won't move the needle. Whether you're a coach, clinician, or leader in an organization, you need the agility to zoom out and zoom in. Seeing the full landscape while recognizing how the individual pieces that shape it is transformational. This skill helps those you support see how external pressures and internal patterns are affecting their overall well-being, performance, and relationships. The same principle applies to your self-reflection. You need to see the whole puzzle, both strategically and emotionally, if you're going to solve the problem effectively.

As human beings, we tend to default to one extreme or the other: obsessing over minutiae or losing ourselves in the abstract. Whether you're guiding a client, mentoring a direct report, or managing your own inner dialogue, cultivating a clear, balanced perspective leads to better outcomes. It may sound counterintuitive, but the more objective you become, the more empathy you can extend, both to others and to yourself—without becoming overwhelmed or misaligned.

CONSIDER THE PHYSIOLOGICAL AND PSYCHOLOGICAL EFFECTS

How is this person's mental, emotional, or physical health being impacted by their current challenges?

Are their experiences interfering with their ability to lead, perform, or engage meaningfully with others?

Are they struggling to focus on work, manage team dynamics, enjoy personal time, or maintain relationships?

What would it take to help them reach a place where those challenges no longer feel detrimental to their well-being or leadership effectiveness?

Sometimes, circumstances show up to signal a turning point. When someone is stuck in a cycle of stress, burnout, toxic patterns, or reactive leadership behaviors, it's a sign that something deeper needs tending. Whether you're supporting a team member, coaching a client, or managing your own inner conflicts, it's essential to identify the root cause. Surface-level strategies won't stick if the person is emotionally exhausted, full of self-doubt, or stuck in survival mode.

REFLECTION: A TOOL FOR LEADERSHIP AND GROWTH

One of the most effective tools—whether in coaching, therapy, or leadership—is the power of reflection. Used wisely, reflective questioning activates introspection, emotional intelligence, and more objective thinking. It helps people step back from their automatic responses and gain a more objective perspective.

We often overlook how deeply a well-placed question or thoughtful paraphrase can shift someone's mindset.

Let's say someone says, "I'm so sick of this situation."

Instead of simply nodding, you might say:

"You've said this situation is draining. What does that look like in your day-to-day life right now?"

With the right tone, timing, and intention, you're not just repeating their words—you're inviting deeper inquiry. You're helping them see their experience through a new lens.

Imagine a team member or client says, "I never get a break."

Instead of brushing it off or reacting emotionally, try an *amplified reflection* rooted in curiosity:

"You mentioned you never get a break. Never?"

This soft challenge creates space for the person to question their own narrative. Often, what feels like an absolute is emotionally true but not entirely accurate. Your role is to create space for re-evaluation without judgment.

In any context, whether you're managing employees, leading a team through transition, or supporting someone in a personal transformation, phrases like "always" and "never" are red flags. They indicate mental rigidity and emotional overwhelm. Telling someone they're wrong only builds walls. Inviting them to reflect builds bridges.

REFRAMING OVERWHELM INTO INSIGHT

Consider a working parent who says:

"I'm trying to get the kids to school on time, but I work overnight, and I'm running on no sleep. I feel like I'm failing everyone."

That's not just a complaint; it's a cry for validation and support.

Whether this is a coaching client or someone on your team, you can use a *double-sided reflection* that blends empathy with strength-based reframing:

"The fact that you're working through the night and still showing up for your kids each morning shows an incredible level of commitment. What does that say about your values?"

This approach doesn't dismiss the exhaustion. Done with empathy and compassion, it reframes the narrative so the person can see their own resilience and feel empowered instead of defeated.

Positive psychology helps us turn emotional, glass-half-empty moments into insights that foster agency and self-compassion. It allows individuals and leaders to pause, reflect, and course-correct without shame.

CHANGING THE LENS CHANGES THE REALITY

As a coach, therapist, or organizational leader, your role isn't to shield others from the chaos of life or work. Even sacred texts remind us that "He causes his sun to rise on the evil and the good, and sends rain on the righteous and the unrighteous." (Matthew 5:45 NIV) Adversity is universal. The difference lies in how we respond to it.

The moment we change the way we *look* at a challenge, the challenge itself begins to shift. Reality is perception. When we take ownership of our perceptions, we take the first step toward changing our outcomes.

Whether you're guiding others or doing your own inner work, tools like accurate empathy, positive intelligence, and compassionate leadership can reshape how people experience stress, growth, and transformation.

POSITIVE PSYCHOLOGY AND TRAGEDY

Navigating empathy and positive psychology becomes more intricate in situations involving traumatic or devastating circumstances.

The last thing you want to hear when you're going through something tragic or traumatic is "be positive." Positive psychology isn't about forcing positivity. It's about managing your thoughts so you can cope with your situation in healthy ways. It's unrealistic to expect yourself or anyone else to find something good in the middle of turmoil, particularly in highly traumatic situations. Grant yourself some grace; allow time and self-compassion to work their magic. By gradually shifting your perspective and acknowledging the small blessings life offers during the storm, you can work wonders. This approach allows you time to heal while adjusting to your circumstances. With the power of deliberate intention, you will find something to be grateful for amid life's challenges.

Let me share something raw from my own life. Like many people in midlife, I found myself in a role reversal that no child is ever really prepared for, parenting my parent. Overnight, it seemed, my mother and I had traded places, and it became one of the hardest seasons of my life.

My mother was diagnosed with early-onset dementia, along with other health problems. At the very same time, I was knee-deep in research on managing my thoughts, dipping my toes into positive psychology, and practicing accurate self-empathy. Life has a cruel irony sometimes. Here I was, learning about resilience and compassion, while watching the strongest, most resilient woman I knew slip away before my eyes.

I recall one particular day, when I drove her to yet another appointment. Another doctor. Another grim report. Sitting there in that cold office, I felt the weight of frustration, fear, and hopelessness pressing down on me. In that moment, self-compassion was no longer a concept in a book. It was pounding on the door of my heart, demanding to be let in.

I thought to myself, *What am I going to do?* I was an only child, adopted, with my father long gone. My mother, once vibrant and fiercely independent, was now fragile, confused, sometimes child-like, and sometimes downright cantankerous. One moment, she tested every ounce of my patience; the next, she broke my heart with her vulnerability.

That was when it hit me. To survive this, I had to change the way I saw it. I had to stop clinging to the role of son and step fully into the role of caretaker. The dynamic had shifted, and I could not afford to resist it. The woman who had once been my anchor now leaned on me, whether she wanted to or not. As painful as that was, I had to rise to it.

Adding to the heartache was the quiet, relentless truth I could not escape: this season was not going to last much longer. With every appointment, every decline, I knew the end was approaching. The day I signed the papers to bring in hospice was the day my worst nightmare became real. I knew then that when my mother passed, a part of my life would go with her.

For my own survival, I knew I had to find a bright spot. My thoughts could no longer stay stuck in *My mother is dying.* Instead, I began to reframe them into *I need to maximize these next few months with her because I will never get them back.* That shift did not erase the pain, but it gave me purpose.

I remember moments that tested every ounce of my patience, like changing her diaper or steadying her frail body as we made our way down the hallway. I would feel frustrated, tired, and even angry. Even with everything I was feeling, I just kept bringing it back to three simple things. One, we had a home to come back to. Two, we were able to get her the help she needed. And three, I got to be the one to give my dear mother dignity in her final moments. That was a gift, really. What mattered most to both of us was that she would spend the rest of her life in the home she had poured herself into creating.

Through it all, one truth anchored me: gratitude. Gratitude that my mother had chosen to adopt me, to give me the life I was given. Without her choice, I would not be the man I was then, nor the man I have become now. That realization reframed everything.

The moral of this story is simple, yet profound. You cannot control everything that happens in your life, but you can control how you see it. When you change the way you see it, you change your life.

If you are in one of these difficult seasons, I want to encourage you to give yourself empathy. Do not try to deny your pain or force yourself into toxic positivity. Instead, take one small step each day to gently adjust your perspective. Find one thing, however small, that gives you a flicker of hope or reminds you that you can take one more step forward.

If someone you know is going through something like this, be their mirror of strength. Show up without judgment, without clichés, and without trying to force them into a smile. Help them notice the pieces of resilience already within them. Most of all, validate their pain, emotions, and humanity because that is exactly what you would want if the roles were reversed.

GUIDING PRINCIPLES FOR COACHING AND BEYOND

Let's look at some of the research-based positive psychology models I use in my coaching practice to help my clients achieve lasting transformation in their lives. I'll illustrate how to use accurate empathy in each of these different approaches for positive outcomes.

1. The Transtheoretical Model of Change

This model identifies where someone is in the process of change. It lays out five phases: pre-contemplation, contemplation, preparation, action, and maintenance.

While coaches can use this to meet their clients where they are, you can also use this model to understand yourself and others in important interactions.

- Pre-contemplation: "I'm not sure I even want to make a change. Why would I?"
- Contemplation: "What if I did make this change? I might, I might not."
- Preparation: "I think I'm ready to start making a change."
- Action: "I'm going to do it. My next step is…."
- Maintenance: "I'm actively doing X, Y, and Z, and the next phase of my plan is…."

Your clients and team members have already taken a courageous step by deciding to pursue change. They may come to you with clear goals, but often they are unsure of the path forward. As a coach or leader, your responsibility is not to hand them a roadmap, but to help them discover why these changes truly matter to them.

Your role is to create the space for exploration, to guide with curiosity rather than prescription, and to empower them to make choices that lead to lasting transformation. During the action and maintenance phases, your commitment to practicing accurate empathy becomes critical. It is what helps them uncover the deeper motivations that sustain progress and transform their vision into lived reality.

When they're in the pre-contemplation and contemplation stages of a goal, using accurate empathy can look like:

- Validating their feelings and acknowledging their struggles
- Helping them establish an objective view of their situation (What problems are not making this change, causing them? What will they gain if they make this change?)

If they're in the preparation stage, your role can include:

- Guiding them to connect their core values to the goal(s)
- Helping them stay grounded so they can come up with realistic steps to achieve their goals
- Establishing a milestone-driven process they can return to if they start straying from those steps

Finally, if they're in the action and maintenance phases, you're there to:

- Check in with them and remind them to check in with themselves (how they're feeling, how they're realistically doing)

- ◦ Support and empower them as they navigate change, ensuring they learn from the process
- ◦ Help them to forgive themselves when they break a commitment or don't keep a promise to themselves or others

Your job as a coach isn't to tell them what to do and when to do it. Using this model in your coaching, along with accurate empathy, requires you to help them see their situation from different angles so they feel confident in their ability to make better choices that will help them achieve their goals.

2. Appreciative Inquiry

This technique focuses on motivating someone by getting them to acknowledge their previous successes. It encourages self-efficacy and self-belief, so they feel able to overcome challenging circumstances. It involves examining a particular issue with curiosity, not judgment, to understand their relationship with it.

The four Ds of this model are as follows: discovery, dream, design, and destiny (Cooperrider and Whitney 2005). The discovery stage involves identifying these strengths and abilities. The dream stage is one of envisioning and outlining a path forward that builds upon what was identified in the first stage. In the design step, you create goal statements for each area to improve and determine the steps that will allow you (your team members or your client(s)) to achieve those goals. The destiny stage is the finalization of a collaborative plan where all parties contribute their unique strengths and resources toward achieving the ultimate goal.

Some of the questions to ask when using this model include:

What is their background with it? What does accomplishing this mean to them? How does accomplishing, or not accomplishing, their desired outcome affect them cognitively, emotionally, or physiologically?

While coaching often highlights what's *not* working, it's equally important to explore what *is* working and to recognize what the individual is already doing well. Focusing on strengths helps maintain motivation and allows them to view their growth process through a more balanced, constructive lens.

This approach doesn't ignore areas that need improvement. Instead, it offers a more objective, bird's-eye perspective, one that invites them to look beyond perceived shortcomings and begin leveraging their strengths as tools for progress. When framed this way, the journey becomes less about fixing what's broken and more about building on what's strong—with self-belief and empathy leading the way.

3. Motivational Interviewing

This is tapping into someone's core values to get them to commit to and work toward a goal.

Ask questions and actively listen to the answers to understand their perspective and gain more clarity on an issue. Ultimately, your goal is to arrive at a generative (or "aha") moment.

In their own words, what are their reasons for wanting to change? How does this goal align with their vision for their life? What do they think are the obstacles blocking their progress? What previous successes can they learn from and build on?

Sometimes, clients come in with goals that don't truly align with their values. This might be due to their limiting beliefs about themselves and what they can achieve, or it might be the result of someone else's expectations or goals for them. Either way, it's not surprising when someone doesn't know what they actually want or value most.

By asking thoughtful, open-ended questions, you guide others toward insights they may not yet be fully conscious of. The coaching process frequently uncovers deeper layers of meaning beyond the initial concern that was brought to the table. To support this kind of discovery, it's essential to create a space where individuals can open up at their own pace.

Even if you have a strong grasp of their motivations, struggles, or growth edges, avoid making assumptions. Offering up what *you* believe to be the answer may inadvertently short-circuit their self-discovery. Instead, give them room to speak freely and process aloud.

If you tend to be more extroverted and feel the urge to interrupt, resist it. Your silence may be the doorway to their breakthrough. Conversely, if you're more introverted by nature, challenge yourself not to shrink back. Ask the hard questions. Gently prompt them to dig deeper. Growth often lives just beyond the comfort zone.

By practicing accurate empathy and asking powerful, well-timed questions, you help people develop a stronger understanding of themselves, even if it doesn't happen immediately. Your role is to plant seeds of awareness. Whether those seeds take root today, tomorrow, or weeks later is not always in your control. What matters is the presence, patience, and trust you bring to the process.

Release your own expectations. Set aside the desire for instant results. Listen with the intention to learn, not to fix. Empathize without inserting your agenda.

ACCEPTANCE AND COMMITMENT THERAPY (ACT)

ACT invites people to become more mindful of their thoughts and feelings, not to fight them, judge them, or push them away, but to name and accept what's present. With your support, they learn that they may not be where they want to be *yet*, but forward movement is still possible even without perfect conditions.

This approach belongs in every coaching conversation. Whether you're working with a client, a team member, or reflecting on your own life, it's essential to first understand where the person is coming from before trying to help them move forward.

CT and accurate empathy are inseparable companions. Together, they help you ask more meaningful questions, validate emotions without judgment, and meet people exactly where they are, not where you wish they were. This kind of presence isn't passive; it's powerful. It allows people to unfold on their own terms, in their own time.

Every person filters life through their own lens. That's true whether you're showing up as a coach, a friend, a partner, a parent, or a leader. Accurate empathy requires that you remove your lens long enough to see through theirs. That means letting go of the urge to project your own expectations or rush someone toward a place they haven't chosen to go yet. Especially when it comes to emotions, yours or theirs, assumptions are the enemy of connection.

Instead of performing empathy, *practice* it. Choose presence over pretense. Let curiosity quiet your inner fixer. Real connection begins where an agenda ends.

Here's the irony: many of us are naturals at offering others the grace to go at their own pace, but we rarely give ourselves that same permission. We say, "Take your time," to someone else, while silently demanding that we hurry up and get over it. We swallow our pain, sideline our needs, and call it strength. Yet, being strong for everyone else while abandoning yourself is not sustainable, and it's not strength; it's self-neglect wrapped in duty.

Who is strong for you while you're carrying the weight of everyone else?

True strength is learning to be there for yourself. That means offering yourself the same patience, compassion, and empathy you give so freely to others. It means acknowledging your hurt without minimizing it, and recognizing that your healing deserves time, space, and tenderness.

Accepting yourself as you are, right now, is one of the most courageous acts of self-empathy. So is letting go of what you cannot change and choosing to shape what comes next. Self-acceptance is not resignation; it is a declaration that all versions of you, past, present, and future, are worthy of care.

Let that be your foundation, because when you embrace all of who you are, you create space to become everything you're meant to be.

1. Cognitive Behavioral Therapy (CBT)

CBT aims to help people break negative mindsets and behavior cycles by adjusting distorted thought patterns. It teaches them to recognize when inaccurate or unhelpful thoughts create negative emotions that lead to patterns of unhealthy behavior. CBT can help them reframe their thoughts and language to transform their beliefs and behaviors. This approach has been found to increase empathy in patients with chronic pain (Song et al. 2018). This study was performed with a very small sample size, however, it serves to emphasize the natural intersection of CBT and accurate empathy. Coaches need to know how to show accurate empathy to help their clients learn how to do so as well.

To help another person uncover and acknowledge harmful thoughts and behaviors, you first must utilize accurate empathy techniques. You must understand them and help them feel safe enough to discover these details about themselves. If you try to "fix" them right away, the lack of trust and a solid foundation will destroy the opportunity for compassionate, meaningful interactions.

APPLYING ACCURATE EMPATHY MOVING FORWARD

Let's bring back your GPS from Chapter Six.

We know that perfect empathy is not possible in every situation. You might apply empathy easily and accurately in one situation and struggle to find the right road the next time. When you make a wrong turn, go back to the beginning instead of trying to skip to the third turn ahead.

Say, for example, that a conversation with your partner ends with both of you saying some hurtful things. Sometimes, we say things we don't mean, but other times, we say things that we do mean in the heat of the moment. While you may mean what you said, you probably didn't mean to say it the way you did.

In this scenario, where do you start?

That's right, at the beginning.

Reflect on where you were coming from in that conversation.

Were you hurt? Angry? What was the match that lit the fire?

Did your partner's feelings trigger something in you because they were wrong, or was it because you know it's true and it's a harsh truth to face? Either way, did you validate your partner's feelings or dismiss them? Did they validate you?

If the conversation became more of a fight, the odds are high that at least one of you was feeling unheard and misunderstood. A lack of accurate empathy was present in that situation, even if your intentions were good. So, lead with curiosity about yourself, your feelings, and how you showed up in the conversation. Then, think about how you might restore trust and improve future interactions with them. While this process isn't one-sided, and both partners need to work on themselves, you can only control *your* thoughts, words, and actions.

Next, depending on what came up for you in the first stage, start working on showing yourself compassion and empathy. Even if you didn't handle everything as well as you could have, your feelings are still valid. Instead of beating yourself up about what has happened, process it and commit to moving forward in a more intentional and empathetic way.

Start by doing some of the self-compassion exercises we talked about in Chapter Six, but don't stop there. Showing yourself compassion and self-empathy isn't a one-and-done deal.

Finally, once you've gone through the stages of observing, reflecting, processing, and forgiving yourself, ask your partner if they're ready to try talking again. If they aren't, having a little patience can go a long way in restoring trust and safety in your relationship. If they are, be honest, open, and ready to show them the empathy you've shown yourself.

Depending on the severity of the conversation and where you started, it may take more than one conversation and one demonstration of accurate empathy to heal things with yourself and your partner. I never said this process would be easy, but if you commit to it, it will change your life and the lives of those around you for the better.

You can't force someone to show empathy to themselves or you, but if you model what it looks like, they may be able to improve their relationship with empathy over time.

Just remember, you can only control yourself.

MAIN TAKEAWAYS FROM THIS CHAPTER

⇒ Positive psychology is one of the greatest tools you have for developing accurate empathy.

It focuses on positive experiences, individual traits, and institutions that support their development.

Whether you're a coach or clinician, the approaches involved in positive psychology can help you and anyone else involved in transitioning from a survival mindset to a thriving mindset.

⇒ There's no one-size-fits-all in positive psychology.

It gives us as coaches the opportunity to dig deeper and utilize more than the typical approaches of our chosen field(s).

Some templates and approaches are useful for certain situations. We've even used general examples in this book to demonstrate accurate empathy in action. However, there's always a need to step outside the box and adjust our tactics and responses to reflect the situation we're in and those with whom we are interacting.

⇒ You've heard the common phrase, "Reality is perception."

This is true, whether you're in a client session or out in the world. If you change your perception, you change your reality. Obviously, you can't change everything that happens to you and others in your life. However, changing your perception is powerful in shaping your thoughts, actions, and finally, your outcomes.

⇒ Three primary steps are required to gain the ability to clearly see your client's (or the other person's) situation.

These approaches are also necessary for giving yourself empathy. If you don't take these steps, demonstrating accurate empathy is nearly impossible.

1. Break the problem down into different aspects of the other person's life.
2. Consider how it's affecting them physiologically.
3. Use strategic reflections.

Before you rush into a solution, understand the problem. Otherwise, the solution likely won't be sustainable or comprehensive enough to create lasting change.

⇒ Reflections are useful for coaching, engaging in self-empathy, and making everyday interactions that require accurate empathy easier.

They help you and your conversation partner see the situation, as well as the thoughts and emotions involved, more clearly.

Using amplified reflections is common in coaching because they offer a path to reflection without making the other person feel like you're disputing their feelings and their side of the story. Instead of invalidating their feelings or saying that their version is only a half-truth, you're leading them to discover how they might be amplifying their emotions based on the truth. This doesn't mean that you're assuming the other person is overreacting. It's simply a path to the root cause and, eventually, a solution rooted in accurate empathy.

⇒ Positive psychology is never about forcing positivity, especially in a traumatic or debilitating situation.

If you or someone you know is going through a tough time, the last thing anyone wants to hear in that type of situation is, "There's always a silver lining."

Trying to force someone to feel positive will likely alienate them further and make them feel misunderstood. If you're the one going through a hard situation, don't try to suppress your negative emotions or immediately replace them with positive ones.

⇒ Positive psychology can be integrated with any field or approach, including those we mentioned above.

There are some common themes of positive psychology and the disciplines we discussed (such as ACT, CBT, and DBT) that make for effective integration. These themes are mindfulness, awareness, curiosity, and empathy.

⇒ Always start from the beginning when an interaction goes south.

Check in with yourself and be honest about where you were during the interaction. Without judgment, consider why you were feeling that way, where the conversation went wrong, and what you could do to improve when you engage with that person again.

Allow them time to do the same. If they aren't ready, don't push it. We all process things in our own time and in different ways, unique to our experiences, beliefs, and personalities.

Chapter Eight

EMOTIONAL INTELLIGENCE AND EMPATHY

IN OUR CONTENT-SATURATED WORLD, EMOTIONAL intelligence (EI or EQ) remains a subject of fascination, yet a thorough understanding and mastery of it eludes many. This situation prompts several key questions: What exactly is emotional intelligence? What defines its absence? Assuming we can answer these questions, the next challenge lies in understanding how to cultivate or enhance your emotional intelligence. Additionally, how does the improvement of EQ impact our ability to demonstrate genuine empathy? The array of questions surrounding EQ can be overwhelming, leading to confusion rather than clarity. However, one thing is certain: EQ is a vital skill that can't be ignored, especially for those aspiring to be exceptional coaches, astute clinicians, or transformative leaders. It's not merely about how you interact with others, but how you make them *feel* during those interactions that truly matters. Success in this area leads to exponential growth. Failure not only undermines your efforts it can also be the primary catalyst of personal and organizational collapse.

To initiate our discussion, let's establish the definition of emotional intelligence. The technical definition of EQ is the capacity to identify, comprehend, and express your emotions and those of others. It bears a strong resemblance to empathy, doesn't it? We often associate emotional intelligence with an individual's ability to interpret another person's emotional state and respond empathetically and appropriately. While this may seem straightforward, it's much easier said than done.

The challenge lies in the absence of a universal standard for measuring EQ. Thankfully, there are assessments available that assist coaches and individuals in recognizing their EQ blind spots. Fortunately, this serves as an excellent starting point for pinpointing areas that may require your attention. In my practice, I employ the Emotional Quotient Inventory (EQ-i 2.0) tool, which we'll delve into later in this chapter. It's widely recognized and utilized as one of the most respected EQ assessment tools today.

One of the most misleading ways to view emotional intelligence is to confuse performance with authenticity. Someone who reads a room well, mirrors emotions, or responds to cues in a way that wins respect or even affection may appear emotionally intelligent. On the surface, they create harmony, soothe discomfort, and seem tuned in. However, this is often more show than substance. True EQ is not about skillfully managing appearances; it is about genuine connection. The difference is like the contrast between an actor reciting lines with perfect timing and a friend who listens with their whole heart. One entertains, the other transforms.

When it is weaponized, it exploits the most vulnerable aspects of our human nature. Think of the politician who taps into fear, prejudice, or wounded pride. They seem attuned, but what they are really doing is exploiting the most vulnerable and damaged aspects of people's psyches. Misery may love company, but so do bias and bigotry.

You must understand what emotional intelligence is and is not to use it appropriately and detect when others are using it for the right reasons. It's also essential to consider how emotional intelligence and empathy intersect, so you can work on a comprehensive approach to improving your relationships and interactions.

In my view, accurate empathy as it relates to EQ is the ability to be present and to act and respond in such a way that you inspire awareness and accountability in yourself and others. Emotionally intelligent people motivate individuals and groups by tapping into the greater good of their psyches.

Before we can begin to understand and respond to our emotions, as well as others' emotions, in an empathetic and emotionally intelligent way, we must know more about emotions in general. Emotions can be positive or negative, mild or strong. You have to learn to adjust your responses based on an emotion's valence and arousal.

VALENCE AND AROUSAL

Valence refers to the positivity or negativity of an emotion, whereas arousal is the intensity or strength of that emotion.

How do you determine these aspects of an emotion, especially if that emotion is not your own?

We know that self-awareness and asking questions that bring about self-awareness for others are huge steps to developing accurate empathy.

Have you ever reacted strongly to something that wasn't as big of a deal as you thought in hindsight? Maybe you've responded too quickly in the heat of the moment and immediately regretted it. I get it. We're only human. However, part of becoming emotionally intelligent is realizing you don't always have to turn everything up to ten when one will do. Be aware not only of the outcome you desire or what you do, but also how you do it.

Studies have shown that valence and arousal impact emotional processing and can activate the region of the brain that engages in interoception, emotional awareness, and other unconscious sympathetic functions. One study looked at the brain's reaction to words of different levels of valence and arousal while participants read (Hamer, Chida, and Molloy 2009). Emotional words were processed first, as opposed to neutral words.

When we look at the effects of an emotional state and how it causes our clients to experience things like depression, we must ask how the level of emotional intelligence displayed by us as clinicians or leaders affects them.

We can also use a valence and arousal approach for our clients as a way of helping them process their emotions. One study showed that naming emotions can have a positive effect on fear and anxiety (Association for Psychological Science 2012). This is one reason we call attention to the nature and intensity of our clients' verbal and physical expressions. I talked about amplified reflections in the last chapter as a way of triggering introspection, which also applies here.

We can measure positive high and low arousal externally and internally. For example, we could give a client a survey on a Likert scale. As they choose "strongly agree," "strongly disagree," or any of the options in between, they can share the impact that is felt about how a clinician treats them. In other words, when our clients or patients engage with us, and we cause them to feel seen, respected, appreciated, and heard, they tend to respond in a high arousal state. This often induces a placebo effect. Your high EQ coaching may help those in your care take their medications, follow through on diet or exercise routines, recover from trauma, or cope in healthy ways. Our ability to connect with people authentically and in a meaningful way can impact their arousal and take them from apathetic and hopeless to hopeful and connected.

In the same way, when leaders or clinicians affect their patients or teams and create a negative high or low arousal state, we see everything go downhill from there.

Throughout my professional journey, I've had the honor of collaborating with a diverse array of individuals and groups, ranging from esteemed legal and healthcare professionals to accomplished professional athletes, entrepreneurs, elected officials, and executives of global organizations. I mentioned that one of the emotional intelligence assessments I employ to introduce my clients to the concept is the EQ-i 2.0. While there are numerous EQ assessments available, I favor this specific tool due to its robust evidence and research foundation, as well as its incorporation of a 360-degree component for organizations. This assessment provides a valuable framework for identifying and evaluating various facets of emotional intelligence. Notably, it pinpoints five key areas that serve as an excellent starting point for understanding and assessing emotional intelligence.

To comprehensively understand Emotional Quotient (EQ), let's explore its five crucial components and their significance for both you and your coachee.

1. Self-perception.

This includes self-awareness, self-actualization, and self-image.

Consider how motivated and disciplined you are in working toward your goals.

How do you perceive yourself? Do you generally see yourself in a positive or negative way?

Is your self-image distorted by external factors, such as your childhood experiences, your interactions with others in adolescence, or previous traumas?

If you want to improve your self-perception, you must be willing to reflect and have honest conversations with others. Therapy can also be enlightening for a lot of people when it comes to their blind spots regarding themselves and others.

As a coach, clinician, or leader, you can encourage the people you care about to develop self-empathy by using reflections and helping them draw from past experiences. We talked about pointing out what they're doing right and what these choices say about them as individuals. This is important in helping them reframe their self-perception from one of guilt, shame, hatred, or pity to one rooted in compassion and empathy.

2. Self-expression.

Self-expression consists of how we communicate our emotions and beliefs, as well as how assertive we are. This also refers to how independent an individual is.

How do you express yourself verbally? What about nonverbally?

You might give someone the silent treatment to get attention, which is a behavior that's low in emotional intelligence. Alternatively, maybe you take time to process your emotions, consider other perspectives, and engage in respectful conversations with others. These are high emotional intelligence behaviors.

As coaches, clinicians, and mental health professionals, we must be aware of how we express ourselves in client sessions and hyper-aware of how our clients express their emotions, since words are not the only indicator of how they feel.

3. Interpersonal functioning.

This involves interpersonal relationships, empathy, social responsibility, and more. We know that we can improve our interpersonal functioning through practice, reflection, and intention.

You can't achieve perfection in any of these areas, but becoming proficient in accurate empathy will improve every area of your life. Embrace the learning curve because every interpersonal relationship is different and will require personalized approaches to empathy.

We have a responsibility to ourselves and our clients to maintain a professional but empathetic presence during sessions. It's also important to tend to our personal relationships so that we don't bring our baggage into sessions.

4. Decision-making.

This looks at how we go about solving problems and how much control we have over our responses. How much impulse control do you demonstrate?

Do you tend to fall apart whenever you have to make an important decision, or do you spend time considering all angles and make an informed decision with confidence? Some decisions are more difficult than others, but establishing strong decision-making skills can make the process less strenuous.

Decision-making skills are crucial during client sessions, but it's also essential that you develop these skills outside of your profession. If you can't make solid decisions in your own life, how can you guide your clients to make better decisions?

5. Stress management.

This refers to things like our flexibility and stress tolerance (how well we cope).

How do you respond to minimal stress and chaos? Do you have a lot of physical symptoms related to high levels of stress?

Some individuals may have a lower tolerance for stress, especially if they've experienced trauma or were raised in a high-stress environment. However, as is the case for all these key areas, your tolerance and responses to stress can be improved.

Stress management is also related to resilience. Do you tend to be optimistic in the face of turmoil? How do you view challenges?

While some people who experience traumatic or stressful events emerge more resilient, others cope by avoiding their emotions and staying inside their comfort zone. Additionally, even if an individual who's faced trauma is more resilient, that doesn't mean they're in touch with their emotions or emotionally intelligent overall. There are a lot of factors that influence the development of resilience following trauma, including one's characteristics and how much access they have to support (Ungar 2013).

As coaches, clinicians and mental health professionals, we often play a crucial role in our clients' development of resilience and healthy coping mechanisms. We can't tell them what to do, but we can be a catalyst for them as they improve their self-awareness, empathy, and emotional intelligence.

I probably don't need to explain how developing stress management techniques yourself is crucial for your role as a coach or clinician. Stress can creep into every area of our personal and professional lives, negatively impacting our clients' outcomes as well as our own.

When we examine these five things, I agree with the EQ-i 2.0 instrument, the leading model for measuring EQ, which suggests that doing these things correctly is a great indicator of EQ. However, I think we can go beyond a scientific measurement and consider things that have more to do with moral and social values.

Morality is defined as an established set of principles related to good and bad behavior. Staying in touch with our morality tends to include thinking about the short-term and long-term effects of our actions and how we respond to others. Empathy and morality are built on compassion, understanding, and doing what's right.

If you're a mental health or allied health professional, it goes without saying that it's not your job to teach morals to your clients. However, you can contribute to their moral health by modeling empathy, helping them determine their priorities and values, and engaging in reflective activities that help them develop self-awareness.

THE DELICATE NATURE OF EMOTIONAL INTELLIGENCE IN COACHING AND LEADERSHIP

We as clinicians and leaders must take the time to measure twice and cut once regarding what we think, say, and do when engaging with our clients and teams. An easy way to think about this is to put yourself in the shoes of the affected party or parties. What would you need from your coach, clinician, or another person to make you feel that you're valued and you matter? How can they show you that they're not dismissive of your perspective, even if they don't agree with it?

In over fifteen years of working with high-level leaders, I've found that most of them are outcome-driven. They often make the mistake of considering how to create an outcome that matches their vision without first talking and listening to those they need the most to achieve that outcome.

The lesson is that to develop greater emotional intelligence and empathy, we must think before we speak. We must listen before we respond. This means truly listening to someone. It doesn't take much to repeat back to someone what they said. It helps them feel you are listening and truly considering their words. It shows them that you respect their perspective. This is especially true when it differs from yours. This process is often the difference between healthy relationships with solid communication and relationships where one or both individuals feel unheard and misunderstood.

When engaging in accurate empathy, it's crucial to consider pitch, tone, and inflection—beyond just active listening. A simple adjustment in tone can significantly alter the course of an interaction and greatly influence the presence of empathy and emotional intelligence in a conversation.

For instance, saying, "Why?" with an upward pitch at the end of the word can often be perceived as condescending, challenging, or dismissive. In contrast, saying, "Why?" in a soft voice with a downward pitch indicates curiosity and receptiveness to the other person's perspective. This non-threatening tone demonstrates your willingness to understand why something may be important and meaningful to them.

This supports the belief that it's not necessarily what you do, but how you do it that truly matters. This is true when we look at a coach or a leader's demonstration of emotional intelligence and empathy.

CONFLICT MODES

In leadership positions and in coach or clinician roles, you have to think about how you're affecting another person's self-worth. This is necessary for any relationship. I'm not saying you're entirely responsible for someone else's self-image. It's impossible and unhealthy to be another person's only source of acceptance and validation. However, if you don't consider the other person at all, they will feel that lack of empathy and understanding.

So, how do we consider someone's self-worth without misusing empathy or engaging in sessions that cross professional boundaries?

Two of the International Coaching Federation's (ICF) core competencies are the ability to create a safe, supportive space and the capacity to remain fully present and conscious during every interaction. These competencies aren't limited to coaching sessions—they also apply when engaging with colleagues, whether you're leading a team or collaborating across levels. Both can be strengthened by cultivating self-awareness and being intentional about how you show up—in your energy, your language, and your presence.

If you have a client who's not ready to open up to you completely in the first few sessions, do you try to convince them to share everything? Of course not. Creating a safe space for them might look like offering some words of encouragement, validating their feelings, and actively listening to what they feel comfortable enough to share.

It's essential to prioritize listening over speaking. For years, I have emphasized in my lectures the significance of having two ears and one mouth. It is my belief that this proportion directly reflects the appropriate balance between listening and speaking. We should listen more than we talk. Our job as coaches and leaders is to bring out the best in other people. When we give people the opportunity to express themselves and feel heard, not only do we increase their respect for us, but we also increase their self-efficacy and contribute to their development of resilience. How can we do that if we fail to bring the best version of ourselves to our interactions with others?

Leadership isn't about barking orders or dominating a situation. It's also not about always compromising or accommodating to get people to like you. Sometimes, we have to engage in conversations and address situations that we don't want to be involved in or have to resolve. However, conflict management is an important part of any relationship. You must understand how you typically respond to conflict and use that knowledge to show accurate empathy in any situation.

An instrument I'm fond of using in my practice, especially when working with corporate groups and healthcare systems, is the Thomas-Kilmann Conflict Mode Instrument (TKI). It's a scientific way of measuring how we handle conflict (Schaubhut 2007). The five ways to handle conflict, in no particular order, are:

- Accommodate
- Compromise
- Collaborate
- Compete
- Avoid

These must be used at different times and to various degrees. Our challenge as human beings is that we usually default to our top three methods. What I like about the TKI is that it measures how much energy we put into our default mode. You would think collaboration and compromise would be the best. You might even believe that you should never avoid conflict or compete. However, sometimes avoiding conflict is the best course of action. You might have to avoid conflict because a situation is dangerous. A more common example is deciding to avoid conflict temporarily and suggesting that you have a serious conversation at a better time. Other times, competing may be the right choice. For example, competing might look like standing up for yourself.

Accommodating and avoiding are on the unassertive ends of the spectrum, whereas collaborating and competing are assertive forms of conflict management. Compromising is in the middle.

If your default mode is accommodating, this can be beneficial at times, but damaging in other situations. It may make sense to accept someone else's point of view to prevent a heated argument occasionally, especially if it's a small, isolated incident. However, if you're doing this all the time, it can lead to built-up resentment and feeling like you're unheard in the relationship. This directly affects your self-empathy and empathy for the other individual.

We desire a compromise in most situations, but it's not always possible.

You must determine which approach will help others understand your perspective and take into consideration what's important to you and why. The approach you choose should also help you understand them better. As we look at these modalities, understanding and managing our default modes is a significant contributor to our emotional intelligence and how we present ourselves, especially in turbulent situations. The bottom line is awareness. As we lead in our respective spaces, it's our awareness that's going to create an intentional outcome. A lack of it will bring an unintended outcome that causes significant negative consequences.

Being intentional and communicating with others in a present and strategic manner with compassion, empathy, and EQ better positions us to bring out the best in our clients.

One of the spiritual texts I read most contains the basis of the well-known phrase, "Do unto others as you would have them do unto you." (Matthew 7:12 (KJV and Luke 6:31(NIV)) Another popular phrase stemming from Matthew 6:45 (NKJV) is, "Out of the abundance of the heart, the mouth speaks."

In my view, these two ideas can be the bookends for emotional intelligence. If we treat others with the same respect, compassion, and humility we wish to receive from them, the odds are much greater that we'll create a harmonious environment where our clients, friends, partners, children, and others in our lives feel respected, validated, and seen.

Remember, thoughts become words. Words become actions and situations. True emotional intelligence begins from the inside out. As we learn to think before we speak and consider how our words and actions affect ourselves and others, we significantly increase our ability to make a positive impact.

Do we have to increase our emotional intelligence before we can truly understand how to show accurate empathy? Let's talk about it.

WHICH COMES FIRST: EMOTIONAL INTELLIGENCE OR EMPATHY?

There's no rule for which one you should focus on first. They go hand in hand and are both a major part of your journey toward improving your connection with yourself and your relationships with others. If you follow the exercises and advice in this book, you'll likely improve your accurate empathy skills *and* emotional intelligence simultaneously.

They're both essential to developing as a professional in the mental health industry. Even if you're not a coach or clinician, they're still completely necessary for your overall happiness and the success of your personal and professional relationships.

While striving for accurate empathy and emotional intelligence in your interactions is essential, it's best to avoid becoming overly fixated on them. Engaging in constant overanalyzing while attempting to perfect these abilities can have detrimental effects on your well-being and relationships. It's valuable to recognize that emotional intelligence and empathy are not static traits, but are skills that evolve through experience and learning.

To better illustrate my point, consider this analogy: Cooking oatmeal on a stove requires some attention, but overworking it is unnecessary. If you stir it constantly, you're putting in more effort than required and wasting time. However, if you don't stir it at all or not enough, it will burn. Similarly, mindfulness and empathy are essential in your interactions with others, but aiming for perfection is unrealistic and a waste of energy. Instead, focus on being intentionally present and adapt your approach to suit each situation.

If you ever get stuck in a situation and you aren't sure how to respond, it's better to take your time instead of rushing to try to solve the problem. There's no shame in telling a client you need to think more about what they said or did. In fact, it'll likely encourage them to do the same. There's no shame in telling your child, partner, friend, or coworker that you want to revisit a conversation at a better time. It's almost always possible to delay a conversation to make sure you're both in the right headspace to interact in an empathetic, rational way.

When it's not possible to postpone a conversation, go back to the basics as best you can. Consider where you're coming from, respond with intention, and reflect later on what you can improve for the next conversation with that individual and in general.

Remember, controlling the thoughts, actions, or reactions of others is beyond your reach. Instead, focus your efforts on setting the tone for every interaction you have. By leading by example, you can potentially inspire others to take responsibility for their actions as well. Individuals need to develop empathy for themselves and cultivate self-awareness. If a person is unwilling to contribute to the growth of your relationship while you are actively working to change, they might not be the ideal person for you. Allow yourself and others time to evolve.

I hope this book will help you identify the beliefs, habits, and relationships that align with your happiness and success, as well as those that are hindering you.

Self-reflection and learning from past experiences are two of the most crucial things you can do consistently to maintain and improve your empathy and emotional intelligence. Together, these can lead to better interactions and deeper connections.

EMOTIONAL INTELLIGENCE AND EMPATHY REFLECTION

It can be difficult to tell if you're progressing in emotional intelligence and empathy. This is why I encourage regular introspection. You also have to be willing to ask for feedback and receive it with grace and humility. Let's review some exercises that will help you stay on the right track in your journey.

1. Engage in introspection. (Did you really think we were going to start anywhere else?)

Consider how you're showing up every day.

Are you moving through life on autopilot, or are you being intentional with your thoughts, words, and actions? Are you actively trying to build the life you want by taking it one powerful habit at a time?

Compare yourself to the person you were a year ago. Can you honestly say you're in a better place? Have you met some of your goals? Did you set any goals in the first place? The purpose of this exercise isn't to be hard on yourself. Don't get down on yourself if you haven't made much progress. Instead, think about the changes you want to make and come up with one habit you can start implementing today. If you truly want to create lasting change, you have to start taking a different approach.

If you're regularly engaging in introspection, you're on the right path. You wouldn't be concerned about how you show up if you didn't care about becoming a more empathetic and emotionally intelligent person.

2. Ask for feedback and consider it as objectively as possible.

There's nothing wrong with asking those close to you how you're doing. This may not always be possible, especially if the people in your life aren't interested in improving themselves.

However, if you have people in your life who are also interested in growing as individuals and in your relationship, they are the ones who can likely give you helpful feedback.

Ask them if you're showing up for them the way they need (this doesn't mean addressing their needs while neglecting your own). Check in with them after negative interactions and find a better way forward together. Make sure you're doing your part by working on yourself and actively contributing to the improvement of your relationships.

There are so many ways to get feedback. It doesn't always have to be you asking, "How am I doing?" It might be as simple as asking the other person, "Do you feel loved and supported by me?" Maybe you could give your team members an anonymous survey that allows them to voice their opinions. The important thing is you're asking. Don't wait for them to come to you. Depending on what type of relationship you have with them, they may never speak up. Try not to fear feedback. It will help you improve your accurate empathy skills and thereby your relationships.

3. Do a relationship audit.

This is another thing you can do on your own. If you don't consistently do this, the previous step will not yield valuable results.

While I encourage you to take responsibility for your role in the success or failure of every relationship you have, it's also crucial to recognize when you can't do more for the relationship. Some people will impede your growth, negatively affect your mental health, and chip away at your happiness, either intentionally or unintentionally. If this is the case for one or more of your relationships, you'll both be better off if you have the emotional intelligence and maturity to end the relationship.

If you can't end the relationship, you can still improve things. For example, let's say you have a coworker with whom you're always butting heads. You can't control their actions, but you can improve your accurate empathy and try to understand their perspective. If they're truly an inconsiderate person, all you can do is cultivate self-empathy and try to utilize emotional intelligence when you interact with them. You can be empathetic toward them, but that doesn't mean you have to accept maltreatment or pretend they're your favorite person.

Alternatively, pay attention to which relationships are healthy. Are you showing up to those relationships with accurate empathy? Are you giving those relationships the attention they need to thrive and grow? Make sure you're asking for feedback from healthy connections.

4. Consider how your life is going as a whole.

Is one (or more) aspect of your life misaligned with your goals and values? Is there something that's taking your time and energy away from the things that truly matter to you?

Similar to the relationship audit, performing a life audit is an important step in improving your emotional intelligence and empathy.

If there's even one part of your life that feels like it's wearing you down mentally, physically, or spiritually, it's either indirectly or directly impairing your ability to show accurate empathy toward yourself and others.

You may not be able to make major changes right away. For example, if you're dreading going to work every day, focus on what you can do. Maybe you can ask for projects that are more interesting to you. You can embrace more challenges that will help you grow. If you truly hate your career, focus on one step every day that can help you get closer to finding another job or field.

If you need to make some changes at home, be honest with your loved ones and try to find a way forward together. Change is difficult, but showing yourself and others accurate empathy will help you see it through without causing irreparable damage to your relationships, health, and life in general.

5. Don't discount your strengths and blessings.

We talk a lot about identifying and addressing areas for improvement. While it's essential to be honest with yourself and others about your weaknesses, noticing and leaning into your strengths is equally important.

As you determine the ways in which you want to improve your life, remember to acknowledge what's going right for you. Be intentional with gratitude during this process. I'm willing to bet you can find one small thing to be grateful for.

Underestimating yourself and your ability to make sound choices will impair your use of accurate empathy and emotional intelligence. Self-awareness, self-belief, and self-compassion are essential to the process.

As we near the end of this book, I want you to reflect on your progress.

Do you find any of the exercises above, or the exercises in previous chapters, difficult to do? Do you notice yourself resisting any part of the process? You can only improve your accurate empathy and emotional intelligence if you're honest with yourself. That's nonnegotiable.

If you discover that you could benefit from working with a qualified professional, please reach out. Sometimes we need someone to hold us accountable and help us stay objective. That's okay. What's important is that you recognize this need and take steps to become someone you're proud of. You can find your way to being honest with yourself and others. Once you do that, self-empathy and empathy toward others will become a lot easier.

MAIN TAKEAWAYS FROM THIS CHAPTER

⇒ We can mistakenly perceive someone as having emotional intelligence, just like we can believe we're skilled at empathy when we're misusing it.

If someone can win over hearts and minds, such as a misguided politician, that doesn't make them emotionally intelligent. They may be tapping into others' desires and needs in a skillful way, but manipulation, or the ability to use others' emotions against them for personal gain, is not a form of emotional intelligence.

⇒ We can use the dimensions of valence and arousal to help our clients be more self-aware.

Even if you're not a coach, labeling your emotions can help you process them more effectively. Valence concerns the positivity or negativity of an emotion, while arousal is the intensity of that emotion.

It's helpful to be aware of how your verbal and nonverbal actions and responses affect the valence and arousal of another person's emotions. This awareness can help prevent misunderstandings and lead to more productive conversations.

⇒ The Thomas-Kilmann Conflict Mode Instrument (TKI) is a useful tool for emotional intelligence development.

Coaches can utilize the TKI to determine their clients' default conflict mode and identify which conflict modes are most appropriate when engaging with them.

Think about which one is your default: avoid, compromise, collaborate, compete, or accommodate. Now think about how this tendency has affected your interactions positively and negatively. Being aware of your habits, especially those related to conflict, can help you have more interactions where empathy and understanding are present.

⇒ We can't increase our emotional intelligence unless we're willing to look at ourselves.

Two major aspects of emotional intelligence are self-perception and self-expression.

The way you think, what you believe, and how you act based on your thoughts and beliefs have a significant impact on your interactions with others, as well as how you feel about yourself and life in general.

Even if you're generally self-aware and empathetic, always take time to reflect on your thoughts and actions, and get in touch with your feelings whenever you're faced with a tough situation. Nobody can carry out accurate empathy perfectly every time, but if you commit to the lifelong process of improving your empathy and emotional intelligence, you'll get a lot of things right.

⇒ Go back to the basics when you get stuck.

There will be times when you don't know where an interaction or relationship went wrong. You'll have experiences that seem to leave you with no way out or forward. When this happens, get curious and focus on yourself first.

Identify your feelings and where they're coming from so you can communicate them properly and minimize the chance of a misunderstanding or misuse of empathy.

⇒ Emotional intelligence and empathy are closely related and often develop simultaneously.

They incorporate self-awareness, reflection, and a willingness to consider others' perspectives and emotions. Those who are emotionally intelligent are usually empathetic and vice versa, but it's still important to work on your relationship with both and make sure your efforts aren't misdirected.

⇒ Here are some steps you can take to stay on track with developing and mastering accurate empathy and emotional intelligence:

1. Engage in introspection.
2. Ask for feedback.
3. Do regular relationship audits.
4. Perform a life audit.
5. Acknowledge your strengths and embrace gratitude.

If you follow these steps and regularly check in with your progress, you won't veer off course.

It can be easy to only focus on the parts of ourselves we dislike or the areas of our lives we want to improve. This can only lead to a perpetual feeling of not being enough or needing more. Recognize what you have and acknowledge that you can't be the person you want to be without the person you are today and the person you were yesterday.

It's essential that you view mastering accurate empathy as a never-ending, but worthwhile, process instead of seeing it as an end goal. You, your loved ones, and the world are constantly changing. You must be willing to adjust your approaches and expectations to allow for growth. Let the fact that there's always room for improvement be exciting and empowering rather than intimidating.

Chapter Nine

NEUROPLASTICITY AND YOUR ABILITY TO MASTER ACCURATE EMPATHY

LIFE IS NOT A STRAIGHT line; it is a living tapestry, woven from threads of evolution and change. These two forces are constant companions, silent architects shaping our stories whether we recognize them or not. Evolution is subtle, like the slow bend of a river carving its way through ancient stone. It is deliberate, unfolding moment by moment through choices we make, lessons we absorb, and the resilience we gain along the way. It asks for our participation, inviting us to become co-creators in our transformation.

Change, by contrast, is less polite. It can arrive like a storm, sudden and disorienting, or seep in like water beneath a door, unnoticed until it has reshaped the entire room. It is the wild card in the human experience, indifferent to plans or preferences. Sometimes it blesses us with unexpected opportunities that elevate everything we thought possible. Other times, it tears through our lives without warning, dismantling our sense of control and forcing us to reckon with what we thought was certain.

Yet within both lies a sacred invitation—not simply to adapt, but to awaken. Evolution asks, "What are you becoming?" while change whispers, "Will you allow yourself to be undone, so something truer can emerge?"

Amidst the chaos of change and the unpredictability of chance, there lies a wellspring of hope and agency. When we find ourselves yearning to break free from the shackles of emotional turmoil, the "what ifs" of regret or our unhelpful default behaviors are signs that we need to reclaim our power. No longer can we afford to be sick and tired of being sick and tired. It's time to take charge of our lives.

This chapter presents a blueprint for mastering your thoughts and emotions. This transformative process will empower you to create a fulfilling life by replacing limiting beliefs and self-destructive patterns with purposeful, intentional actions.

If you continue to go through life in the same way, being reactive as opposed to being proactive, accepting mediocrity and lackluster connections and outcomes, the world will continue to change around you, but you will not evolve.

Alternatively, if you choose to grow and embrace change as an opportunity to learn, you and your outcomes will evolve into something far better than you could have ever imagined.

I want you to know that not only are you capable of growth, but you can master how you go about it. You're capable of cultivating love and respect for yourself and accurate empathy for others, which can significantly improve your relationship with yourself and your personal and professional relationships.

Believe it or not, your brain is capable of great change. There's no reason to believe that you're incapable of turning your life around, especially since you're reading this book right now. You know, maybe deep down, that you can take your outcomes into your own hands. I call this living by intention.

So, in this second-to-last chapter, we'll discuss how to challenge our default-mode processing and use the principles of neuroplasticity to create lasting, positive change in our lives and the lives of others.

Before we move on, I want to celebrate you for taking this step toward improving your life. This book is only the beginning, but it creates a solid foundation for emotional regulation and cognitive evolution. Now it's time to put everything you've learned into action and commit to a lifetime of learning. It may sound a bit scary or time-consuming, but it's worth every second of uncertainty and discomfort to get to a place where you're happy, healthy, and wealthy (whatever that means for you). This book is here to guide and support you every step of the way.

PROCESS-ORIENTED BEHAVIOR: CHALLENGING YOUR DEFAULT MODE PROCESSING

Understanding the connection between our behavior and our emotions can be empowering. It allows us to gain a deeper understanding of ourselves and our actions. Ultimately, it can motivate us to make positive cognitive and behavioral changes.

In this chapter, we'll explore techniques and teachings that I've crafted from my personal life journey and countless hours of clinical engagement with hundreds of coaching clients. Across two decades of transformative work, I've witnessed firsthand the extraordinary impact of these approaches in empowering a diverse array of individuals and groups struggling to navigate life's challenges with renewed resilience and purpose.

These techniques target the underlying factors contributing to low self-worth, anticipatory trauma, and generalized stress and anxiety disorders. They empower individuals to break free from the clutches of these conditions and develop a sense of clarity. By acknowledging the need for empathy, compassion, and emotion-focused coaching approaches, individuals can embrace their vulnerability and embark on a path of self-discovery and healing. I offer practical self-regulation tools, equipping coaches and clients with the skills to manage their emotions and responses effectively. Prioritizing self-compassion, my approaches cultivate a profound sense of inner acceptance and kindness, fostering self-care and emotional well-being. They encourage individuals to treat themselves with the same kindness and understanding they would offer to a friend in need, promoting a sense of self-worth and self-esteem.

Additionally, I want to emphasize the importance of savoring the present moment, which can enhance your capacity for gratitude and empathy toward yourself and others. I encourage individuals to focus on the positive aspects of their lives, appreciate the simple joys, and cultivate a mindset of abundance. These elements are essential for building meaningful and authentic connections with others.

EQ IS NOT COMMON

Contrary to popular belief, common sense and emotional intelligence (EQ) are not innate qualities ingrained in our default mode of processing information. Instead, our tendency to adhere to familiar patterns and behaviors is deeply rooted in the ego's protective nature. The ego has noble intentions, aiming to ensure our safety and survival. However, issues arise in its approach to achieving this objective.

The ego operates primarily on fear-based instincts, leading it to prioritize self-preservation and immediate gratification over long-term growth and well-being. While necessary for basic survival, this protective mechanism can become detrimental when it dominates our decision-making and limits our potential for personal development.

Our ego's protective nature often manifests in our resistance to change, our tendency to judge ourselves and others harshly, and our struggles with demonstrating self-compassion and empathy. Its defensive nature acts as a shield, guarding our fragile sense of self from perceived threats. However, this shield can come at a significant cost. One of the ways in which the ego defends itself is by suppressing or disregarding our emotions. This suppression can be a subconscious mechanism, as we may not even be aware that we're doing it.

When we suppress our emotions, we're essentially denying a part of ourselves. This denial can lead to an accumulation of negative energy within us. This buildup can manifest in various ways, both physically and mentally.

Physically, we may experience symptoms such as headaches, stomachaches, or fatigue. We may also be more susceptible to illness. Mentally, we may feel anxious, depressed, or irritable. We may also have difficulty concentrating or making decisions.

In addition to affecting our physical and mental health, suppressed emotions can also damage our relationships. When we're unable to express our true feelings, we may come across as distant or inauthentic—this can lead to misunderstandings and conflict.

A warning signal that you may be suppressing your emotions is when you, or someone close to you, constantly broods over unresolved issues. This brooding can be a sign that you're not allowing yourself to fully process and release your emotions. Another warning sign is chronic anxiety and depression. Several factors can cause these conditions, but suppressed emotions are often a contributing factor.

If you suspect you're suppressing your emotions, several strategies can help you approach the issue.

1. Practice mindfulness meditation.

Engage in mindfulness meditation to enhance your awareness of emotions and embrace them without judgment. This practice can facilitate emotional connection and acceptance.

2. Journal your thoughts and feelings.

Keep a journal to objectively examine your emotional processing. Reflect on how your thoughts influence your emotional state. Describe how your actions and reactions affect those around you.

3. Seek professional support.

Consider meeting with a qualified coach or therapist, especially if you're a leader, clinician, or coach. A skilled professional can help you identify the root of your emotional suppression and develop healthy strategies for expressing and managing your emotions.

Overcoming the limitations of the ego and cultivating a more balanced and compassionate approach to life requires intentional effort and practice. As we continue through this chapter, I'll provide practical tools and strategies to help you understand your ego's influence on your thoughts, feelings, and behaviors. You'll learn how to recognize the ego's protective instincts and distinguish them from your true self. The experiential exercises and reflective practices in this book are designed to help you develop the skills to navigate your inner landscape with greater awareness and compassion. By understanding and working with your ego, you'll unlock your potential for personal growth, emotional healing, and more fulfilling relationships.

WHERE DOES OUR DEFAULT MODE COME FROM?

Cultural norms, often communicated through language and parental models, have a profound influence on people's behavior. These norms shape our thoughts, feelings, and actions, even when we're not consciously aware of them. Adherence to cultural norms, even when they may be ineffective or outdated, highlights the powerful impact of how we perceive ourselves within our culture.

Several factors contribute to conforming to cultural norms and expectations. We talked about several of these factors in Chapters One and Two. One of the primary factors is the significant influence of parents and caregivers. From a very young age, we soak up the cultural norms of our families, observing the behavior of our parents and other influential adults. We mimic their actions and internalize their values, beliefs, and attitudes, and this process shapes our expectations and behaviors. The main issue here is that our caregivers and role models may be dysfunctional. In many communities, people mistakenly equate being self-sufficient with being self-aware.

When confronted with behaviors or events that threaten their sense of self, individuals might minimize the significance of those disruptions. This minimization serves as a defense mechanism to protect the integrity of their self-concept. For example, an individual who prides themselves on being independent might downplay the importance of relying on others for emotional support or assistance.

Another strategy employed to cope with disruptions to one's identity is justification. In this process, individuals assign positive or acceptable reasons to behaviors that deviate from their own core beliefs or values. For instance, a person who values honesty might justify a dishonest act by claiming it was necessary to avoid hurting someone's feelings or to meet an unmet need.

The tendency to rationalize or dismiss disruptions to one's identity can be particularly pronounced in dysfunctional, codependent relationships. In such relationships, one or both individuals sacrifice their needs and desires to maintain the approval and validation of the other person. This dynamic often stems from a deep-seated fear of abandonment or rejection.

In codependent relationships, individuals might engage in excessive caretaking behaviors to maintain the connection with their partner, even at the expense of their own well-being. They might overlook or minimize their partner's harmful actions to avoid disrupting the relationship. This pattern of behavior reinforces the codependency and perpetuates the cycle of dysfunction.

Additionally, this conflict can manifest as inner turmoil, as we struggle to reconcile our true selves with the expectations placed upon us. This turmoil can lead to anxiety, depression, and other psychological distress.

It's important to recognize the powerful influence of parents and caregivers, and critically examine what we have internalized. While conforming to expectations can provide a sense of validation, we must maintain our sense of self and challenge norms that no longer serve us. This process of self-reflection and individuation allows us to break free from the constraints of external expectations and live more authentic and fulfilling lives.

CULTURAL INFLUENCES

Another factor that contributes to the influence of cultural norms is our cultural surroundings. The culture in which we live is made up of the shared beliefs, values, and practices of its members. These cultural norms are communicated through a variety of channels, such as language, education, and the media. We're constantly exposed to these norms, and they gradually become internalized, shaping our thoughts, feelings, and actions.

Television and other media yield a major influence. The media can portray certain behaviors as desirable or undesirable, and this can influence our own behavior. For example, if we see a character on a popular television show behaving in a certain way, we may be more likely to adopt that behavior ourselves.

Numbing ourselves with apps, television programs, and social media posts that resonate with our broken parts is one of the significant ways we cause ourselves to suffer. Without realizing it, we're attempting to escape from our emotions, experiences, and thoughts by using media as a distraction. In our efforts to eliminate negative thoughts and suppress self-destructive urges, we engage in counterproductive habits that further exacerbate depression and create more cognitive dissonance in the process. These habits can include excessive drinking, overworking, using prescription or illicit drugs, engaging in promiscuous sexual encounters, and even immersing ourselves in cultlike religious and political groups, just to name a few.

Although we frequently resort to avoidance patterns to cope with negative thoughts and behaviors, we do possess the ability to modify these patterns in more constructive and beneficial ways. By tapping into the cognitive architecture of our brains and our internal language system, we have the potential to establish new guidelines for how we interact with our emotions. This process empowers us to override self-sabotaging emotional default programming, thereby creating new neural pathways toward embracing positive change and personal growth.

REFRAMING: REALITY IS PERCEPTION

In clinical terms, this process is known as reframing or reformulating self-instructional control. Self-instructional control refers to the instructions we give ourselves. To better comprehend this concept, take a moment of quiet reflection. Try to refrain from thinking or engaging in any activity. Soon, your mind will break this tranquility and begin hijacking your thoughts. This illustrates the necessity for self-awareness and intentional pursuit, especially when you're already stressed out or dealing with tough issues. The tendency to get frustrated early and give up is common. If you find yourself doing this, it's okay. The way you resolve this is to simply accept the fact that you're a normal human being, and no matter how much of a pain in the ass this is, you're not going to give up. Your mindset and perspectives weren't created overnight, and they won't change overnight either. This is about commitment and consistency. You must practice self-compassion and self-empathy daily. As the old saying goes, "How do you eat an elephant? One bite at a time!"

To achieve positive transformation, we must embark on a dual journey involving internal dialogue and environmental control. Firstly, we must reshape our internal dialogue through self-instructional control. This means challenging negative self-talk and replacing it with positive affirmations and self-compassion. We should practice mindfulness to become aware of our thoughts and emotions and catch ourselves when we engage in self-limiting patterns. Secondly, we should consciously select environments and relationships that foster our growth and well-being. This means surrounding ourselves with supportive people who encourage us and provide us with opportunities for personal growth. It also means creating a physical environment that's conducive to relaxation and self-care. This holistic approach empowers us to break free from self-limiting patterns while cultivating emotional resilience. We must recommit daily to creating a life aligned with our core values. This means living according to our deepest beliefs and desires, even and especially when it's incredibly difficult.

Change is an unavoidable aspect of life, and it's not without its challenges. Adapting to a fresh perspective requires willpower and persistence. Moreover, it demands a willingness to confront one's ego and venture beyond the familiar comfort zone. Navigating the complex terrain of change is further complicated by the tendency to surround ourselves with individuals who share similar dysfunctional beliefs, circumstances, and behaviors. While these people may initially seem like friends and a support system, in reality, they are more accurately described as comrades.

A comrade is not a true friend. They are someone who is struggling alongside you. They're fighting what you're fighting, hating what you hate, and coping the way you cope. Your relationship with them is likely born from shared misery rather than genuine connection. The adage "misery loves company" aptly captures this phenomenon, as we often attract what resonates within us into our lives. Consider this: If your only connection to someone is because you're both mentally or emotionally incarcerated, they are a fellow inmate, not a friend. Friendships should uplift and inspire, not enable you or drag you down. True friends challenge you to grow and become the best version of yourself. They celebrate your successes and support you through your failures while holding you accountable. They are there for you through thick and thin, offering a listening ear, a shoulder to cry on, and a helping hand when you need it most.

Surrounding yourself with positive, supportive people is essential for your well-being. When you have friends who are genuinely on your side, it makes navigating life's challenges easier. They will encourage you to step outside of your comfort zone, try new things, and pursue your dreams. They will also be there to pick you up when you fall and help you dust yourself off.

If you find yourself surrounded by comrades instead of friends, it's time to make a change. Seek out people who share and live your core values. Seek out those who are willing to support you on your journey. These are the people who will help you grow and become the best version of yourself.

FAMILIAR BUT UNPRODUCTIVE BEHAVIORS

When faced with recurring difficulties, people often resort to familiar but unproductive behaviors. This default mode behavior, driven more by habit than choice, perpetuates stress and anxiety. The inability to interact differently with our dilemmas prevents us from discovering new solutions. This is because our brains are wired to seek out familiar patterns, even if those patterns are not helpful. When faced with a difficult situation, our brains automatically default to the behaviors we've used in the past. However, if those behaviors aren't effective, we need to be able to break out of that cycle and try something new.

Individuals who lack behavioral variability, particularly in challenging situations that demand it, needlessly suffer again and again. This is because they're unable to adapt their behavior to the changing demands of their environment. As a result, they're more likely to experience stress, anxiety, and depression.

Imagine the possibilities if we abandon following the behavioral rules we've adopted and revise that old mental and emotional processing with new thoughts, approaches, and behaviors that we haven't tried yet. This is possible through Acceptance and Commitment Therapy (ACT), which is a type of psychotherapy that helps people accept their difficult thoughts and emotions and commit to living a meaningful life. ACT teaches people to be present in the moment, to connect their actions to their values, and to take action even when they're feeling afraid or uncomfortable. By following the principles of ACT, we can break free from our old patterns of behavior and create a more meaningful life.

Our culture and media often sell the illusion that good mental and emotional health means the absence of discomfort. According to this narrative, a healthy person should not experience painful memories, distressing emotions, interpersonal tension, or difficult urges. As a result, when these very human experiences arise, many of us believe something is wrong, and we scramble to get rid of them or avoid them altogether.

But here's the paradox, what we resist internally often grows louder. The more we try to suppress or ignore our thoughts and emotions, the more intrusive and overwhelming they can become. Avoidance may offer temporary relief, but it comes at the cost of long-term resilience. Instead of gaining control, we often feel even more out of control, disconnected from ourselves and our ability to respond with clarity.

Our brains do not grow through avoidance, they expand through engagement. It is in facing challenge, not fleeing from it, that we develop insight, wisdom, and emotional strength. Growth begins when we stop pathologizing discomfort and start seeing it as the gateway to deeper understanding.

AWARENESS AND INTENTION

Developing empathy requires both awareness and intention. Although it may not seem immediately achievable, improving your relationships with yourself and others through empathy is within your reach. With dedication and effort, you can grasp the opportunity to transform your interactions.

So be prepared to encounter challenges on your path to self-actualization and accurate empathy, and know that *you can change your outcomes if you put your mind to it.*

NEUROPLASTICITY AND HOW IT APPLIES TO YOUR ACCURATE EMPATHY DEVELOPMENT

The human brain is a master of adaptation. Neuroplasticity, its innate ability to rewire and reshape itself, allows it to evolve with every experience we encounter. Whether the moment is joyful or traumatic, deliberate or accidental, the brain is always learning, always adjusting, always doing its best to protect us.

One of the most fascinating features of this adaptation is something called scaffolding. When areas of the brain begin to decline or weaken, it compensates by developing new neural pathways, adding layers of support to keep functioning intact. Here's the catch—if we continue repeating the same behaviors or patterns that once led to a painful or unhelpful outcome, the brain may recreate that same result, not because it is broken, but because it is loyal to what it knows.

As we move through life, our brains absorb information constantly. They are shaped by every interaction and experience, often without our conscious consent, and without regard for whether we are tired, anxious, hopeful, or depleted. This remarkable capacity is both a gift and a burden. It means we are never truly stuck, but it also means we must be intentional about what we expose ourselves to, because the brain is always listening.

Neuroplasticity doesn't take any of that into consideration. In fact, it's an automatic sympathetic process. The brain does what it does to protect itself first and the human body second. However, there's a bright cloud inside of this thunderstorm of happenstance.

When we're intentional, we can convert neuroplasticity from being oppositional to being our friend.

The more the brain experiences, the more it adapts. We know from neuroscience that there is no one area of the brain that does everything. The old assumption is that the right side of the brain is more artistic, while the left side is more logical. Then the concept of a reptilian brain was often used as an excuse to justify our primal instincts, urges, and reactions. The truth is that the brain is mechanistic in its approach to problem-solving. We look at the prefrontal cortex, which is often associated with being mindfully present and intentional. We look at the somatic region of the brain when it comes to anything physical or physiological. We look at the deeper structures of the brain such as the amygdala, the hippocampus, and the limbic system for helping us survive in threatening situations.

What's wonderful about all this is that we have a much better understanding of neurochemistry than ever before. We know that we can affect how people position themselves to react to fight-or-flight circumstances by increasing serotonin or regulating dopamine. We know certain chemicals, like cortisol, increase in our brains when we're stressed.

We see the evidence of how malleable our brains are in pharmacology. Many clinicians prescribe drugs that diminish undesirable responses. As a holistic coach and clinician, I agree with my internal medicine colleagues that if something can be measured in bloodwork or seen on a scan, there may be justification for pharmacological intervention. However, I also believe that we can have a self-generated placebo effect through cognition and awareness when we pay attention to the outcomes we desire while being mindful of our circumstances. Neuroplasticity avails itself to this premise.

When we think before we act, we have an opportunity to get more desirable results. Happenstance is not a good precursor for creating an intentional outcome. In fact, I've said time and time again that people don't plan to fail; they fail to plan. An example is professional athletes. Science has confirmed that when athletes visualize their desired outcome, the odds are much greater that they'll attain that outcome than if they don't visualize it. The same applies to us in our pursuit of accurate empathy. So, when we pay attention to our desired outcomes, the chances of manifestation are far greater.

If you don't actively work on carrying out self-empathy and empathy toward others, it's unlikely you'll get the results you desire. It's also unlikely that you'll inspire the other person involved to engage in introspection and self-improvement. Being intentional in any situation, especially one that requires accurate empathy, benefits all involved.

Neuroplasticity is a gift because it allows us to learn from our mistakes and explore with curiosity to determine what we did to create those outcomes. It helps us to learn from the outcomes that we didn't want but occurred anyway.

How does this work?

There are certain things one can do to reinforce brain states while pursuing evolution. Here's a personal example.

Throughout my career, I've had to take several credentialing exams. I took matters into my own hands by looking at how the brain learns to find what I could do mentally and physically to create an optimal environment and achieve my intended result.

I recall studying for my National Board Health and Wellness Coach exam. The exam is proctored. You can't leave the room during the exam, and the only thing you're allowed to bring in besides your test-taking materials is a peppermint. Trust me, the peppermint part is relevant.

Given the difficulty of the exam, and the sting of having previously missed a passing score by only two questions, I knew something had to shift. I needed to find a way to optimize not just what I knew, but also how my brain would perform under pressure. That meant treating my mind like an elite athlete in training. Every detail mattered.

One of the first changes I made was to shape my environment to mirror the testing conditions. I understood that the brain thrives on familiarity, especially under stress. Since the exam room would be brightly lit, sparse, and outfitted with folding chairs, I recreated those same conditions in my study space. I sat in a folding chair beneath harsh lights, surrounded by plain white walls. The only comfort allowed during the test was a peppermint, so I kept one nearby while studying or used peppermint oil to train my body to associate the scent with calm and focus. Over time, this became a subtle signal to my nervous system that it was safe to relax and recall what I had learned. By normalizing the discomfort, I removed the intimidation from the equation and gave my brain a reliable anchor.

I also leaned into what I had learned about myself as an audio-visual learner. For material that felt difficult to retain, I recorded myself explaining key concepts aloud, then played those recordings as I drifted to sleep. This wasn't just about memorization, it was about immersion and repetition in an altered state, where the subconscious mind is more open to receiving and storing information.

You have probably picked up on the deeper lesson here. I was not simply studying, I was training my brain to recognize patterns, build cognitive associations, and reduce resistance to performance. I was using intention to override fear, and structure to disinhibit myself from the noise of my environment. These changes may have seemed small on the surface, but they created the conditions for my mind to do what it was designed to do—learn, adapt, and deliver under pressure. By the way, I passed with an exceptionally high score.

Neuroplasticity picks up on our responses without our consent or permission because we're usually operating on autopilot.

However, if we're aware of this process, we can use it to our advantage.

What happens when you do things with foresight rather than hindsight? I catalyzed the attainment of a mindful state to optimize my performance in a situation that naturally causes most people, myself included, a lot of stress and anxiety.

You can do the same. You have the power to take dominion over your thoughts and create the outcomes you desire by learning how your brain works.

We understand that the amygdala plays a significant role in how things are embedded into the hippocampus, which is basically the brain's library. In its own way, the amygdala looks at validation, reward, pleasure, and pain and creates a neurochemical signature that causes us to have an enhanced awareness about anything that resembles what created those feelings. We can influence how our brains react by deliberately creating rewarding cues in our environment that help our brains evolve and develop in a way that matches our vision.

Intentionally cultivating the right skills and being mindful about showing accurate empathy when you enter a conversation will improve your outcomes and more often than not, the other person's outcomes.

We can use neuroplasticity to cultivate awareness of ourselves, our responses, and our role in situations that either go right or wrong. If you can take a more objective viewpoint of your own state and improve your ability to recognize where others are coming from, you can learn to show empathy to yourself and others.

WHAT'S THE BEST PATH FORWARD?

The exposure method I used is not unique to personal development. It is widely applied, in varying degrees, across both medical and military training. For example, in traditional medical residencies, interns were often required to work through long shifts with minimal sleep. The assumption was that if they could function under extreme fatigue and stress, they would be better prepared for the real-life pressures of patient care. While that model may now be considered outdated or even harmful, the underlying principle still holds value.

At its core, the idea is simple—train yourself to become familiar with discomfort so that unfamiliar environments lose their power to destabilize you. By voluntarily exposing yourself to the very conditions that would typically trigger anxiety or fear, you are giving your brain a chance to build resilience. You are teaching it to stay focused on the task, not the tension.

This practice is not about glorifying struggle, it is about preparation. The goal is not to become numb, but to become clear. When your internal state is steady, your performance becomes consistent, regardless of what is happening around you.

We can harness neuroplasticity to improve our approaches to success. I believe that we can train our minds using a reward system instead of punishment. There's something to be said about developing a sustainable one-bite-at-a-time approach to reduce needless stress and anxiety. How is throwing ourselves into the deep end without a floaty a good idea?

To achieve greater effectiveness in our daily lives, cultivating a mindset of gratitude serves as a powerful starting point. By acknowledging and appreciating the positive aspects of our lives, we can shift our focus away from feelings of negativity and overwhelm.

This simple act of gratitude can change our emotional and mental state, making us more receptive to positive experiences.

Additionally, practicing patience with others is essential for fostering harmonious relationships. When we're patient, we allow ourselves the time and space to understand the perspectives and experiences of others, rather than reacting impulsively. Patience also enables us to handle challenging situations with greater ease and grace, reducing the likelihood of conflict and misunderstandings.

Accepting and embracing both what we can and cannot control is another key component in managing our stress and anxiety effectively. By acknowledging our limitations and letting go of the need to control every aspect of our lives, we can cultivate a sense of inner peace and serenity. This acceptance allows us to focus our energy on the things that are truly within our power to change, rather than wasting time and resources on what we can't control.

In my professional practice as a coach, I've witnessed firsthand the transformative impact of these principles on my clients. By incorporating gratitude, patience, and acceptance into their daily routines, many of them have reported significant improvements in their ability to manage stress, cope with anxiety, and cultivate a greater sense of well-being.

By implementing these simple yet powerful strategies, we can unlock our full potential and experience greater fulfillment and joy in our daily lives.

Like everything else I've taught you in this book, it's easier said than done. However, neuroplasticity shows us that it's possible. As you continue this pursuit toward accurate empathy, taking dominion over your reactions and thoughts will help you become the best person you can be.

Your brain is designed to help you survive tumultuous circumstances and evolve. It'll do so without your permission, and if you're not conscious of it, it might take you in a direction you don't want to go.

Doesn't it make sense to be aware of this process so you can learn from it and use that information to improve your life and others' lives? Of course it does.

I want to leave you with some exercises you can do to embrace neuroplasticity and have it help rather than hinder you with your accurate empathy.

TAKING NEUROPLASTICITY INTO YOUR OWN HANDS

We're often frustrated or disappointed about things that happen that are beyond our control. These events range from getting stuck in horrible traffic to experiencing the death of a loved one.

So here are some exercises for the next time you're faced with a minor inconvenience or major challenge.

1. I invite you to identify three things these difficult circumstances are drawing out of you—qualities, insights, or strengths that might have remained dormant without this challenge. Adversity has a way of introducing us to parts of ourselves we would never meet in times of ease.

This is not a time for self-criticism; it is a time for honest, constructive reflection. Rather than letting a monkey wrench derail your progress, imagine using it to tighten loose bolts, reinforce your foundation, and build something more resilient than before. What feels like an interruption could be an invitation to recalibrate.

Allow yourself to feel what you feel without letting those emotions trap you in loops of negative thinking. This is not about slapping on a smile or pretending everything is fine. It is about recognizing that your discomfort may be a doorway to growth. When you stay curious instead of reactive, you interrupt the cycle of emotional hijacking and reclaim your power to respond with clarity.

2. When you find yourself ruminating or emotionally triggered, especially about something valid, pause and ask what the moment is trying to teach you. What is it revealing about you, your relationship with the other person, and the situation itself?

Perhaps you are still replaying a difficult exchange with your partner, or struggling to communicate with your child about something they did or failed to do. These moments are not just interruptions to your peace; they are invitations to deepen your understanding of yourself and those you care about.

If your partner shares their feelings openly and with clarity, it is important to honor the truth in their words, even if it stirs up something uncomfortable in you. Instead of immediately reacting from a place of defensiveness, take a step back and ask why that reaction is rising within you. Ask yourself, what do I gain by being offended? In most cases, the answer is nothing.

Your ego, designed to protect you, may be responding to what it perceives as a threat. That response may be automatic, but it is not always accurate. A defensive posture might feel like strength, but in reality, it often blocks resolution and intimacy. In those moments, your greatest strength is in reflection, not reaction.

Explore what lies beneath the surface of your emotional response. Why does this particular issue bother you? Is there a past wound, an unmet need, or an internal belief shaping your sensitivity? When you uncover the root of your reaction, you gain more than insight—you gain choice. You create the space to respond with wisdom rather than reflex.

Remember, the goal is not to silence your partner or invalidate their experience. The goal is to engage with empathy, to meet the moment with humility and a willingness to grow. Open communication paired with self-awareness forms the foundation of a healthy relationship. When you reflect instead of retaliate, you not only strengthen your connection, you also expand your capacity to love and be loved.

Every interaction holds the potential to teach you something new about who you are. Ask yourself, how are these circumstances shaping my evolution? How can I make sure that neuroplasticity is working in my favor?

What was once meant to burden you can become the very thing that blesses you—if you are willing to shift your mindset, examine your perspective, and lean into the discomfort with curiosity rather than resistance. Growth rarely feels comfortable, but it always leaves you stronger on the other side.

3. Give yourself more space and time.

Have you ever been to a restaurant that's open 24/7? I don't want to turn you off your favorite restaurant, but think about this: Can you thoroughly clean a restaurant when it's open all hours of the day, every day? Is there ever a time when you can thoroughly clean the entire restaurant?

As far as that example goes, I'm not quite sure if I'm right or wrong, but I do know that if you don't shut down your brain sometimes, it's not getting "clean."

Your brain and mind need downtime and rest to clean up your thought process. To maximize the positive potential for neuroplasticity, you can take these general steps.

4. Relax your brain.

You don't have to bring out a yoga mat and sit in a lotus position. It can be much simpler than that. During the day, about every four hours or so, stop and do nothing. Close your eyes if possible and breathe. Set aside your phone and just be.

5. Get a good night's sleep.

Sleep is crucial for maintaining your overall health and well-being. Your brain and body undergo several crucial processes while you're asleep, but it's not only about staying in bed for eight hours. You must sleep well to think and perform well.

There are so many habits and conditions that can negatively impact your sleep. Some of these are within your control, such as minimizing bright lights (putting the phone down) a few hours before bed, avoiding that afternoon cup of coffee or other caffeinated beverage, relaxing your brain (avoiding mentally stimulating activities a few hours before going to sleep), and exercising. Above all, don't drink, smoke, or use controlled substances to sleep.

6. Get into an exercise routine.

Any amount of exercise is better than none. Numerous studies have demonstrated that regular physical activity can improve overall well-being, resilience, productivity, and lifespan. It can also boost your self-esteem and relationships. Most healthcare professionals, including myself, recommend at least thirty minutes of exercise five days a week. If you're under seventy years old, I suggest exercising for an hour each day, incorporating resistance training daily, and adding twenty to thirty minutes of cardio on three of those five days. Research has confirmed that following these guidelines can significantly improve and extend your life.

7. Embrace new experiences.

Everything we have covered so far comes back to one essential truth—if you want to grow, you must be willing to learn. True learning requires more than good intentions. It calls for awareness, humility, and a mindset that actively seeks growth rather than waiting for it to happen by accident.

Many people make the mistake of rushing past their experiences. They move on quickly, without pausing to ask what went right, what went wrong, and what could be improved. This habit of glossing over both the wins and the losses cuts off the opportunity for wisdom to take root. When you fail to reflect, you limit your chances of achieving better outcomes in the future.

Far too many self-improvement books promise that one method or strategy is all you need to succeed. The truth is that no matter what approach you use, intention matters. Without intentional effort, even the best tools will fall flat. Furthermore, without consistency, even the most brilliant insight will fade. This is why it is so important to ensure that your goals are in alignment with your values and with the vision you hold for your life.

Look for practices that ground you in mindfulness and purposeful action. Your brain is constantly evolving and constantly adapting to the information and experiences you feed it. That is the power of neuroplasticity. You can direct it in ways that improve your empathy, strengthen your relationships, and sharpen your thinking, or you can leave it to operate on autopilot with no guarantee that it will serve your best interest.

You hold more influence than you think. Use it well.

MAIN TAKEAWAYS FROM THIS CHAPTER

⇒ Your brain will automatically respond and change based on your experiences.

If you're not intentional and mindful of neuroplasticity and your ability to control the direction of your thoughts, beliefs, and actions, you won't change your outcomes for the better.

Your brain changes with every experience you have, but you have some control over how you respond and how it impacts your future responses.

⇒ Recognizing and changing your default mode processing can be challenging, but it's not impossible.

Adjusting your perception of change and challenges is essential, and this process takes time.

Five steps to making this shift:

1. Mindful connection:
    - Cultivate a deep understanding of your personal values, long-term goals, and the specific outcomes you desire to achieve.
    - Regularly reflect on these elements to ensure alignment and make necessary adjustments as your life evolves.
    - Embrace the dynamic nature of your values, goals, and outcomes, acknowledging that they may shift over time due to various life experiences and evolving perspectives.
2. Regular revisiting:
    - Establish a routine for revisiting your values, goals, and desired outcomes.
    - Consider setting aside dedicated time for this reflection, such as weekly or monthly.
    - Be open to making changes when necessary, as these elements are not set in stone.

- Embrace a growth mindset that allows you to adapt and evolve your aspirations as you gain new insights and experiences.

3. Perception adjustment:
    - Recognize that change and challenges are inherent parts of life and personal growth.
    - Shift your mindset from viewing change as a threat to perceiving it as an opportunity for learning, growth, and adaptation.
    - Embrace challenges as opportunities to develop resilience, problem-solving skills, and inner strength.
    - Practice reframing negative thoughts and emotions associated with change and challenges into positive perspectives.
4. Time investment:
    - Understand that adjusting your perception of change and challenges is a gradual process that requires patience and consistent effort.
    - Be willing to invest time in developing a more positive and adaptive mindset.
    - Engage in practices such as mindfulness, meditation, and journaling to cultivate a deeper awareness of your thoughts and emotions.
    - Seek support from mentors, coaches, or therapists who can guide you through this transformative process.
5. Continuous learning:
    - Commit to ongoing learning and personal development to expand your knowledge, skills, and capabilities.

- Actively seek opportunities to learn from diverse sources, such as books, online courses, workshops, and conversations with others.

By taking a comprehensive approach that involves mindful connection, regular revisiting, perception adjustment, time investment, and continuous learning, you can create a more meaningful life aligned with your values, goals, and desired outcomes.

⇒ FACT: Our thoughts and beliefs influence our behaviors.

Refusing to believe this fact or do anything about it to improve your outcomes is where many people go wrong. Being stuck on stupid is *never* a good idea.

We're all capable of shifting our thought process, but it requires being aware of our default responses and consistently working on reframing negative, unproductive thoughts and beliefs.

⇒ If you can measure something in bloodwork or see it on a scan, there's usually justification for pharmacological intervention, but most of the time:

We can take an approach based on awareness, mindfulness, and positive psychology to minimize unwanted thoughts, beliefs, and behaviors, replacing them with those that are productive and beneficial to us and our outcomes in life, work, and love.

⇒ We can use neuroplasticity to our advantage in developing and mastering accurate empathy.

We often mistake empathy for a trait that can only be taught or developed at a specific stage of life. However, there's always potential for growth and learning.

Our thoughts can be redirected, and our beliefs can be shifted or changed completely. Therefore, we can change our behaviors and outcomes as well. When you change how you show up to things, the things you show up to change.

⇒ If you feel triggered or upset about something, consider what these circumstances are teaching you about yourself.

Engaging in introspection, particularly after an argument or a problematic event, can be eye-opening and teach you so much about yourself and how you typically respond.

When you're willing to work on developing an objective view of yourself and your circumstances, you're much more likely to take away something that will help you in future situations.

⇒ Rest is crucial not only for your body, but for your mind as well.

Lying down may be resting your body, but it doesn't mean your brain is truly resting. For many of us, especially those who are highly strung, it can be difficult to turn our brains off and stop thinking about work and life, even when our heads hit the pillow. If the only time you're truly relaxed is when you're asleep, that's a sign you need to engage in self-empathy and find ways to rest throughout the day.

Set aside time to be mindful and present. This can mean meditation or yoga, but it can also mean taking a few moments out of your day to breathe and not do anything else.

⇒ Never try to force positivity at the expense of processing and learning from your negative emotions.

However, do try to shift your perspective so that it's more productive and you're restoring your power in the situation. Negative emotions are a normal part of life, but getting stuck in a cycle of negative thoughts and feelings is a problem you need to address.

⇒ To increase neuroplasticity, be willing to:

Try new things, take care of your mental and physical health, and embrace learning in every area of your life.

Your brain can only change so much, but it can change *a lot*. Don't underestimate your ability to improve your self-awareness, compassion, and accurate empathy. Try not to underestimate others based on their past mistakes or shortcomings if they're also trying to improve themselves. Everyone is capable of growth.

Everyone can develop and master accurate empathy.

Chapter Ten

IMPLEMENTING WHAT YOU'VE LEARNED

FROM INSIGHT TO INTEGRATION

Congratulations. You have made it to the final chapter of this book, but more importantly, you have arrived at the beginning of something deeper. What you've read was never just about gaining knowledge, it was about reclaiming your power to authentically, intentionally, and compassionately connect with others and with yourself.

Throughout this journey, you've explored the transformative role of accurate empathy and the radical necessity of self-compassion. You've examined what it means to be fully present, to listen without agenda, and to show up in a way that honors both your values and your humanity. Here's the truth—none of this sticks until you choose to live it. This final chapter is about that choice. It invites you to reflect, integrate, and begin applying these insights in ways that create real, lasting change.

When I first set out to write this book, I thought I was speaking directly to coaches and clinicians. Yet, somewhere along the way, it became clear this message is for anyone who has ever felt stuck. Anyone who has walked away from a difficult conversation wondering, *What just happened? What did I miss? Where did it go wrong?* It's for those moments where connection broke down, not out of malice, but out of misunderstanding. Moments where good intentions collided with old wounds and clarity gave way to confusion.

Even still, one of my core goals remained the same. I wanted to create a resource for those in helping professions such as coaches, clinicians, and leaders who are committed to becoming more people-centered in their work because the truth is, it's not enough to mean well. We must also lead well, listen well, and love well, and that starts with being honest about the barriers we face.

Not long ago, during a conversation with the Applied Neuroscience Community, I was asked how stress impacts coaches and clinicians—not just in their work, but in their ability to show up as whole human beings. My response was simple and direct: "It's a major problem."

We all know the weight of it. Balancing personal demands while trying to support others is often overwhelming. That internal pressure has a ripple effect. It touches our relationships, our clarity, our presence, and our capacity to lead from a place of integrity.

If you work in the public sector, you may feel the weight of politics, funding restrictions, and constantly shifting priorities. If you work in healthcare, you've likely seen how profit can sometimes take precedence over people. Often, the decisions that shape patient care are made by executives, not clinicians. For those of us navigating the system as individuals, we're often left caught between providers and insurers, each with their own agenda—none of which prioritize our well-being in the ways we need most.

Across all of these spaces, one truth rises above the rest. Whether you are a leader, a healer, a parent, or simply someone doing their best to show up with heart, there is no substitute for human-centered engagement. The systems around us may be strained, but that does not mean we have to become mechanical in how we relate to others.

To protect what matters most—your peace, your people, your purpose—you must return to the core of what makes you whole. This book was written to help you do exactly that. To equip you with the mindset and the methods to move from performance to presence. From reacting to responding. From burnout to breakthrough.

Now, the question becomes—how will you use what you've learned?

WHAT WE ALL HAVE IN COMMON

As I dug deeper into this topic, I realized that these challenges extend far beyond the realm of health professionals. They touch every aspect of our lives. This isn't just an issue for a select few; it's a human problem that resonates with all of us. Each of us has the power to navigate these difficult interactions and emerge stronger, and that's what this book aims to explore. By sharing insights and strategies, I hope to help you transform uncomfortable moments into opportunities for growth and deeper connection.

Regardless of our field, we all encounter the challenges of everyday life. Yet, we often overlook the deeper humanity in each other, focusing solely on the roles we play. For coaches, clinicians, and leaders in business, this tendency is particularly detrimental.

When coaches and clinicians view their clients as mere cases, they risk missing the unique stories and struggles that shape each individual. This lack of empathy can hinder the effectiveness of their support, leaving clients feeling isolated and undervalued. We know that patient adherence is much greater when they like their clinician. We also know that the placebo effect has an opposite, called the nocebo effect. If your clients and patients don't like you or how you make them feel, the odds of them complying with the simplest of protocols and seeing positive results are significantly compromised.

In a business context, leaders who focus solely on performance metrics rather than the people driving those results can create a culture of disengagement. Employees may feel like cogs in a machine rather than valued contributors, leading to decreased morale and productivity.

This disconnection adversely impacts our ability to connect with one another at a human level. When we prioritize titles over humanity, we create barriers that keep us from understanding each other's struggles, strengths, and aspirations. It fosters an environment where empathy is scarce, and relationships become transactional rather than meaningful.

Embracing our shared humanity enables us to create environments where everyone feels valued, heard, and empowered to contribute. Ultimately, this shift can lead to more impactful coaching, improved patient care, and stronger teams in the business world, resulting in a more compassionate and connected society.

Your mastery of accurate empathy is also crucial for your personal relationships, including the one with yourself. As we've discovered, you can't have truly healthy, functional, and successful relationships without compassion and accurate empathy. You can't lack respect or love for yourself and expect to be able to give those things to others in a way that makes you both happy and fulfilled.

Once you finish reading this book and go through the process of developing self-empathy, I encourage you to focus on one relationship at first. Don't overwhelm yourself by going out and trying to fix every relationship you have. You probably started reading this book with a particular relationship or area of your life in mind. There's no better time than now to start implementing everything you've learned to improve your life and your influence on those around you.

CHAPTER ONE RECAP

If you truly want to stop feeling lost in life and love, you must understand yourself and learn to love yourself first.

This requires honest, thorough self-reflection. Who you are today is an accumulation of all the past versions of you. Therefore, you have to be willing to get uncomfortable and revisit parts of your past that you may have intentionally or unintentionally buried.

Whenever you feel stuck or whenever you discover something new about yourself, revisit the questions we went over in Chapter One.

1. How old are you? Which generation were you born into?
2. What is your gender? Race? Nationality?
3. What's your current socioeconomic status versus what you were born into?
4. How did the aforementioned position you in the society in which you lived as a child and how you live currently?
5. What kind of environment were you exposed to from birth to adolescence?
6. How was your environment outside of your home?

The first step in resolving feelings and challenges is understanding why we have them in the first place. While it will likely make you feel vulnerable, this process is crucial for mastering accurate empathy. On the surface, these questions seem unrelated to your ability to show compassion and empathy. However, when you dig deeper (which we did in the last few chapters), you start to realize how relevant they are to your relationship with yourself and your interactions with others.

If you skipped this exercise the first time around, I urge you to go back and go through it now. At this point, you know that trying to master accurate empathy without this stage would be like trying to build a house without any tools. You'll only get so far before the weak foundation starts to crumble.

The Three Types of Empathy Revisited

The other thing I want to remind you of is the difference between sympathy and empathy. Empathy isn't just feeling bad for someone or being kind to them. It's feeling their emotions with them, to an extent that doesn't harm your health and well-being. You feel motivated to take action to help them, even though you likely don't have all the answers.

There are three main types of empathy you need to be aware of: cognitive, emotional, and compassionate empathy.

Cognitive empathy involves understanding someone's thoughts and emotions. With this type of empathy, you don't necessarily share their feelings, but you can grasp them.

Emotional empathy goes one step further. With emotional empathy, you do share their emotions.

Finally, compassionate empathy requires both compassion and empathy and is characterized by taking action to help. This type is essentially cognitive empathy, emotional empathy, and compassion all in one. Compassionate empathy, when practiced correctly, enables you to relate to others on a deeper level without absorbing their emotions in an unhealthy, unproductive manner.

We looked at examples of the three types of empathy with different dynamics. Through this exercise, it became clear that applying accurate, compassionate empathy is helpful in a variety of roles and relationships, whether you're a parent talking with your child, a boss interacting with your employee, a supportive shoulder for your struggling friend, or a therapist offering support to a client in a session.

There are drawbacks to applying compassionate empathy inaccurately, which is why setting boundaries is necessary. For instance, imagine you're feeling overwhelmed and a friend reaches out for support. If you're not in the right headspace, trying to be empathetic might lead to saying things you don't mean or not being fully present. This can strain relationships with clients, team members, or even those close to you, potentially resulting in misunderstandings, feelings of neglect, or a loss of trust.

For coaches, clinicians, and leaders in both clinical and business settings, this can create extremely negative consequences. When you're not fully engaged, you might miss critical cues from clients or team members, leading to misdiagnoses or ineffective strategies. A coach who isn't in tune with their own feelings may struggle to motivate their clients, resulting in stagnation rather than growth. In clinical settings, a clinician who overlooks their emotional state might unintentionally project frustration or disinterest, which can leave clients feeling dismissed or invalidated.

Moreover, in leadership roles, failing to acknowledge your own limits can foster a toxic environment. If you're constantly pushing through without addressing your feelings, it can lead to burnout, affecting your performance and the morale of your entire team. They may sense your detachment and respond with disengagement of their own, creating a cycle of ineffective collaboration and poor communication.

To avoid misusing empathy, you can regularly check in with yourself and your emotions, learn to differentiate between relationships that uplift you and those that hold you back, and acknowledge your limits. Recognizing your limits doesn't mean accepting your weaknesses instead of working to improve them; it means understanding that you may not always be in the right mindset to wield empathy effectively. In situations like the one with your friend, it's a good idea to reschedule the conversation until you're better equipped to engage. Do what you can to be helpful without compromising your long-term well-being. Get the support you need as you try to support others in the way they need to be supported. Taking the time to care for your own emotional well-being not only helps you, it also creates a positive ripple effect, fostering healthier connections and more effective leadership.

While you have to assess each situation to determine which type of empathy is needed, I'm encouraging you to master compassionate empathy so you can be consistently accurate in your application of it. With the right tools and approach, you can use accurate empathy to develop self-confidence and respect, and improve your personal and professional relationships. Applying accurate empathy to every part of your life is the best thing you can do if you want to be happy, healthy, and successful. It takes time and intention, but it will be the most fruitful endeavor of your life.

Now, let's revisit the dangers of misusing empathy, as well as what can predispose you to incorrectly applying it.

CHAPTER TWO RECAP

Our efforts to engage in empathy can either take us in the direction of empathic concern or empathic distress. By now, you have the tools and approaches to help you show accurate empathy and avoid empathic distress.

As we discussed in Chapter Two, empathic distress is associated with burnout, apathy, high levels of stress, and other health issues. Empathic distress is highly likely if you don't set boundaries and you lack self-awareness. This is common for individuals in a care profession, such as the healthcare industry, where they're dealing with others' emotions and experiences almost every day.

Inaccurate empathy can also lead to codependency and learned helplessness. These states make it even more difficult to show empathy to yourself and others—It becomes a vicious cycle.

Relationships that are sustained on codependency or learned helplessness inherently involve a lack of self-empathy and accurate empathy toward the other person. This is unsurprising given that these types of relationships usually develop because one or both people have low self-esteem, have experienced trauma or abuse, or were likely exposed to similar unhealthy relationships as children.

Misusing empathy can be harmful in any context, but it's especially risky for coaches, clinicians, and mental health professionals. When empathy is applied inaccurately or inconsistently, it can lead to serious consequences for both the practitioner and the person they're supporting. While burnout and emotional detachment are the more visible outcomes, another serious risk is *transference neurosis.*

This occurs when the individual begins to project unresolved emotions onto their therapist or coach—feeling intense affection, anger, or even distrust that may have little to do with the present relationship. In some cases, they may develop romantic feelings or deep resentment toward their provider. Although transference can't always be avoided, its impact can be minimized through mindful presence and the intentional, appropriate application of empathy.

When empathy is rooted in clarity and boundaries, not emotional overidentification, it helps maintain a healthy dynamic. Misattunement, on the other hand, can compromise both parties. Transference neurosis benefits no one—not the practitioner, and certainly not the person seeking support.

The Impact of Different Backgrounds

In Chapters One and Two, we reviewed the influence of background on one's ability to show accurate empathy. Your unique experiences can contribute to your relationships, including the one with yourself, in unwanted ways, which is why we focused so much on self-awareness and self-care throughout this book.

Everyone falls into one of two categories:

1. You didn't receive empathy and compassion as a child.
2. You were shown love, empathy, and compassion as a child.

However, your childhood experiences aren't the only factors that shape your relationships. Every experience you've had since childhood has influenced your habits and outcomes. This includes interactions with not just your caregivers, but also extended family, classmates, teachers, and other authority figures. Each of these interactions contributes to how you view and engage with others, impacting your ability to form healthy connections and navigate relationships as an adult. Understanding this broader context can help you recognize patterns in your behavior and relationships, leading to personal growth and better interactions.

We've explored numerous examples of experiences that can either enhance or obstruct your ability to empathize with yourself and others. However, it's crucial to approach this with a mindset of curiosity rather than confinement. Just because you didn't receive empathy as a child, that doesn't seal your fate; it doesn't mean you can't cultivate self-empathy as an adult. Conversely, receiving empathy doesn't automatically equip you with the tools to extend that same understanding to others.

Think of it this way: imagine two people raised in the same household. One may thrive despite a lack of empathy from their parents, while the other may struggle despite being showered with affection. Their journeys are uniquely their own.

We are all shaped by our distinct experiences, yet the principles we've discussed are universally relevant. Reflect on this: How well do you know yourself? Before you can genuinely offer empathy to others, it's essential to cultivate self-awareness, self-respect, and self-empathy. Consider your own narrative. What lessons can you draw from it that might deepen your understanding of both yourself and those around you?

Remember, accurate empathy is both an action we take and a skill we develop. We expanded upon this idea in Chapter Three.

CHAPTER THREE RECAP

Empathy isn't an inherited trait; it's a skill—one that anyone can cultivate with intention and practice. You might demonstrate empathy beautifully one moment and fail miserably in another. Think of it like riding a bike: just because you've learned to balance, that doesn't mean you can ride on autopilot—not considering your environment. You could easily run over someone, run into a pothole, or get hit by a car. In the same way, accurate empathy requires conscious, intentional effort.

American psychologist Carl Rogers developed the term "accurate empathy," which involves genuinely understanding others' perspectives. Imagine your significant other sharing a frustrating experience from their day, feeling overwhelmed by work, or lacking support from their colleagues.

Your partner opens up about feelings of inadequacy, guilt, or remorse. You think you understand what they're going through—maybe based on your own experiences or past interactions—so you impulsively jump in with advice or criticism. This reaction can be incredibly damaging. Instead of feeling supported, your partner may feel like you're brushing aside their emotions, leaving them feeling alienated and judged rather than understood. This can create a significant divide in your relationship, making them hesitant to share their vulnerabilities with you again. The trust and intimacy that should bind you together could be shattered, and you'll be left wondering how the hell it all went so wrong. Instead of jumping in with your own story, things would go much better if you took a moment to listen deeply and ask questions. This is accurate empathy—valuing the other person's unique perspective and fostering a safe space for expression.

The stakes are even higher in clinical and coaching settings. If a coach assumes they understand a client's feelings without truly listening, it can stall progress and foster distrust.

For example, a client struggling with anxiety rooted in past trauma may feel misunderstood if their coach or therapist jumps to conclusions, making them less likely to open up in future sessions.

Each person is the expert on their own emotions. Lean into curiosity instead of making assumptions. Ask questions and invite sharing. This shift can transform superficial exchanges into meaningful connections.

So, next time you assume you understand, pause. Reflect on how your assumptions might do more harm than good. Accurate empathy is a powerful tool for fostering a deeper understanding and connection in every relationship, whether at work or at home.

Application in Coaching

As a health practitioner or life coach, you have a responsibility to observe, listen deeply, and work to understand the lived experiences of the individuals you support. Fulfilling this responsibility requires you to be fully present and appropriately invested in each interaction. Note: That kind of presence is nearly impossible if you haven't first cultivated empathy and understanding toward yourself.

As coaches and clinicians, we must be attuned not only to the verbal and physical cues of those we serve, but also to our own internal responses. If you're distracted, disconnected, or carrying unresolved tension into the session, it shows. People can sense when you're not fully engaged. If you're irritated, emotionally unavailable, or simply going through the motions, the impact is palpable. That's why emotional awareness (both inward and outward) is essential for creating compassionate, effective, and meaningful sessions.

We're often reminded to practice what we preach—and that reminder couldn't be more relevant in this profession. Failing to do so can have serious consequences for the practitioner and client. At the end of the day, we're human too. We require grounding, emotional regulation, and a sense of connection to show up well in our personal and professional lives.

Introspection is not just a tool for those we help—it's essential for us as well. Being mindful of the emotions, thoughts, and beliefs you bring into a session (and those that arise within it) enables you to hold space with clarity and compassion. It allows you to offer support without projecting, judging, or reacting based on bias. Yes, your training gives you a deep understanding of emotional patterns, but that doesn't mean there isn't something to be learned from the person across from you. They are the expert on their experience, and there is wisdom in recognizing that.

Reflective Practices to Support Your Work

1. Check in with yourself regularly.

Assess where you are emotionally, physically, and mentally. How can you help someone reflect on *their* internal state if you're avoiding your own? If you enter a session carrying emotional baggage you haven't acknowledged, can you truly afford to pretend it's not there? The answer is simple: you can't. Not without compromising your ability to be fully present and helpful.

2. Invest in your personal and professional development.

A "do as I say, not as I do" mindset has no place in this field. If you expect those you support to do the hard work of change and growth, then hold yourself to that same standard. Commit to your own evolution.

As a professional who holds space for others, continually seek out ways to strengthen your emotional capacity, deepen your skill set, and refine your approach. If your motivation to grow has waned, go back to the first step. Pause, reflect, and ask yourself why. That's where the real work begins.

3. Be willing to explore and adapt.

If you're not motivated in your current field or with your personal pursuits, that might be a sign that your priorities or passions have changed. Give yourself the time and space to consider what you want and need during this season of your life. Sometimes you need to step back to move forward.

4. Be open with yourself.

Recognize when you don't have the emotional or physical capacity to pursue a specific goal or work with a certain client. A huge part of mastering accurate empathy is committing to self-empathy.

If you consistently take these steps, you'll be well on your way to mastering accurate empathy and becoming an even more effective coach or clinician.

CHAPTER FOUR RECAP

In Chapter Four, we went over the dos and don'ts of accurate empathy for high-capacity coaching, but we also determined that these apply to every personal and professional interaction (meaning: even if you're not a coach).

Let's refresh our memories. The essential dos of accurate empathy include:

1. Reflect on your inner state so you can understand your outer presentation.
2. Engage in active listening and do your best to set your judgments aside.
3. Show them you're present by building on what the other person says and leading with curiosity.
4. Revisit these steps and reflect regularly.

Then, there are the don'ts that you need to remember.

1. Don't ignore your own biases.
2. Don't overlook signs that you're misusing empathy.
3. Don't assume that you have any more to learn and no room to improve.

These might seem simple, but we tend to go through a lot of life on autopilot. We try to *get through* tasks and conversations instead of being fully present and mindful. We accidentally do the bare minimum in our relationships when worrying about work and other stressors. While doing this every once in a while is human, it's important to train your mind to recognize when you're neglecting real connection and presence.

You'll misuse or neglect accurate empathy every now and then, but the compounding consequences of not mastering accurate empathy are too great to ignore. Over time, this neglect leads to the disintegration of the core components of every relationship: trust, respect, compassion, and commitment. However, if you're in a relationship that's hanging by a thread, I want you to know it's not impossible to restore these foundational aspects with accurate empathy.

Bringing It Back to Coaching

The dos and don'ts of accurate empathy also apply to you as a coach. You know that the way you show up to client sessions has a significant impact on client outcomes. Therefore, you have a responsibility to yourself and your clients to be just as aware of your own thoughts, feelings, and blind spots as you are of theirs.

The self-awareness tools we went over in Chapter Four were:

1. Note any physical sensations and emotions you have before and during the session.
2. Observe your thoughts and how they affect your mindset, body language, and overall presence.
3. Remind yourself of your motivations (regarding the client session, your profession as a whole, and any external challenges).
4. Reflect on your interactions to identify areas of improvement.

Follow these steps if you want to improve your well-being and client outcomes.

I want to emphasize that demonstrating accurate empathy in coaching involves the dos mentioned above. An effective coach listens to and validates their clients before guiding them to discover their own answers using the tools and abilities they've identified during sessions. By demonstrating accurate empathy, you serve as a role model for your clients.

One of the most common mistakes coaches make is not being fully present. When presence is lacking, you're likely to miss both verbal and nonverbal cues that reveal where someone truly is, especially on an emotional level. This is where Carl Rogers' framework of accurate empathy becomes essential. It invites us to slow down, listen deeply, and get genuinely curious about not just *what* is being said, but *how* it's being said.

Asking clarifying questions and using reflective techniques are covered in detail in later chapters. These evidence and research-based strategies can open the door to meaningful introspection and pave the way for genuine breakthroughs.

One of the most important details to remember from this chapter is that mindfulness and awareness are the keys to improving your capacity for accurate empathy toward yourself and others. Put your judgments and assumptions aside to make room for growth and learning.

CHAPTER FIVE RECAP

Your brain has the capacity to learn new skills, particularly empathy, which can help you change your outcomes for the better.

The connection between the orbito-ventromedial PFC (emotional control) and the dorsolateral PFC (cognitive control) is evidence of the relationship between our emotions and behaviors. Therefore, we know that if we exercise more control over our thoughts and emotions, we'll also be able to exert more control over our actions.

When it comes to engaging in true, accurate empathy, you need to take a top-down approach instead of a purely bottom-up approach. Both of these approaches are rooted in neuroscience.

Bottom-up elements include certain aspects of brain health, like:

- Genetics
- Hormones
- Lifestyle choices

Top-down elements are things like:

- Beliefs
- Thoughts
- Core values

There are also outside-in factors such as:

- Education
- Family environment
- Traumatic experiences
- Other social and environmental factors

While these factors heavily influence the way we think, act, and respond, we don't have to let them continue to affect us in negative ways. That's why there are so many introspective exercises in this book. Your past is not your present or future. You have control over so many of these factors. It can be painful to hear that you're more in control of your outcomes than you think. However, it's crucial that you don't sit in that pain. Use this knowledge to get inspired and motivated to change your life for the better.

Your ability to demonstrate accurate empathy is heavily influenced by your thoughts and emotions, making a top-down approach critical. Bottom-up processing is involuntary. You want to avoid living on autopilot, especially when interactions require empathy. The last thing you want to do is become complacent and neglect awareness and mindfulness in your relationships.

Embracing a top-down approach also helps you break free from negative thinking patterns. For many of us, doom thinking is our default. I got stuck in this cycle because I was becoming over-embedded in my clients' issues and failing to give myself empathy and compassion. I lacked boundaries. I wasn't practicing self-awareness as often as I should have been, so it took me a while to realize my need for it. I eventually did realize it and started putting my well-being first so I could improve my life, as well as my clients' outcomes.

Let's recap the introspection exercise from this chapter. It's an effective way to get in touch with your past and present and prepare for a more productive and happy future (one that aligns more closely with your values and goals).

1. Identify the positive and negative aspects of your life right now.
2. Consider what you've experienced in the last five to ten years and how those experiences might still be affecting you.
3. Determine what you can't control (as well as what you couldn't control in the past).
4. Think about what you can control and plan on showing yourself empathy moving forward.
5. Show yourself the same compassion and empathy you'd show a loved one (pretend you're talking to a loved one or write it down).

This exercise is something you can do regularly. It's helpful any time, not just when you're going through a tumultuous period. There's always room for improvement, but make sure you're not neglecting gratitude in your quest for growth and betterment.

One of the aspects of your life that you can control is your relationships. Be mindful of what and who you allow into your inner circle. If you're spending time with those who don't respect you or have entirely different values than you do, ending or pausing those relationships is within your control. It can be difficult, but parting ways with toxic, immature, or generally unkind people is one of the best things you can do for your mental well-being. When you start cultivating self-empathy, you'll realize that these types of relationships aren't worth keeping.

CHAPTER SIX RECAP

One of the ideas I repeat the most in this book is, "You can't show others accurate empathy unless you learn self-empathy first." Trust me when I say that repeating this again and again was deliberate.

In Chapter Six, I asked you to reflect on the last terrible day you had. From there, you engaged in some reflection regarding your emotions, thoughts, and responses on that day. Hopefully, you connected the dots between your responses and how the rest of your day went. Self-reflection exercises like this one are key to overcoming default-mode processing and creating better outcomes. Following this exercise, I emphasized the importance of observing and reflecting upon your emotions and responses without judgment. Leading with curiosity, humility, and accountability, without putting yourself or others down, leaves space for personal growth and evolution.

For coaches in particular, cultivating self-awareness and self-empathy allows you to achieve your professional goals and maintain a balance between your work and personal life. The benefits also extend to your clients, who see you model what you preach.

For all you non-coaches out there, let's dive into a vital truth that often gets overlooked. We'll use a common situation as an example. You're a parent juggling work, kids, and a household. You're so focused on meeting everyone else's needs—packing lunches, attending meetings, and managing schedules—that you forget to carve out even a moment for yourself. Over time, you start to feel drained, resentful, and maybe even a bit invisible. Your family may not see it, but that emotional fatigue affects everyone, creating a tense atmosphere at home.

Now, if you're thinking to yourself, *I always put others first, and I can show them empathy and compassion without any problems*, let's pause for a moment. Sure, you might be able to lend a listening ear to a friend in distress or help a colleague meet a deadline. However, when you're running on empty, how genuine and deep is that empathy? Think of yourself as a phone battery that's always on low power. You might still function, but you can't support anyone else's needs when you're barely hanging on.

What you might think of as true empathy could actually be sympathy or misplaced compassion. It's like you're at a party, smiling and engaging with others while feeling completely overwhelmed and alone on the inside. If you neglect your own needs, you're not only hurting yourself—you're also depriving others of the authentic connection they crave.

So here's the essential truth: Focusing on yourself first isn't selfish; it's a critical act of self-preservation. By taking time to recharge, whether it's enjoying a quiet cup of coffee, going for a walk, or simply saying no to an extra commitment, you're not just caring for yourself—you're positioning yourself to be there for others in a meaningful way.

When you prioritize your well-being, you create a strong foundation for genuine relationships. Think about it: When you're filled up, you have so much more to give. So take that time for yourself. It's the best gift you can offer—not just to yourself, but to everyone in your life.

Do you remember where you need to start to ensure you have a healthy, thriving relationship with self-empathy? Like any process, you start at the beginning. Consistently reflect on your background and experiences. There's always something to learn about yourself, and you'll likely be surprised by the discoveries you make when you're in a new and different stage of life.

Everything we've gone over in this book should help you be mindful and prepared for intentional and unintentional changes in your life and the lives of your loved ones. Therefore, even though you can't change where you started, you have more control than you think over where you go next.

So, if you haven't gone through the process of cultivating self-empathy yet, or you start neglecting yourself and your well-being, go through these steps:

1. Once again, get curious about your experiences.
2. Reflect on recent interactions that didn't go well (especially those that required more empathy from you).
3. Take a self-compassion break.
4. Abandon any perfectionist beliefs that you hold and accept your flaws (while also working on improving those areas).

Remind yourself that this process isn't self-indulgent. It will help you become the person, parent, partner, leader, and/or friend you want to be—someone who's happy and secure, and spreads that happiness and security to others.

Potential Consequences

The last thing I wanted to do with this book was engage in fear-mongering. However, I don't shy away from the truth, and you shouldn't either. There are real, severe consequences to neglecting self-empathy.

Some of these consequences include:

- Resentment
- Uneven relationships
- Abusive or toxic relationships
- Codependency or learned helplessness
- Being stuck on stupid (I just love the way that sounds)

Failing to take your own happiness and well-being seriously is guaranteed to negatively impact you and those around you, regardless of how hard you try to protect the people close to you.

CHAPTER SEVEN RECAP

Putting accurate empathy into action can be easy in one interaction and incredibly difficult in the next. Therefore, utilizing the tools and approaches we've gone over is crucial to your mastery of this skill.

Positive psychology approaches and the approaches to accurate empathy that I teach overlap in many ways. Instead of solely directing our energy and attention toward our weaknesses and failures, we want to view every interaction as a learning experience. We want to focus on our areas of improvement and prioritize our well-being first. Positive psychology and accurate empathy require being intentional and mindful about where we put our energy.

Positive psychology focuses on our:

- Virtues
- Strengths
- Core values

These elements are crucial for accurate empathy. They're closely related to one's identity, self-esteem, and more. We know that low self-esteem, identity issues, and adverse experiences contribute to a lack of self-compassion and empathy, which makes it difficult to show these things to others.

I encourage everyone, especially coaches and clinicians, to embrace some of the core teachings of positive psychology in their pursuit of better, healthier, and more genuine relationships and interactions. Helping those who you support to develop a healthy relationship with change and chaos can equip them to manage their reactions and create better outcomes. Learning to view challenges as opportunities for growth rather than world-ending experiences is a difficult yet rewarding process for all involved.

Positive psychology is crucial for several reasons. First, it acknowledges the reality of our emotions. When we face devastating events, it's easy to get lost in negativity or feel like we must suppress our feelings to appear strong. However, embracing positive psychology and self-empathy allows us to validate our experiences and emotions, which is essential for genuine healing.

Second, these practices promote mental resilience. By focusing on coping strategies and understanding our emotions, we can build a stronger foundation to navigate life's challenges. This resilience doesn't mean ignoring pain; instead, it equips us with tools to face it head-on, ultimately leading to healthier responses rather than falling into despair or harmful behaviors.

Finally, extending grace and empathy (both to ourselves and to others) fosters deeper connections. When we practice self-empathy, we become more compassionate toward those around us, creating an environment where vulnerability is welcomed and shared. This communal support can be incredibly powerful, reminding us that we are not alone in our struggles.

Ultimately, embracing positive psychology and self-empathy during tough times is about finding a balance. This allows us to honor our pain and open ourselves up to the possibility of healing and growth.

Positive psychology seamlessly integrates with different coaching models, including:

- Appreciative Inquiry
- Motivational Interviewing
- Cognitive Behavioral Therapy (CBT)
- The Transtheoretical Model of Change
- Acceptance and Commitment Therapy (ACT)

Appreciative Inquiry encourages curiosity instead of judgment. This approach consists of reflecting on one's previous successes to cultivate motivation and discipline when faced with challenges. Prioritizing curiosity over judgment is a critical step in developing self-empathy and overcoming negative beliefs about yourself and your capabilities.

Motivational Interviewing draws on one's core values for motivation and commitment. This approach overlaps with accurate empathy in that it encourages you to understand yourself better. It helps you become better connected to your goals and values, setting you up for a greater chance of happiness and success.

CBT is more concerned with the reframing process we've discussed many times throughout this book. It helps you identify negative thought patterns and transform them into patterns that serve your growth. If you're stuck in a cycle of negative thinking without reflection and reframing, accurate empathy is absent.

The Transtheoretical Model of Change breaks the process of change down into five different stages: pre-contemplation, contemplation, preparation, action, and maintenance. Your experiences with change, both expected and unexpected, are heavily influenced by your ability to show accurate empathy to yourself and others. Accurate empathy, when integrated within this model, can involve helping clients by validating their emotions, guiding them to develop a more objective view of their situation, reminding them of their core values and how they connect to their goals, and checking in with them to make sure they're learning throughout the process.

Finally, Acceptance and Commitment Therapy (ACT) involves observing, naming, and accepting thoughts and emotions. This goes back to understanding where you're coming from, or in this case, where your client is coming from, to get a clearer idea of where you want to go.

Self-empathy isn't possible without identifying, understanding, and validating your emotions before you act. As a coach or clinician, helping the person you're supporting with this will strengthen their self-empathy and capacity for managing their emotions in future challenging situations and conversations.

All of these approaches involve helping the client feel safe, validated, and empowered. This is achieved by helping them accept their feelings and situation, look at everything objectively to increase their understanding of themselves, and reframe their thoughts and beliefs to be more positive and productive.

Accurate empathy is essential for the practitioner regardless of their area of specialization. Combining accurate empathy and positive psychology with your care style benefits you and your clients.

CHAPTER EIGHT RECAP

Emotional intelligence and accurate empathy are closely related. Ideally, you're improving both at the same time. Those with low emotional intelligence are far more likely to misunderstand and misuse empathy. The process of mastering accurate empathy will also improve your emotional intelligence.

Before we recap how to improve your emotional intelligence and why it's crucial to your accurate empathy development, let's revisit its definition. Emotional intelligence (EQ or EI) is the ability to determine, understand, and express your emotions (and others') in a mindful, healthy way.

Accurate empathy, as it relates to EQ, is the ability to act and respond in a way that encourages self-awareness, compassion, and accountability in yourself and others. Emotional intelligence does not mean manipulating people by using their emotions against them.

Part of being mindful of your emotions, as well as the emotions of those you're interacting with, is understanding valence and arousal.

You may realize that someone is upset, but unless you get curious and dig deeper to understand how that emotion impacts them, the reasoning behind it, and how significant it is, you'll struggle with determining how to show accurate empathy in that situation.

Therefore, it's a good idea to understand valence, how positive or negative an emotion is, and arousal, the strength of an emotion. Coaches and clinicians can determine valence and arousal by validating their clients and asking them follow-up questions that help them get to the root of their experiences.

Let's simplify this concept with an example.

Imagine Alex walks into a café looking upset. Jamie notices Alex's frown and how he's staring at the ground. Jamie knows something isn't right, but instead of just asking, "What's wrong?" he thinks about the emotions involved.

Valence is about whether the emotion is positive or negative. Here, Alex's emotion is negative because he looks sad.

Arousal is about how strong that emotion is. If Alex is crying, the arousal is probably high. If he's just a bit quiet, the arousal is likely low. However, we've learned to dig deeper and not make assumptions.

Jamie decides to approach Alex with empathy. He says, "Hey, I can see you're feeling down. Want to talk about it?" This shows he cares and opens the door for Alex to share more.

By understanding that Alex is experiencing a negative emotion (valence) and noticing how intense it is (arousal), Jamie can better support him. This way, they can have a meaningful conversation that helps Alex feel understood.

The Importance of Understanding Conflict Modes

To effectively carry out accurate empathy in interactions with our clients, partners, children, and others, we must understand how we handle conflict. Being aware of your default behaviors so you can identify your areas of improvement benefits everyone. You can model this awareness and growth mindset, inspiring others to work on themselves.

According to the Thomas-Kilmann Conflict Mode Instrument (TKI), the five types of conflict management are:

- Accommodate
- Compromise
- Collaborate
- Compete
- Avoid

Determining your top two to three default modes is crucial to developing a greater understanding of how you might have fallen short of accurate empathy in previous interactions. Each of these conflict modes can be effective. When you lean into emotional intelligence and accurate empathy, you improve your ability to determine which of these approaches is most beneficial for a particular interaction.

Checking Your Progress

To make sure you're moving forward in your pursuit of accurate empathy and greater emotional intelligence, we went over the following exercises.

1. Engage in introspection.
2. Ask for feedback and truly consider it.
3. Assess your current relationships and make the necessary changes.
4. Try to look at how your life is going as objectively as possible.

5. Recognize and practice gratitude for your strengths and everything that's working well.

Committing to regular introspection, communication, and gratitude can only improve your relationships and overall well-being.

Those who are in tune with themselves and others have a greater capacity for empathy and are less likely to misuse or neglect it. So keep trying to learn more about yourself and those around you so you can act and respond in ways that deepen your relationships.

CHAPTER NINE RECAP

Although you just finished Chapter Nine, I want to make sure we cover the crucial points again.

We're able to change our default thoughts and actions by embracing neuroplasticity. Neuroplasticity is an automatic process in which your brain changes and evolves with every experience you have. The problem is that your brain prioritizes its safety first and your physical safety second. This doesn't sound like a problem, but it is since we often need to exit our comfort zones to grow.

Being aware of the way your brain responds to change and "threats" is your starting point. As I mentioned before, your brain is trying to protect you, but that doesn't mean the way it protected you during previous experiences is helpful now.

Your ego is also trying to protect you, but it's primarily driven by fear. Its priorities are instant gratification and self-preservation. However, you're driven, or you *want* to be driven, by your long-term happiness, success, and well-being. These things naturally clash.

While we can trace our default functioning to our cultural and familial influences, we can't use those experiences as excuses forever. You are fully capable of changing your thoughts, behaviors, and outcomes. You can show yourself and others accurate empathy even if you've never gotten it from others. Finally, you can learn to give your own emotions and experiences as much weight as you give to your loved ones' feelings.

Showing ourselves empathy involves addressing our own emotions and acknowledging their importance, rather than ignoring or dismissing them. However, one of the ways your ego tries to protect you is by suppressing emotions. This can lead to adverse emotional and physical health consequences.

The potential side effects of neglecting yourself and your emotions are so great that I believe it's imperative to go over the exercises from this chapter again.

If you find yourself regularly suppressing your emotions, I want you to try adding one or more of these activities to your routine.

1. Practice mindfulness meditation.
2. Journal your thoughts and feelings.
3. Seek professional support.

Lastly, revisit the self-compassion exercises from Chapter Six. Try to remember that at the end of the day, you're human too. You need and deserve just as much love, understanding, compassion, and empathy as everyone else.

FINAL THOUGHTS FOR MY FELLOW COACHES, CLINICIANS, AND MENTAL HEALTH PROFESSIONALS

I can truly say that everything I've talked about in this book has not only helped me become a better person, but also a more effective and impactful coach.

Although accurate empathy is still underestimated and underutilized in many settings and industries, such as in healthcare and other corporate environments, you know that its potential is too great to ignore for your own business and life.

Whether you're just starting in your career, or you've been in business for longer than I have, investing in cultivating and mastering accurate empathy toward yourself and others will be one of the most significant contributors to your growth and success.

It's no coincidence that when I first started as a coach who didn't truly understand accurate empathy, I had no boundaries, poor well-being, low-quality relationships, and less money. While a lot of factors played a role in helping me get where I am now, developing accurate empathy was, without a doubt, the best thing I did for my business and life. Those around me, including my family, friends, and clients, have also benefitted from my decision to take care of myself and extend that same care to others. I've let go of relationships that drained me and welcomed new relationships that fill my cup. Most of all, I've improved my relationship with myself, which has transformed the way I live, love, and work.

If you're still doubting the importance of implementing accurate empathy at home and in your practice, which I sincerely doubt after reading this book, I challenge you to consider the potential consequences of moving forward without it. If you're not happy with where you are now in life and business, I can guarantee accurate empathy is missing. You can't afford to keep moving forward in the same way because you will get the same results. Let this empower you instead of intimidating you.

I believe in you. This is your time. On that note....

THANK YOU

Each chapter of this book has been focused on helping you gain the tools necessary to look within before you face your attention and energy outward. How we show up has a great deal to do with what we get back from others. The challenge is, how do we show up for ourselves? As discussed in every chapter, the failure to be self-compassionate and accurately apply empathy toward yourself is the source material for all dysfunctional, codependent relationships. Thankfully, the opposite occurs when we allow ourselves to be imperfect and treat ourselves with empathy and compassion. Many of us need to stop taking ourselves so seriously, but of course, that doesn't mean we shouldn't be intentional toward our self-improvement and the pursuit of our goals.

Vulnerability is a strength. It's often seen as a weakness of the human condition, but nothing could be further from the truth. People embrace imperfect people because they remind them of themselves. When coaches and clinicians are authentic, their clients immediately sense it. The same is true for leaders in organizations. The more relatable the leader, the more stakeholders will feel a sense of community and buy into the vision and mission of the organization.

As we conclude our time together, I hope you leave as a different person than you were when you arrived. There's nothing wrong with admitting what you don't know. However, once you know better, you can do better.

We all know the phrase, "Knowledge is power." I'd like to add to that knowledge is only power when it's applied. It's one thing to be well-educated, but it's another thing to be intelligent. Many studies have proven that people who relate and communicate well with others are the most successful. Nobody cares about how smart or well-connected you are if you're incapable of acting like a human being and treating others like they're human beings. Many powerful, wealthy people ultimately fail because they don't treat others with decency or respect. Even those who appear successful on the outside are not always happy or fulfilled. You want to be happy and fulfilled, and I'm here to tell you that you can and will be if you commit to this process.

As you turn these final pages, I ask two things of you:

1. Revisit this content frequently for your own improvement and growth.
2. Recommend this book or make it required reading for your organization, colleagues in your practice, your teams, or your college curriculum.

As we transform ourselves, we must understand that positive transformation is the result of deliberate action. All of us long to break free from emotional turmoil and evolve past our autopilot behaviors. Hopefully, you now have a blueprint that can help you be a better person, cultivate the capacity to love and respect yourself, and show accurate empathy toward others so you can attain your highest potential while inspiring others to do the same.

Accurate empathy is still underestimated by many individuals and groups, but we know better than to downplay its potential.

"You are so much stronger than you think. Thank you for taking this journey with me. May you live long and well. I love you madly, most sincerely I do."—Dr. D Ivan Young, MCC, NBC-HWC

References

Association for Psychological Science. 2012. "'That Giant Tarantula Is Terrifying, but I'll Touch It' – Expressing Your Emotions Can Reduce Fear." https://www.psychologicalscience.org/news/releases/that-giant-tarantula-is-terrifying-but-ill-touch-it-expressing-your-emotions-can-reduce-fear.html.

Cooperrider, David L., and Diana Whitney. 2005. *Appreciative Inquiry: A Positive Revolution in Change*. Berrett-Koehler Publishers. https://www.taosinstitute.net/files/Content/5692967/whitney_Appreciative-Inquiry-Positive-Revolution-in-Change.pdf.

Gaiswinkler, L., Paul Kaufmann, Ewald Pollheimer, Andrea Ackermann, Sandra Holasek, Hans-Peter Kapfhammer, and Human-Friedrich Unterrainer. 2020. "Mindfulness and Self-Compassion in Clinical Psychiatric Rehabilitation: a Clinical Trial." *Mindfulness* 11 (2): 374–83. https://self-compassion.org/wp-content/uploads/2019/08/Gaiswinkler2019.pdf.

Germer, Christopher K., and Kristin Neff. 2015. "Cultivating self-compassion in trauma survivors." In *Mindfulness-oriented interventions for trauma: Integrating contemplative* practices, edited by Victoria M. Follette, John Briere, Debra Rozelle, James W. Hopper, and David I. Rome. 43–58. Guilford Press. https://self-compassion.org/wp-content/uploads/2015/08/Germer.Neff_.Trauma.pdf.

Hall, Judith A., Sarah D. Gunnery, and Katja Schlegel. 2025. "Gender and Accuracy in Decoding Affect Cues: A Meta-Analysis." *Journal of Intelligence,* 13 (3): 38. https://doi.org/10.3390/jintelligence13030038.

Hamer, Mark, Yoichi Chida, and Gerard J. Molloy. 2009. "Psychological distress and cancer mortality: A meta-analysis." *Journal of Psychosomatic Research,* 66 (3): 255–58. https://www.sciencedirect.com/science/article/abs/pii/S0022399908005278.

Moyers, Theresa B., and William R. Miller. 2013. "Is Low Therapist Empathy Toxic?" *Psychology of Addictive Behaviors,* 27 (3): 878–84. https://pmc.ncbi.nlm.nih.gov/articles/PMC3558610/.

Song, Man-Kyu, Soo-Hee Choi, Do-Hyeong Lee, Kyung-Jun Lee, Won Joon Lee, and Do-Hyung Kang. 2018. "Effects of Cognitive-Behavioral Therapy on Empathy in Patients with Chronic Pain." *Psychiatry Investigation,* 15 (3): 285–91. https://pmc.ncbi.nlm.nih.gov/articles/PMC5900372/.

Sares-Jäske, Laura, Mercedesz Czimbalmos, Satu Majlander, Reetta Siukola, Reija Klemetti, Pauliina Luopa, and Jukka Lehtonen. 2023. "Gendered Differences in Experiences of Bullying and Mental Health Among Transgender and Cisgender Youth." *Journal of Youth and Adolescence,* 52: 1531–48. https://doi.org/10.1007/s10964-023-01786-7.

Schaubhut, Nancy A. 2007. *Technical Brief for the Thomas-Kilmann Conflict Mode Instrument: Description of the Updated Normative Sample and Implications for Use.* CPP, Inc. https://kilmanndiagnostics.com/wp-content/uploads/2018/04/TKI_Technical_Brief.pdf

Seligman, Martin E. P., Tracy A. Steen, Nansook Park, and Christopher Peterson. 2005. "Positive Psychology Progress: Empirical Validation of

Interventions." *American Psychologist,* 60 (5): 410–421. https://greatergood.berkeley.edu/images/uploads/Seligman-PosPsychProgress.pdf.

Sokolov, Arseny A., Samuel Krüger, Paul Enck, Ingeborg Krägeloh-Mann, and Marina A. Pavlova. 2011. "Gender Affects Body Language Reading." *Frontiers in Psychology,* 2: 16. https://pmc.ncbi.nlm.nih.gov/articles/PMC3111255/.

Teles, Ricardo Vieira. 2020. "Phineas Gage's great legacy." *Dementia & Neuropsychologia,* 14 (4): 419-21. https://pmc.ncbi.nlm.nih.gov/articles/PMC7735047/.

Ungar, Michael. 2013. "Resilience, Trauma, Context, and Culture." *Trauma, Violence, & Abuse,* 14 (3): 255–66. https://michaelungar.com/files/15contributions/5._Resilience,_Trauma,_Context,_and_Culture.pdf.